ALIEN
WORLD ORDER

"In *Alien World Order,* Len Kasten provides a coherent account of the history and imperialistic activities of Reptilian extraterrestrials on Earth and the Milky Way galaxy over millennia, using the work of Robert Morning Sky, Stuart Swerdlow, Alex Collier, and other primary sources. The scope of Reptilian influence over human elites and society is breathtaking and provides an explanation for many of the historical ills afflicting humanity. Kasten peels back the layers of secrecy even further to reveal the dire situation we collectively face today—where our political leaders are vassals for imperialistic Reptilian aliens—and the need for an informed citizenry to take back their sovereign destiny."

MICHAEL E. SALLA, PH.D., AUTHOR OF
INSIDERS REVEAL SECRET SPACE PROGRAMS &
EXTRATERRESTRIAL ALLIANCES

"Veteran UFO researcher Len Kasten has built a terrifying scenario of his findings about the aliens' historical background and their future intent to control Earth. Along with different alien types, Kasten's book focuses on the often reported reptilian-like beings and their nefarious plans. This book should be read by all those concerned with putting the pieces of the alien puzzle together."

DAVID M. JACOBS, PH.D., AMERICAN HISTORIAN AND
AUTHOR OF *WALKING AMONG US:*
THE ALIEN PLAN TO CONTROL HUMANITY

"Len Kasten's *Alien World Order* makes a compelling, well-documented case for the historical and ongoing competition between the Reptilian Draco Empire, with its program of hate, and the Galactic Federation, with its program of love. I urge you to read this book; the more of us who do, the more likely we'll prevail against the Dracos and, with help from the Galactics, lift Earth to a planet of peace, cooperation, and encouragement for all."

SASHA (ALEX) LESSIN, PH.D., AUTHOR OF
ANUNNAKI: GODS NO MORE

"As a researcher and historian, I am always grateful when a fellow author documents true information for the public. I commend Len for his outstanding dedication and analysis of truth! I look forward to many more books from Len."

STEWART A. SWERDLOW, AUTHOR OF *TRUE WORLD HISTORY: HUMANITY'S SAGA* AND *MONTAUK: THE ALIEN CONNECTION*

"The information within these pages allows us to take a giant leap forward to a deeper knowing that has always been encoded within our DNA. This hidden history has been patiently waiting to be revealed when we are ready to face the deep spiritual and psychological questions that arise from this knowing. Are you ready?"

JASON QUITT, COAUTHOR OF *FORBIDDEN KNOWLEDGE: REVELATIONS OF A MULTI-DIMENSIONAL TIME TRAVELER*

"As always, Len Kasten writes in an articulate, thoughtful, and compelling manner. *Alien World Order* presents a profound and cohesive 'look behind the scenes' at the massive, sinister alien agenda that is interwoven with planet Earth's long history. I highly recommend Len's new book!"

EDWARD T. MARTIN, AUTHOR OF
KING OF TRAVELERS: JESUS' LOST YEARS IN INDIA

"Len Kasten has his hand on the pulse of historical truth regarding the most denied reality on planet Earth today."

CARRIE L'ESPERANCE, AUTHOR OF *SOUL BREATHING: SPIRITUAL LIGHT AND THE ART OF SELF-MASTERY*

"A psychedelic overview of the alien agenda. From ancient aliens to the New World Order and secret space programs—it's all here in a rip-roaring read."

XAVIANT HAZE, AUTHOR OF *ALIENS IN ANCIENT EGYPT*

ALIEN
WORLD ORDER

THE Reptilian Plan TO Divide AND Conquer THE Human Race

LEN KASTEN

Bear & Company
Rochester, Vermont • Toronto, Canada

Bear & Company
One Park Street
Rochester, Vermont 05767
www.BearandCompanyBooks.com

Text stock is SFI certified

Bear & Company is a division of Inner Traditions International

Library of Congress Cataloging-in-Publication Data

Names: Kasten, Len, author.
Title: Alien world order : the Reptilian plan to divide and conquer the human race
    / Len Kasten.
Description: Rochester, Vermont : Bear & Company, 2017. | Includes
    bibliographical references and index.
Identifiers: LCCN 2016032801 (print) | LCCN 2016047576 (e-book) |
    ISBN 9781591432395 (pbk.) | ISBN 9781591432401 (e-book)
Subjects: LCSH: Extraterrestrial beings. | Reptiles. | Eschatology.
Classification: LCC BF2050 .K38 2017 (print) | LCC BF2050 (e-book) |
    DDC 001.942—dc23

LC record available at https://lccn.loc.gov/2016032801

Printed and bound in the United States by Lake Book Manufacturing, Inc.
The text stock is SFI certified. The Sustainable Forestry Initiative® program
promotes sustainable forest management.

10 9 8 7 6 5 4 3 2

Text design and layout by Debbie Glogover
This book was typeset in Garamond Premier Pro with ITC Avant Garde Gothic Std,
Digitalium, and Gill Sans MT Pro for display fonts

Cover collage images courtesy of IngImage, iStock Photo, and Wikipedia

All images courtesy of Creative Commons, unless otherwise noted

To send correspondence to the author of this book, mail a first-class letter to the
author c/o Inner Traditions • Bear & Company, One Park Street, Rochester, VT
05767, and we will forward the communication, or contact the author directly at
www.et-secrethistory.net.

Contents

PⴹRT III

Modern World Wars and Beyond

INTRODUCTION

From Prophecy
to Reality

The science-fiction classic *The Time Machine* by H. G. Wells was first published as a novel in 1895. It was based on his short story "The Chronic Argonauts," written in 1888 while Wells was a student and published in his college newspaper. Written, as it was, prior to the scientific and technological breakthroughs of the early twentieth century, it would be expected to be weak in terms of scientific speculation. But remarkably, the story contained a complete description of the concept of space-time, designating time as the fourth dimension of space, twenty years before Einstein unveiled his theory of special relativity! It also offered some interesting social insights. In his visit to the distant future in *The Time Machine,* the inventor–time traveler encounters a civilization of simple-minded, pleasure-seeking young people, the Eloi, who live in an earthly paradise of beauty and leisure. But underground there is a different society. There lives a race of apelike creatures, the Morlocks, who run the machinery that permits the pleasures of the surface world to exist. The time traveler at first assumes that this subsurface worker race has been enslaved by the Eloi to do all the hard labor necessary to keep their paradise functioning. However, the time traveler discovers that periodically the Morlocks put the Eloi into a trance, and then batch consignments of the young people are brought underground to become food for the cannibalistic Morlocks. The Morlocks allow the

Fig. I.1. Movie poster for The Time Machine

Eloi to enjoy their surface playground, but they are being kept like cattle in a pasture, for food.

Although it appeared to be pure science fiction, the novel seemed to have its origins in Wells's pessimistic views about the future of humanity. Some critics claim it reflected a socialist orientation since its bleak view of the future appeared to be an indictment of industrialization and capitalism. It is true that Wells was a socialist, later joining the Fabian Society, a British organization that endorsed socialism as the answer to the economic ills of the time. He even sought to become the president of the society. In a visit to Russia in 1920, he met with Vladimir Lenin and Leon Trotsky, the progenitors of the Russian Revolution, and a decade later he met with Josef Stalin. Given his communist leanings, it would be logical to conclude superficially that *The Time Machine* is a vision of the likely final days of capitalism. And Wells appears to admit as much when he says on the last page, "He, I know—for the question had been discussed among us long before the Time Machine was made—thought but cheerlessly of the Advancement of Mankind, and saw in the growing pile of civilization only a foolish heaping that must inevitably fall back upon and destroy its makers in the end." Yet, this sordid ultimate chapter in the history of mankind on this planet doesn't really make sense as any sort of acceptable prognostication of the far future. How anyone of Wells's intellect could believe that we would come to such an end is inconceivable. If Wells had lived after the advent of the atomic bomb, it might be believable that he thought that we would destroy civilization in a final catastrophic war. But the idea of the human race reverting back to troglodytes and simple, senseless, inarticulate little people is absurd. As a race, in general, we are already approaching a state of advanced spirituality and scientific sophistication.

Certainly we could not revert back to apes and idiots in eight hundred thousand years! More likely, we will be godlike beings colonizing other planets or distant stars. So, since it really makes no sense from a prophetic viewpoint, how could this novel have remained a classic for more than a century, spawned two Hollywood films, and inspired countless sequels and spin-offs? As we will see, we may have underestimated Wells's prophetic powers, and there may be much more to this story than is immediately apparent.

Fig. I.2. H. G. Wells. Photo by George Charles Beresford (1903)

THE WAR IN THE AIR

As a prophet, Wells was really unrivaled in his time. Many of the descriptions in his writings were remarkably accurate glimpses of events and situations many years in the future. Perhaps most astounding was his novel *The War in the Air,* written in 1907 and serialized and published in a British magazine in 1908. By 1907 the Wright brothers had just achieved noteworthy short flights under power. They had taken six flights in *The Flyer III,* from seventeen to thirty-eight minutes long, the farthest flight distance reaching twenty-four miles. Outside of the brothers' home base of Ohio, this news was widely greeted with disbelief and skepticism. A major Paris English-language newspaper said in a 1906 headline about the flights, "FLYERS OR LIARS?"* Yet, in the Wells novel, in a scenario highly suggestive of the Japanese attack on Pearl Harbor, a mighty armada of huge German flying machines launches a surprise attack on New York City. Wells says:

> At that time Germany was by far the most efficient power in the world, better organised for swift and secret action, better equipped with the resources of modern science, and with her official and administrative classes at a higher level of education and training.... Once again in the history of progress it seemed she held the decisive weapon [a strange reference before World War I]. Now she might strike and conquer before the others had anything but experiments in the air. Particularly she must strike America, swiftly, because there, if anywhere, lay the chance of an aerial rival. It was known that America possessed a flying-machine of considerable practical value, developed out of the Wright model; but it was not supposed that the Washington War Office had made any wholesale attempts to create an aerial navy.

---

*This was a headline in the Paris edition of the *Herald Tribune* in 1906 regarding the first powered flights in 1904–05. The Paris edition of the *New York Herald* said on Feb. 10, 1906, "The Wrights have flown or they have not flown. They possess a machine or they do not possess one. They are in fact either fliers or liars. It is difficult to fly. It's easy to say, 'We have flown.'"

But the American attack was only the beginning. He says further, "The attack upon America was to be the first move in this tremendous game. But no sooner had it started than instantly the aeronautic parks were to proceed to put together and inflate the second fleet which was to dominate Europe and manoeuvre significantly over London, Paris, Rome, St. Petersburg, or wherever else its moral effect was required. A World Surprise it was to be—no less a World Conquest."

Incredibly, this was precisely the German state of mind thirty-two years in the future in 1939, when also the German Air Force was to be the key to blitzkrieg and victory in Europe. And, in Wells's story, while the German military knew that America was a "sleeping giant," they knew it was totally unprepared for an attack from the air. In actuality, when Germany declared war on the United States in December of 1941, the Amerika-Bomber had been on the Nazi drawing boards for three years. In a speech on July 8, 1938, to German aircraft manufacturers, German Air Marshal Hermann Goering said, "I completely lack the bombers capable of round-trip flights to New York with a 4.5-tonne bomb load. I would be extremely happy to possess such a bomber, which would at last stuff the mouth of arrogance across the sea." This plan to bomb New York more than three years before Pearl Harbor leaves no doubt whatever about the early German war designs.

But most prophetic of all of Wells's World War II scenarios was his description of the new German leader, a perfect portrait of Adolph Hitler. Wells says:

Prince Karl Albert was indeed the central figure of the world drama. He was the darling of the Imperialist spirit in Germany, and the ideal of the new aristocratic feeling—the new Chivalry, as it was called—that followed the overthrow of Socialism through its internal divisions and lack of discipline, and the concentration of wealth in the hands of a few great families [Krupp, I. G. Farben, Tyson!]. He was compared by obsequious flatterers to the Black Prince, to Alcibiades, to the young Caesar. To many he seemed Nietzsche's Overman [a common comparison to Hitler] revealed. He was . . . splendidly non-moral.

But there was something of Goering also in Prince Karl.

The Emperor . . . placed him in control of the new aeronautic arm of the German forces. This he developed with marvellous energy and ability, being resolved, as he said, to give to Germany land and sea and sky [*liebensraum!*]. The national passion for aggression found in him its supreme exponent, and achieved through him its realisation in this astounding war. But his fascination was more than national; all over the world his ruthless strength dominated minds as the Napoleonic legend [Hitler was frequently compared to Napoleon] had dominated minds. . . . He made the war.

What is perhaps most amazing about this novel is the fact that while Wells may have gotten some of the details wrong, he did identify the participants and did capture the entire panorama of World War II. It was indeed a "war in the air," in which the Germans almost decimated London with bombs and rockets, and in which the Allies achieved victory by the total destruction of the major German cities by round-the-clock B-17 raids. He wrote this at a time when the Wright brothers were in the very earliest stage of development of the airplane. This level of accurate prognostication thirty years before the fact implies that

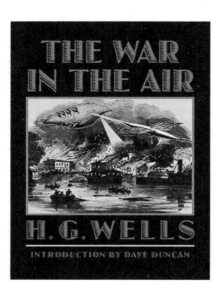

Fig. I.3. Cover for H. G. Wells's book The War in the Air

Wells had some sort of crystal ball. To simply say that he was psychic is not enough because psychics are rarely so accurate. It really makes him something of a modern-day Nostradamus.

STAR WARS

It has now been well established that the extraterrestrials (ETs) inclusively referred to as the Reptilians, or alternately the Reptiloids, have been living here on Earth for thousands of years and that they consider the Earth to be their ancestral home, since they claim that they were the original occupants in prehistoric times. They were contemporaneous with the dinosaurs, who were also reptilian-based creatures, which means that they supposedly lived on the surface of Earth between two hundred million and sixty-five million years ago, at which time the dinosaurs became extinct. That period, known as the Jurassic, is based on carbon dating, which is notoriously unreliable. There is contrary evidence that the age of the dinosaurs may have been no more than one million years ago. We do know that the Reptilians preceded the appearance of the human race on this planet. It is believed that they came here from planets in the Draco star system. Draco is approximately three hundred light-years from our solar system.

The humans in this galaxy were predominantly concentrated in the star system of the Lyra constellation. The Draco Reptilians and their allies in Orion and Rigel attacked and enslaved the inhabitants of planets in twenty-one star systems in this sector of the galaxy, while the humans in the Lyra system established peaceful and flourishing civilizations based on agriculture on several planets. Then, the Draco, having developed fearsome weapons, invaded the Lyra system. The Lyran humans, essentially peace loving, were not prepared for such a massive invasion. The Draco utterly destroyed three Lyran planets: Bila, Teka, and Merok. Fifty million were slaughtered. The Lyran survivors fled to other star systems, primarily Arcturus, Antares, the Pleiades, Cygnus Alpha, Alpha Centauri, Cassiopeia, and the Andromeda galaxy, creating a human diaspora in that galaxy as well as our own Milky Way galaxy.

Alex Collier claims to have been in telepathic contact with humans from the star system Zenetae in the Andromeda Galaxy since the age of fourteen. The humans in Zenetae may have originally been refugees from Lyra. He says, in his book *Defending Sacred Ground,* "As the human race fragmented, the races moved, traveled, and settled many different planets in many systems as space travel evolved. The human became aware of other planetary civilizations in these systems. Different cultures met and grew. Belief systems clashed or spread. New thoughts of Philosophy or technologies came into being. Mankind was evolving. A very strong social community developed between all in [from] the Lyra."

Human colonies developed in 110 different star systems, most having spacefaring technology. They banded together to form the Galactic Federation of Light and jointly learned to repel Reptilian invasions. In this, the Sol solar system, they colonized Mars and a large planet between Mars and Jupiter called Maldek. The Reptilians came and destroyed Maldek as they had the Lyran planets. It exploded into fragments, which became the asteroid belt. As their planet-sized Death Star passed Mars, it stripped the planet of its atmosphere, forcing the humans on Mars to take refuge underground.

THE HUMANS FIGHT BACK

On Earth, the Reptilians colonized the continent of Lemuria, which occupied most of the Pacific Ocean at that time and was tropical. The Federation fought back. They sent a fierce human refugee race from Lyra, then inhabiting a planet in the Pleiades, to Earth. They were known as the Atlans. The Atlans built a high civilization with spacefaring technology and sophisticated weaponry on the continent of Atlantis in the mid-Atlantic. They bombarded Lemuria with electromagnetic pulse weapons, and most of the continent sank beneath the Pacific Ocean. The Reptilians retreated underground. They took over a massive underground multilevel cave and tunnel system beneath the Indian subcontinent, stretching from central Tibet near Lake Manasarovar to northeast India, near what ultimately became Benares and then Varanasi on the banks of the Ganges. There, they established their underground capital city of Bhogovita. This civilization was referred to as "Patala" or "Snakeworld" by the surface natives. It became known as the home of the Nagas, or serpent people. Another group of Reptilians remained under Antarctica, which then had a moderate climate.

The Reptilians learned how to shape-shift to appear human, and they infiltrated the Atlantean civilization of prehistoric humans, who were blonde-haired and blue-eyed. They abducted humans and created Reptilian hybrids. This technique of infiltration and hybridization of another civilization prior to an all-out attack has been the hallmark of Reptilian conquest right up to the present day. The infiltrators slowly get control of the levers of power in the targeted population, and the enemy becomes weakened from within. It was used very effectively by their protégés, the Nazis, prior to World War II, when its practitioners, called fifth columnists, were sent to Europe and America in the 1930s. This term was coined in 1936, during the Spanish Civil War, by Nationalist General Emilio Mola, who told a reporter that he had four columns of troops attacking Madrid and a "fifth column" of supporters within the city. The fifth column had already infiltrated the enemy ranks. As will be seen in chapter 20, this same time-tested Reptilian technique is being implemented in America today. The Atlanteans discovered the deception and began pointing their weapons downward. Ultimately, this caused Atlantis to sink beneath the Atlantic, one segment at a time. Then, the Reptilians unleashed an experimental "super weapon," which caused the poles to shift. A Reptilian woman called Lacerta, interviewed in a video posted on YouTube, says that this was some sort of "fusion bomb." The final part of Atlantis sank in one night. Antarctica became a frozen wasteland, and the Gobi turned into a desert. This was probably the event that wiped out the dinosaurs. The Atlanteans had been given adequate notice by their prophets and had migrated to Egypt, the Mediterranean, and Central and South America. Psychic Edgar Cayce called this the migration of "the Children of the Law of One."

GENESIS

Our solar system was not again invaded by the Draco-Orionites because we now had assembled powerful human allies and supporters in many other star systems who were concerned about the fate of the humans on Earth—the Galactic Federation of Light. No doubt this discouraged another Reptilian attack. To bring peace to this planet, a council convened on the planet Hatona in the Andromeda galaxy to resolve the problem. The council decided to create genetically a new race to inhabit this planet. This would become their planet to inhabit for perpetuity. The DNA from twelve human races and the Reptilians was donated to create the new human race about forty thousand years ago. The Reptilians on this planet remained underground. Since they do not propagate as rapidly as the human race, their numbers have remained small, while we have grown to a huge population of more than seven billion. It has been estimated by Alex Collier that the population of Reptilians now living on Earth, in deep underground colonies, numbers only about 1,800. However that estimate is not up to date, and it is likely that the number is now considerably larger. Also, it is known that Reptilian DNA never changes. It is still the same as it was in the Jurassic period, whereas human DNA has been "tweaked" and has evolved consequently due to twenty-two modifications from our stellar friends. We humans on Earth, *Homo sapiens sapiens,* are a great experiment. We have been developed and watched over by advanced star beings that are waiting for us to evolve in consciousness and technology until we can take our place in the human-galactic alliance. This development, of course, has been opposed by the Reptilians, who fear

Fig. I.4. Galactic Federation of Light insignia

(justifiably) that we will eventually help to subdue them on the planets they have conquered and free their human slaves.

THE VAMPIRES FROM DRACO

All the literature about the Reptilians is in complete agreement that the Reptilians drink human blood and eat human flesh. Prolific author and writer Andrew Hennessy, in his article "The Reptilian Blood Legacy," states, "The reptilians and their crossbreeds drink blood because they are drinking the person's life-force and because they need it to exist in this dimension. They will often shape-shift into reptilians when drinking human blood and eating human flesh, I am told by those who have seen this happen. Blood drinking is in their genes and an Elite high priestess or 'Mother Goddess' in the hierarchy, who performed rituals for the Brotherhood at the highest level, told me that without human blood the reptilians cannot survive in this dimension."

They are known to bring human children into their underground realms and sacrifice them in occult rituals and then consume their blood and eat their bodies. Hennessy says in the same article, "Phil Schneider, a builder of US underground bases, told the writer and researcher, Alex Christopher, that when children reached the point where they could not work anymore in the slave conditions underground, they were consumed by the reptilians." Collier says, "They prefer human children best, for two reasons. The first is that children don't have the accumulation of pollutants in their bodies that adults do, and when children are put into a state of fear, their energy field and adrenalin just explodes. The reptilians get a 'rush' from this stuff."

In his book, *Missing 411—North America and Beyond: Stories of People Who Have Disappeared in Remote Locations of North America and Five Other Countries,* author David Paulides documents cases of thousands of disappearances, mainly from national parks and remote locations. These are primarily young people, and they are never recovered despite extensive search efforts. Paulides has identified certain geographic "clusters" where there have been multiple disappearances. Some of these are Lewiston, Idaho; Evergreen, Colorado; Schroon Lake,

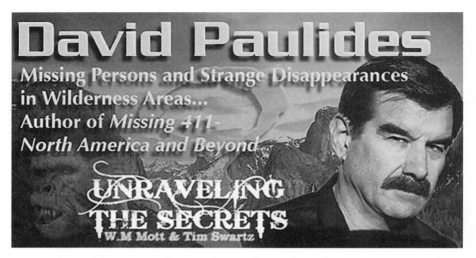

Fig. I.5. *Publicity poster for David Paulides, author of* Missing 411—North America and Beyond: Stories of People Who Have Disappeared in Remote Locations of North America and Five Other Countries

New York; Sequoia National Park, California; and Wasilla, Alaska. Strangely, the national park rangers were usually not cooperative in assisting Paulides in obtaining information about these cases, most of which display an odd similarity. Paulides frequently had to resort to National Park Service reports obtained through the Freedom of Information Act (FOIA) to get the facts of these cases. In a typical case, lone camper Kevin O'Keefe, thirty-six years old, vanished from his campsite in Glacier Bay National Park, Alaska, in October 1985. The park rangers found his sleeping bag and personal items outside his tent. After a fruitless two-hour flyover of the area, the rangers went back to the campsite and found his boots and a hat about one-half mile away. Paulides says, "It appears that everything Kevin needed to survive was at his camp. He had survival books and pamphlets, film, food, a toothbrush, soap, cigarettes, vitamin C, a compass, a flashlight, and other assorted items that you'd expect to find in a campsite where someone was staying for over one month."

The rangers found no evidence of an animal attack, and there was no blood found at the campsite. Paulides says about this case, "Alaska is a location that is not forgiving; you must have shoes if you are to survive. . . . Why would Kevin take his boots off? Did Kevin voluntarily take the boots off?" He says further, "Rangers never answered the obvious question of why Kevin's sleeping bag and other items were outside his tent. This makes no sense." This book by Paulides is a treasure trove of information about a phenomenon that gets little national attention. Most people have absolutely no knowledge about these eerie similar cases. Is there some sinister source of repression of publicity about this information? Do these people become food for the underground Reptilians, who exert enough political influence in the surface world to manage to keep the disappearance stories quiet? Collier claims in the *Letters from Andromeda* newsletter* that the Andromedans have told him through a channeled communication that more than thirteen thousand children have been taken by the Reptilians over the last twenty-five years.

So, as with *The War in the Air*, it seems that *The Time Machine* was fundamentally prophetic as well. Certainly, the beastlike, flesh-eating Morlocks bear a reasonable resemblance to the scaly-skinned, crocodile-resembling Reptilians, and the innocent Eloi young people are analogous to the youthful national park campers and explorers. It could happen that if the Reptilians prevail over the human population of Earth and manage to slaughter most of us, they might very well set up precisely the sort of society described in *The Time Machine*. They are known to have hypnotic powers over humans, clearly evidenced in most of the abductions. And we do know that they are very, very patient. Perhaps they are perfectly willing to wait eight hundred thousand years to obtain the sort of conditions on Earth that they require to develop. It is certainly a very sad prospect that a small contingent of Reptilians could possibly ultimately erase the glories of human civilization and reduce the planet Earth to a worldwide feeding ground! They might even bring back the dinosaurs. Already, prehistoric creatures such as the mammoth are being re-created using viable DNA found in their remains.

---

*See http://www.bibliotecapleyades.net/andromeda/lfa/lfa.html (accessed September 20, 2016).

Fig. I.6. Early poster for Star Wars

    In this book I have attempted to tell the entire story of the inception of this "take no prisoners" battle for the Sol solar system in which we now find ourselves in the twenty-first century. I have traced the struggle from its earliest days to the present. This war against the Reptilians is an emblematic struggle that has attracted the attention of star visitors from throughout the galaxy because it is the first time that this new race, the human race, created and tweaked by twenty-two human civilizations, has dared to confront the ancient and all-powerful Reptilian Empire. We are currently at a stalemate as the human race expands its consciousness and begins to understand how it has been hypnotized, duped, and enslaved and begins to employ its higher spiritual powers to defeat an enemy that cannot reach into the higher dimensions for assistance, as we can. We have finally taken to heart the pleas by Yoda and Obi-Wan Kenobi to Luke Skywalker, "Use the Force, Luke, use the Force!" We are now using the Force, and the final victory may soon be in sight. We will take back Mars, as did our Atlantean ancestors, and then begin to cruise the galaxy on the massive spaceships bigger than the *Enterprise* that we already have! We will then take it upon ourselves to join our galactic friends in freeing the slaves, as Abe Lincoln would have wanted. It may just be the first time that H. G. Wells was wrong.

PART I

The Era of
the First Star Wars

1

The Green World
and Beyond

We are not alone.
The astronomers are wrong. The scientists are wrong.
They are here, but we cannot see them because they
hide. They hide . . . in plain sight.
We are their servants, we are their slaves, we are their
property . . . we are theirs.

ROBERT MORNING SKY

Robert Morning Sky is a very unusual historian. Part Apache and part Hopi, he brings not only a rare Native American perspective to researching prehistory, but also he has inherited much of his knowledge from a unique source. He was given esoteric information that was very carefully passed down from his grandfather. It all began with an ET survivor of a New Mexico UFO crash, sometime before the Roswell crash. Six young Apache men found the wounded ET in the crash wreckage. They brought him to a desert camp on the reservation and nursed him back to health over several months. We are led to believe that this survivor was humanlike and that his rescuers were able to communicate with him in a language they both understood. This encounter brings to mind the similar meeting of George Adamski with Orthon from Venus in the California desert in 1954 (see my book *The Secret History of Extraterrestrials,* chapter 1). In that case, they were able to communicate successfully by telepathy. It is now commonly known that many extraterrestrial craft land in remote locations on Native American reservations in the United States and that their occupants communicate with the residents, who have zero interest in revealing these meetings to government authorities of any stripe.

One of the six rescuers gave Morning Sky's grandfather the detailed information about Earth's ancient history revealed by the ET. It is an astounding story that appears to validate many of the conclusions of Erich von Daniken in the Chariots of the Gods series of books,* but really goes way beyond those speculations. The alien eventually left the desert camp and was able to live as a human, as many humanoid extraterrestrials do routinely. However, he remained in touch with his six friends and over time related to them the whole story of human prehistory on this planet. They called him "Star Elder." They later learned his real name—Bek'Ti.

THE KHEB

Bek'Ti spoke of the evolution of life over millions of years on a planet he referred to as "the Green World," somewhere in this galaxy, which he called "Eridanus." He said that a race of reptilian humanoids he referred to as the Kheb evolved from dragonflies over millions of years on the Green World and became the dominant species. Morning Sky is not any sort of anthropologist or paleontologist, so his conclusion that the reptilian Kheb race evolved from the dragonfly on the Green World was strictly speculation based on what he was told. That type of development, superficially at least, seems highly improbable, since it stretches even Darwinian evolution, which is highly speculative in itself, to the breaking point. Since other evidence about the appearance of the Reptilian race, especially that given by Stewart Swerdlow, who will be referenced in the following chapters, contravenes that of Morning Sky, I am inclined, at this point, to disbelieve that aspect of his story. Swerdlow claims that the Reptilian race appeared fully developed in the Draco star system. He speculates that they may have come from

---

*See *Chariots of the Gods* by Erich von Daniken, published by Berkley Books, 1970.

another universe, dimension, or time period, but he is adamant that there is absolutely no evidence of their evolution from a simpler species in this galaxy. That being said, Morning Sky's history beginning from the point of a fully developed reptilian species intuitively seems correct, knowing what we now know about them, and it is definitely worthwhile to present that narrative here. It casts a bright light on the nature of the Reptilians and fully explains their character.

This story by Morning Sky reads, in places, like a fairy tale, and a reader might be tempted to discard it entirely based on that impression. However, it correlates with information from other researchers such as Alex Collier and Wes Penre, so that it fills many gaps in our knowledge about the prehistory of this planet with information not elsewhere available. While several other writers on these subjects, especially David Icke, do talk about the Reptilians, this is the only source of information on their history and deserves to be given serious consideration.

In his book *Eden, Atlantis, and the UFO Myth,* Morning Sky, speaking as the wise teacher Per to his pupil Matu, much like Socrates speaking to Plato, says:

> The early "kheb" humanoids were tall and rather slender, but their slim build was deceptively powerful. They were very limber and fast, capable of running on narrow trails and passing through thin passages. And they could fly, up and down, side to side and so fast that they seemed a blur. . . . They also had long sharp claws on the hands that they were developing. They could cut and rip with savage quickness, and they had large square jaws with sharp-ridged teeth that could cut a limb off with one snapping bite. They had powerful legs that let them run quickly and leap through the air with extraordinary speed and agility. Their emotionless black eyes could intimidate the hardiest enemy warrior . . . and remember, Matu . . . they could fly. The drone "kheb" were among the most vicious creatures of the Green World. . . . They were efficient and deadly hunters . . . and they were cold-blooded killers. Of all the species that would evolve on the Green World, it was the reptilian bee-humanoids, the "kheb," who would rise to become the most dominant life-form of the world.

Fig. 1.1. Robert Morning Sky

As the millions of years of their evolution continued to go by, the "kheb" people lost most of the very distinct reptilian and insect features of their ancestors. But not all their physical traits disappeared entirely. Though their height began to vary slightly, the "kheb" people generally remained tall and quite slender. And, as is the case with all beings born of reptilian ancestors, they possessed little or no hair on their bodies and they had very little hair on their heads. Their torsos retained the hour-glass shape of their long-ago dragonfly-bee ancestors. Males had broad chests with narrow waists, large and powerful buttocks with strong thighs and tapering calves. Reptilian females had the same shape but with a more delicate and feminine curve to their bodies. Their faces were still triangular, tapering to a pronounced yet soft point. They had large dark eyes, larger than most humanoids, and they possessed an almost hypnotizing beauty. Their mouths were also larger than most beings but with smaller lips. When closed, the mouth of the reptilian people seemed almost to disappear. And though they had lost the extremely large fangs of their ancestors, their "eye" teeth were still long and sharp . . . and quite functional. The long proboscis used to drain the blood of their victims was also gone; it had given way to an angular nose, sharp and narrow, and it too was strangely appealing.

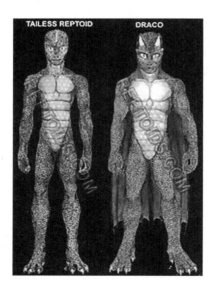

Fig. 1.2. Reptilian types (courtesy of John Rhodes at Reptoids.com)

It may surprise you, Matu . . . but the reptilian people were a physically beautiful people. Their limbs were graceful, their bodies were alluring and shapely. And with their large dark eyes and fluid walk, the reptilian females were known to be some of the most beautiful women in the galaxy. The reptilian people were handsome and fearsome, beautiful and deadly . . . and they could fly. In ceremony, when dressed in their flowing robes, in the best finery their world had to offer, the male and female reptilians could hover lightly, as if on angelic wings . . . but they were the Hand of Death itself, hidden in shining gossamer.

There were many wars between the various Reptilian warrior species in the Green World, but the Kheb rose to ultimate power. The ability to fly made the major difference in their victories. Morning Sky says:

Without fail, the success or failure of the reptilian armies always hinged on the extraordinary ability of the drone warriors to maneuver in flight. Males and females alike could fly on wings that seemed far too delicate to carry their lanky bodies. They were exceptionally quick on the ground, but in the air the reptilians had no peer. . . .

From a distance, the approaching armies of flying warriors looked like a huge black cloud of giant dragonflies, a faint angry buzzing betraying their intent. But even though the enemy might visually detect them while still some distance away, in the blink of an eye the reptilian winged warriors covered the ground that separated them from their enemies. In less than a heartbeat, the viciousness of the reptilian warrior descended on its enemy like the wrath of a cruel and bloodthirsty God.

THE ASCENDANCY OF THE NEKH

One particular group of the Kheb, called the NEKH, were the most powerful. They eventually rose to the top of the heap. According to Morning Sky, "The balance of power swung back and forth between many aspiring realms. Empires and Kingdoms rose and fell. But in time, one race of reptilian people surfaced as the dominant people of the planet. They were known as the NEKH, or the fearsome 'Black Ones.' Through the victories of the Black Warriors and the political manipulations of the Black Kings, the world of the Reptiles was eventually united under one King and one Kingdom."

As the conquests by the NEKH piled up, the need for efficient administrative control of their empire became a paramount consideration. This has always been a thorny problem for conquering armies. It caused major problems for the Roman and British colonial rulers. Always, it eventually becomes clear that slavery is not a lasting solution. It is best to have the conquered civilizations govern themselves and pay tribute to the rulers. The medium of exchange, or money, becomes the vehicle for total control. Morning Sky tells us:

Life advanced quickly under the hand of the Reptilian NEKH Kings. . . . Science and technology, originally developed to assist in the Wars of Conquest by the Kings, leaped forward by leaps and bounds. While weaponry and the science of conquest continued to have the highest priority in research and development, the inventions and tools that resulted from the new technologies were often adapted for everyday use by the average "kheb" human. . . . In time, the "Kheb" Kings abandoned their destructive Wars of Conquest and focused their attention on new wars for power. These wars were not fought on the battlefield; they were fought in the marketplaces of the Green World. Begun as a cooperative effort to achieve a profitable united front throughout the globe, the "Kheb" Monarchs began to work together, not for the sake of peace, but for the sake of monetary gain. Wars of destruction would no longer be tolerated in the major Kingdoms of the New World, peace and order would reign; prosperity and happiness would belong to everyone. Business became the new battlefield. The New World Wars, officially known as the NEKH World Wars, were fought in the business centers of the Green World. Assassinations and murders still took place, but they were no longer a result of heated passions and sheer hatred. . . . "It wasn't personal . . . it was business."

In the new world, one family of Kheb beings surfaced to control the wealth and power bases of the entire globe; they were the first descendants of the early NEKH kings and were known as the NEKH-KHEB. Under their manipulations, peace was achieved, and a new era was realized. All of the kingdoms of the Green World fell under the flag of the Association of Kheb States, another way of saying the Association of Reptilian States. The strength of the New World could be expressed in a simple phrase, "And a profit shall lead them."

This concept of rulership by money is characteristic of all the planets governed by Reptilian overlords and, as will be seen, is particularly apropos in their influence on Earth, where they operate through their puppets, the Illuminati bankers.

THE KINGS OF HEAVEN

With all the states of the Green World incorporated into the association and firmly under the control of the NEKH, the kings looked for new worlds to conquer. They were never satisfied with peace and tranquillity, and it was always in their nature to fight and dominate. They were never really comfortable with a stable, agrarian-based society. Morning Sky says:

With the institutions of the New World Era in place, the NEKH Empires began to look to the skies above. They began, as human beings of Earth have, to explore their moons. They carefully developed their technologies, landed on the surface of their moons and began to establish footholds. Generations later, their moons were colonized and exploited, mined for their resources, and became fully equipped stepping-stones to the planets and worlds beyond. The Reptilian NEKH astronauts reached out and conquered the worlds of their own solar system, establishing new bases and more colonies, exploiting and developing the many new satellites of their neighbors. The NEKH established a solar system community of Reptilian beings, the first Association of Reptilian Worlds.

Once again, never satisfied with peace, the NEKH kings looked beyond their own solar system out into the cosmos. Soon their space technology allowed them to exceed the speed of light by traveling through wormholes, and they began their conquests in other star systems.

The NEKH Kings began to reach out beyond the boundaries of their solar system Empire into the outer reaches of other solar systems and their worlds. Possessed of extraordinary technology and weaponry, with vast resources and coldly calculating Star Warriors, the NEKH Kings began to explore and exploit Other Worlds. As they had done on the Green World, and as they had done in their own solar system, they began yet another series of Wars of Conquest. And it was on these Wars of Conquest that the reptilian people confronted the other humanoids of the Galaxy of ERIDANUS. . . .

When the NEKH Star Ships made first contact with beings of Other Worlds, they were predictably cautious, of course . . . but to the surprise of the reptilian Star Warriors, the Other World beings welcomed them with open arms. Since the Other Worlders had not managed to develop their own space technology, the new civilization looked with awe and near reverence on the ships of the NEKH. Conquest of their planet was simple. . . . As the Other Worlds fell to the NEKH Star Warriors, the Kings were quick to establish their own puppet governments with their own NEKH Administrators in the seats of power. All Other Worlds would function under the same systems established in the NEKH Empire. All newly conquered populations would obey and live by the institutions of the NEKH Worlds, and all conquered populations would pay homage to the NEKH King of the Stars who sat on the Throne of the NEKH Empire. . . . All Hail King NEKH! All Hail the King of Heaven!

THE END OF AN ERA

As the NEKH attacked other distant star systems, they were surprised as they began to encounter stiff resistance, which they were not accustomed to. Morning Sky says, "As the Reptilian Star Warriors continued to move onto unknown worlds, they soon found that there were other species of warriors that were not so easily defeated. Some star races were defended by warriors with exceptional physical strengths and abilities that the reptilian warriors had never seen before. To the dismay of the NEKH kings, some wars of conquest were lost."

Thus, now vigorously opposed, the star warriors found themselves at a crossroads. That point in time was a marker in Reptilian history. It became known as the end of the era of the first star wars. At that point, they could have reformed and chosen to focus just on the internal problems of their now expansive empire. However, that was just not in their DNA. This slowdown in the pace of conquest caused the NEKH kings to reevaluate their military systems and armaments. They realized that they had overlooked a very effective weapon in battle—female warriors. Morning Sky says:

Even with all of their advanced technologies and the inherent viciousness and cold-bloodedness of their reptilian Warriors, the NEKH Kings found themselves taken to a higher level of intensity and deadliness in War. Tactics and weaponry had to be reevaluated

. . . as did the make-up of the warrior on the battlefield. As a result of the demands made by these ultra-level "Star Wars" no reptilian Warrior could be summarily dismissed or ignored . . . regardless of gender. In reviewing the history of the successful wars of the Empire, it soon was recalled that Reptilian females had once fought side by side with the drone warriors in the Wars of the Green World. Their participation played no small part in the victories of the old wars. There was no reason to believe that they could not contribute to victories in the new wars. As had once happened many, many years earlier, reptilian females were once again recruited and placed on the battlefield beside their male counterparts.

THE FEMALE WARRIORS

Several factors had contributed to permitting the female Reptilians to be now ready and prepared for battlefield action—and to become deadly warriors. Of major importance was the cessation of the menstrual cycle. On their home worlds the females' menstrual cycle was regular and predictable because of the solar radiation. However in the faraway solar systems of the conquered planets, this regulation was absent. About this, Morning Sky says:

On their home world, females were bathed constantly with harsh solar radiation from their multiple suns. Pulsing solar storms forced a rhythmic fluctuation in their reproductive cycles, forcing them to produce a chemical in their bodies that would assist in regulating the birth and conception process. But in the vast reaches of space, away from the home world suns and away from the forces that generated internal bodily cycles, the female fluctuation stopped . . . entirely! The menstrual cycles of the female reptilians ceased altogether! In space, reptilian females could still conceive and bear children, but only through the direct and deliberate stimulation of the conception hormones. What this means is that reptilian women had no menstrual cycle. They could completely choose when and if they wanted to become pregnant!

Being free of menstrual-cycle limitations, the females were able to join in military operations. But to the surprise of the NEKH kings, the female warriors were even more deadly than the males, thanks to the transformation of the naturally produced venom in the female hormonal system. No longer necessary for reproduction,* the venom became available as the defense mechanism for which it originally was intended. Morning Sky says:

> But . . . to everyone's surprise, the natural venom of the reptilian females became even more deadly than it had ever been before! . . . Under battlefield conditions, the rush of adrenaline running through the bloodstream of women added to the potency of the venom. To the pleasant surprise of the Kings, and to the misfortune of their enemies, because of the natural transformation of the venom, and because of the added adrenaline influence, the naturally produced venom of the reptilian females rendered them far more dangerous . . . and far more deadly than any of the male reptilian warriors. Still capable of spitting a hot deadly poison at the eyes of their enemy, the new venom now virtually assured death to any soldier on the battlefield who confronted the reptilian females.

NO SENTIMENT

In his text Morning Sky continues the dialogue between Per and his pupil Matu. "And of course, Matu . . . the females were also more naturally vicious. When provoked to battle, the females did not permit logic or sentiment to interfere with their goal . . . total and complete victory was their end-all. The females were not fighting for glory or conquest; they were fighting for their world and their lives. When angered, no one was deadlier than the reptilian female. These factors changed the course

---

*Recent discoveries by biological scientists have shown that the venom genome is very ancient and preceded the evolution of reptiles by 100 million years! Venom has now been shown to have many physiological functions, and many new drugs are being developed from venoms. It is certainly not far-fetched at all to believe that venomous proteins may have had important functions in childbirth in certain creatures—and maybe still do!

of many battles between the races of Star Beings of our galaxy."

The advent of the female warrior had many unintended consequences and benefits. Since the females were used exclusively to administer the conquered territories and planets, they now were far more effective in that role. According to Morning Sky:

> And so too, Other World populations yielded to the presence of the reptilian female guards put in place to control the new governments. Hostile crowds were easily controlled by reptilian females who were armed with little more than long-bladed knives and spears. When puppet governments were installed no diplomat dared to challenge the authority of any reptilian female left in charge of the newly established administrations. The legends of the deadly potency of the venom in reptilian women were spread far and wide. Few beings of Other Worlds had not lost a friend or relative to the venom of a reptilian female.

For the kings, this allowance of female influence into the halls of royal power had more severe and unintended consequences. The queens, who had been administering all the colonies and conquered territories, had become powerful in their own right, and covertly they were not pleased to be dominated by the men when they were really the ones running the empire. They began to view the males as figureheads, while they, the females, really held the reins of power. It was not surprising, therefore, that they conspired to take over the rulership and to subjugate the males. Morning Sky says:

> By the time of Other World expansions, it was the Queens and their loyal female administrators who were the real center of power in the Empire. In any Empire run by a "secret power" figureheads are always the loudest and the most highly visible. The Empire is even given to believe that the issuance of commands comes solely from the figurehead. In truth, sometimes the figureheads even believe that they really are issuing the royal commands. But it is the person who actually sees to the execution of those commands who truly holds

the reins of power. And in every case, it was a female administrator who was responsible for the enforcement of Royal commands.

The queens began to push for more direct control of policy and for more visibility with the people. We learn from Morning Sky:

> With the new status of the Empire as a powerhouse in the stars, the female reptilian Queens began to press the throne for a more visible position in the ruling of the Empire. In order to avoid difficulties at home and to placate the Queens and the reptilian women administrators, the reptilian Kings grudgingly granted the Queens new responsibilities. The Queens became more visible, and became a greater part of the State ceremonies that the people always relished. Minor programs were handed over to the Queen and her loyal female forces . . . but in the control of the Empire, the Kings would never relinquish their authority. . . . It would have to be wrested away. . . . In the eyes of the King, the Queen of the Empire sat on the throne as the head female of the Empire. Her duties were very simple: it was her task to present to the other worlds of the Reptilian Kingdom and to Other Worlds of the Ninth Sector the very clear and emphatic impression that all of the females of the reptilian Empire were solidly and passionately behind their King. Even the Queen's High Court was ordered to present the same image to the worlds of the Ninth Sector. And since all females, including the Queen, answered directly to upper-level male representatives of the King, the King was persuaded that the Queen's role was one of grand illusion and little influence. To the King, the Queen was an ornament for the Court and a decoration for the Monarch to fawn over . . . her presence was purely perfunctory.

CROCODILE TEARS

Morning Sky continues his dialogue:

> The legend of the "Night of Tears" tells us the following, Matu . . . the daily early morning meeting of the King's Royal staff was called

to order. The affairs of the Empire were always the first priority in the morning. Members of the Royal Staff were surprised when the Queen entered the chamber instead of the King. Soldiers of her Royal Elite female guards followed close behind her. As the female soldiers lined the walls of the Royal Chamber, the Queen sat down, not in her chair, but in the King's chair! Several of the King's staff jumped to their feet and loudly protested her outrageous action. When the Queen's Elite Guard stepped forward, the males sat down and remained silent.

The announcement was quick and simple: The King had been assassinated in the middle of the night. The Queen herself had barely managed to escape the assassins. Were it not for her loyal Elite Guard, the Queen might not have survived the night. Though the male murderers were immediately killed, they could not be recognized nor could the source of the assassination plot be ascertained. In order to keep order, in order to prevent riot and pandemonium, the Queen had immediately seized control.

To avoid a coup by the unscrupulous unknown male power who must have been behind the assassination, the Queen issued commands to all female reptilian commanders and administrators to take control of their appropriate circles. To avoid a take-over by this unscrupulous and unknown male power, all males were to be removed from their positions of control . . . for the sake of the Empire! Until the Queen could reasonably insure the safety of the Empire and its people, the Reptilian realms would be run by the female administrators who were already in place. When the Queen was satisfied that peace and security were assured, she would relinquish authority to the King's heir apparent.

And so, the royal coup was complete. In the annals of Reptilian recorded history, this became known as "the Night of Tears." Clever Matu referred to them as "crocodile tears" as he listened to the story from Per.

2

The Empire of Death

THE QUEEN'S EMPIRE

The queen acted quickly to solidify her control over the Reptilian Empire. Morning Sky tells us:

> Over the course of the next few time periods, many of the highest level male commanders and administrators died under the most mysterious circumstances. . . . Descendants and heirs of the reptilian King were also mysteriously assassinated. High-level representatives of the King in key positions on other worlds of the Empire also died. The plot was ruthless and thorough.
>
> She assured the peoples throughout the Empire that she was in complete control, and there was nothing to worry about. Several of the assassinated male administrators and royalty were autopsied and traces of female venom were found in their bodies. The Queen explained this by claiming that male conspirators were now attempting to overthrow the Queen. She told the people that "the devious attempt to turn reptilian male against reptilian female would not work, the Queen would see to that." The Queen promised to lead her people through their time of crisis. The "Night of Tears" would not bring down the Empire, the Queen vowed to her people! "Your Queen shall not fail you," she promised them!

Meanwhile, she continued with the "housecleaning." All males who were even remotely related to the king by blood and all male aspirants to the throne were either found murdered or they mysteriously disappeared. The queen tightened the security for all military and administrative functions and placed them under strong female domination. Under the queen's leadership, the empire became an efficient and highly regimented operation. With all internal threats removed, the executive governmental apparatus was now under firm female control.

Externally, enemies of the empire, sensing weakness of leadership, were now emboldened to take advantage of the situation and attack the empire's outposts. Invariably, that was a huge mistake. The queen's armies fought back with renewed vigor and pushed the invaders way back, taking over new territories wherever they went. The male warriors, seeing the victories of the females, began to admire the queen's leadership and joined in the campaigns with enthusiasm, "for the glory of the empire."

Morning Sky says, "The Empire of the reptiles became a realm of complete and total female domination and control. Where once the reptiles had lived and prospered under the Era of the reptilian Warrior Kings, during the Dynasties of the Reptilian Queens, the Empire expanded as never before, and it leapt to the forefront as the most powerful of all of the Star Empires in the Ninth Realm of ERIDANUS. The fierce Empire of the reptilian NEKH Kings had become a nearly invincible Dynasty of NEKH-T Reptilian Queens."

MIND CONTROL

The advent of the queen's dynasty brought with it more reliance on drugs used to enhance military effectiveness. The queen charged her bioscientists to develop a drug to make her royal guards more fierce, ruthless, and violent so that she would never have to worry about being harmed or assassinated. She was already surrounded by the most able female warriors. This elite guard was called the Assassim, from which the word *assassin* is derived. Under the influence of a drug called *hashashim,* they were on a hair trigger, watching with keen observation all activity around the queen. It is fascinating how these Reptilian practices were carried through to their Nazi protégés in World War II many centuries later. German soldiers were issued a drug called Pervitin to maintain alertness and "wakefulness." It has been estimated that about two hundred million pills were given to the Wehrmacht soldiers during the course of the war. Pervitin was an early brand name for what now is called crystal meth, a form of the drug methamphetamine. Hitler himself used the drug liberally.

Drugs became an important component of the reign of the Reptilian queens. The elite warriors guarding the queen were known as the MAKH. These warriors were originally all males, but they were replaced with fierce female warriors after the Night of Tears. (Hitler was surrounded by a very similar elite military guard of specially trained warriors called the Waffen-SS, a corps that became enlarged as the war progressed.) The queens realized that there was a better way to control conquered civilizations than the "submit or be killed" doctrine. Too many captives chose the latter option, and consequently too many able-bodied individuals were wasted when they could have been put to work for the empire.

Morning Sky says, "In the Era of the Queens, it was an early matriarch who realized that the destruction of conquered populations was also the destruction of a potentially productive work force. Turning to the scientists of her elite forces, the MAKH forces, she instructed them to actively research and develop the science of mind manipulation. The early Queen had hoped that rather than destroy the dissenters, the MAKH scientists could find some way to 're-program' the minds of the conquered populations."

These early matriarchs began the research and development, and eventually the practice became refined and standardized. Morning Sky tells us, "At first, through the simple use of electromagnetic stimulation of the brain, the MAKH were able to create a 'reward and punishment' system that could be used to control the resistant masses. But over many millions of years of research and development, the manipulation of the brain was successfully accomplished, through many different techniques. From long-distance influence and control, to the immediate

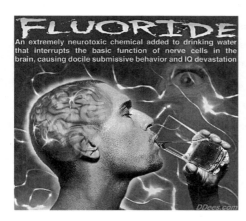

Fig. 2.1. Mind control through fluoridation

programming of minds in the laboratory, the MAKH mind-altering technologies became the foundation of the administrative programs put into practice on the newly conquered worlds."

THE EMPIRE OF SLAVERY AND DEATH

Morning Sky continues:

> The military forces of the conquered worlds were always the first subjects to undergo the re-programming of their minds. After their minds had been altered, the conquered forces obediently professed their complete loyalty and dedication to the Queen. Once tested and confirmed, all warriors and military forces of conquered worlds were placed into the combined warrior forces of the reptilian Empire. As newly dedicated soldiers of the Queen (TT-TT), they were trained to become the most vicious and skilled warriors in the Ninth realm, and were given some of the most advanced lethal weapons and death-dealing technologies. As a result of their training and the available weaponry, the warriors of the Queen's forces became the unquestioned champions in the delivery of Death on behalf of their Matriarch. The combined forces were known as the "Queen's Death," the mighty and invincible TT-TTKHAA, or more simply . . . the TAKH.

This was the initiatory stage of the development of Reptilian mind-control technology, which has since been used in all their conquered territories. It should be noted that the German and Japanese conquering armies attempted to brainwash the civilian populations of conquered countries using very sophisticated propaganda techniques. Also, there is evidence that they used mass drugging. According to an article in *Nexus Magazine* in 1995 by Ian E. Stephen titled "Fluoridation: Mind Control for the Masses," fluoridated water was first used by the Nazis in concentration camps. The article includes an excerpt by one Harley Rivers Dickenson from an Australian government document called *the Victorian Hansard, of August 12, 1987.* It says, "Repeated doses of infinitesimal amounts of fluoride will in time reduce an individual's power to resist domination by slowly poisoning and narcotising a certain area of the brain and will thus make him submissive to the will of those who wish to govern him." The excerpt says further "Both the Germans and the Russians added sodium fluoride to the drinking water of prisoners of war to make them stupid and docile." The Reptilian influence on these dictatorships is evident. Many other mind-control substances have been added to our food, water, air, and medical drugs. Noteworthy in this regard are the high levels of particulate aluminum being sprayed into the atmosphere all over the world. Recent atmospheric lab tests in Phoenix, Arizona, showed readings 6,400 times the toxic level! High aluminum levels in the brain are commonly associated with Alzheimer's disease.

The rulership of the conquered worlds was harsh and brutal. The female administrators in every colony were strict, by-the-book workers. The punishment for deviations from the rules was death, in many cases by instant execution. Morning Sky says:

> It is important to remember that the female representatives of the Reptilian Queen ruled with an iron hand. No one on any Other World could ever do anything without her approval. Any deliberate transgression was punishable by death. . . . As the Empire of the reptilian Queens grew to include thousands of Other Worlds, it became necessary to streamline the institutions of government for maximum efficiency with minimal maintenance. To avoid difficulties, a

single form of government was instituted throughout the Empire. The day-to-day duties of running the business and military affairs of the worlds of the Reptilian Empire were always handled by the SSS-T reptilian females who had been appointed by the Queen. Any and all female and male assistants to the SSS-T were held to strict and rigid measures of control. No detail, however minute, would go unscrutinized by the SSS-T female administrators. And no government was permitted to deviate in any way from the institutions set in place by the Reptilian Empire. Any and all assistant administrators to the female Head of State on the Other Worlds were known as the SSS-T-IM. They had to perform the duties assigned to them, exactly and without deviation. In fact, Matu, deviation from the standard meant death to those who committed the sin. In time, the term SSS-T-IM was applied to not only the assistant administrators but to the institutions themselves. In this way, Matu . . . the SSS-T-IM, or the "system" was born.

The very term applied to the Reptilian warriors who administered the territories contained the root for "death." They became known as the SAKH, which literally means "death from Reptilian beings." On this subject, Morning Sky says, "Again, over the course of many eons, as it has happened before, though the title is actually appropriate to the SSS warriors, people of Other Worlds came to use the term SAKH for both the reptilian warriors and the reptilian people. So too, the stars and the home worlds of the reptilian beings would become known as the SSAKH stars and the SSAKH worlds."

The word *SAKH* became part of the title of Reptilian administrators at every level. The queen became known as "Her Majesty, the Queen SAKH-SAKH." In the Reptilian language, the repetition of a title confers supreme respect. In her role as the commander in chief of the warrior force, she was addressed as SAKH-SAKH-AN. Heads of state on other worlds were known as the SAKH-AN, and assistants to the heads of state were called SAKH-I, or as a group they became the SAKH-IM, designating a plural term. Thus, the root meaning "death from Reptilian beings" was incorporated into every title, always reminding subjects about their fate for infractions. Instant decisions for life and death were made by military commanders. When this was layered on a populace that was already mind controlled to obey all laws, the result was a very efficient and thorough form of slavery. This is further evidence that the human organizations that exhibited strikingly similar tactics of administration of conquered peoples during World War II, such as the Nazis and the Japanese, were essentially under Reptilian control.

THE QUEEN MOTHER

We can begin to discern other Reptilian-derived human customs when we learn more about the queen's maternal and social conventions and traditions. The Reptilian species reproduces by laying eggs. The Reptilian female produces eggs, which remain in a sac until she decides to deliver them, fertilized by a male or unfertilized. Fertilized eggs become females. Unfertilized eggs become males. Over many generations of the matriarchy, the queens developed a procedure for choosing the male who would have the honor of becoming the father of the royal daughters. The early queens started hosting difficult athletic events exclusively for males. The winner would become the royal father. Reptilian females could store the males' semen until they were ready to conceive, and could thus bring forth their daughters at propitious times. Thus the queen would carry the semen of the triumphant male for her entire life and could give birth whenever she chose. Clearly, the Olympic games, which were also exclusively male contests at their origin, were derived from these Reptilian athletic contests. Unfortunately, in the Olympics, the victor had to settle for a simple laurel wreath instead of the royal bed.

For a long time after the advent of the matriarchy, it had been a custom to terminate the life of the queen when she could no longer conceive or administer, so that her duties could be turned over to a younger and more vigorous queen who could bear more royal daughters. Very often this meant that a daughter had to terminate her own mother. This system was changed by an innovative queen who realized that her sac of eggs and semen could be transplanted to the aging

*Fig. 2.2. Queen Elizabeth, the British Queen Mother,
lived to age 101.*

Queen Mother, who could then attend to the problems of maternity, while the new queen could focus on the administration of the vast stellar empire.* Thus, the important role of Queen Mother was born. Of this, Morning Sky says, "To take advantage of her experiences, however, the new Queen would always keep the Queen Mother on the Councils and Courts of the Empire, providing the Queen and the Realm with the benefit of her many years on the Throne. Pampered and waited on hand and foot, her every need fulfilled and her happiness paramount, the status of Queen Mother was not without its benefits."

---

*This system was adopted to avoid the necessity of having to terminate an aging queen in order to replace her with a younger, more vital one. This system was carried out while both she and her mother were relatively vital, so that she could live a long, productive life, and die a natural death. It was for this same reason that the MAKH scientists later found ways to extend the queen's life to amazing lengths. The important point was to avoid having "replaceable" queens. The more "immortal" she could appear to be to the populace, the more she would be respected and obeyed. They wanted to make her appear to be "divine." Motherhood interfered with that perception.

It is fascinating how the spirit of this tradition, if not the actual practice, seems to have somehow descended to the British royal family, in which the Queen Mother continues to be honored and revered although she is no longer required to perform the arduous duties of parturition. How did this unique and amazing convention somehow leapfrog to Earth from the distant stars of Orion? (See plate 3.) This argues for Reptilian influence in the British Empire, which will be explored in later chapters. Certainly no other earthly empire has been ruled by powerful queens who actually had a meaningful role in administration and were respected, even venerated, throughout the realm.

THE SEVEN SISTERS

To differentiate the two queens, the current sitting queen was known as Queen AYA, while the Queen Mother was called Queen BI. The administration and rulership of the empire was complex and difficult. The system for appointing rulers of the seven realms of the empire was very carefully designed to obtain maximum power, efficiency, and loyalty. In Morning Sky's book, Per explains this to his young disciple Matu thusly:

> To aid in the administration of the Empire, Queen AYA chose seven of her Princess Daughters to help her administer to the Empire. Though numerous eggs would be born, only the seven females who showed extraordinary abilities, incredible beauty, ruthless cunning . . . and a cold-blooded willingness to execute the will of the Queen . . . would be permitted to remain on the Central Worlds to assist with the running of the Empire. While the Princess Daughters assigned to Other Worlds could hardly be distinguished from their sisters on the Central Worlds, nevertheless, only seven were chosen to assist the Queen of the Empire directly. . . . As reptilian females, the Seven were SSS-TT. But as the daughters of Queen AYA, they were the "First and Foremost" UR females of the Royal Court, surpassing all other females except the Queen herself. As such, each

Fig. 2.3. The Seven Sisters. The Dance of the Pleiades
by Elihu Vedder (1885)

Princess was known as a SSS-T-UR. "The 'Seven Sisters,'" Matu
nearly jumped! "Master . . ." he had to ask. "The 'Seven Sisters' . . .
the 'Seven Sisters' is a name given to the stars of the Pleiades, Master,
not the stars of Orion. How can that be?"

"That is true, Matu," Per nodded with a devilish grin. "What you
do not know is that the original title of the 'Seven Sisters' was given
to the stars of Orion. The two shoulder stars, the two stars of the
lower skirt and the three belt stars were originally symbolic of the
Seven SSS-T-URs. On our world, at a much later date, the name
'Seven Sisters' was transferred to the stars of the Pleiades."

Although there was a royal court, the Seven Sisters were all-
powerful and acted as a supreme council of governance for the entire
empire, while also ruling their individual realms. Morning Sky says:

The seven Princesses, as the highest representatives of the Queen
had the power to administer death sentences to anyone they might

choose, for any reason they desired. They were the final judges of their realms. So too the Queen Mother had the right to execute anyone who did not serve her every need or who might interfere with her duty as the Queen Mother. Of course, the Queen herself had the power of administering death to anyone at any time for any reason. In short, Matu, all of the Royal Females had the power to administer death. Because of this, the people of the Other Worlds, and the reptilian people of the Home Worlds called the House of the SSS-B by another name . . . to them, it was the House of the SSS-B-AN Judges, the House of the SSS-B-K, and the House of Reptilian Death.

This cannot help but bring to mind the Queen of Hearts in *Alice in Wonderland,* famous for ordering "off with their heads" for any subjects who displeased her. Another very apropos quote from her in the book is, "I warn you my child . . . if I lose my temper, you lose your head." Perhaps the concept of whimsical death sentences administered by Reptilian queens filtered down to the consciousness of author Lewis Carroll somehow. He may have obtained it the same way as the idea of a Queen Mother occurred to the royal family.

THE DIVINE QUEEN

Because the reigning queen was so all-powerful, eventually she became invested with divinity in the eyes of her subjects. Morning Sky says:

Even in the Era of the Kings, it was accepted that the Void, the Great KHAA, which gave birth to all things . . . was feminine in essence. Only a female essence could give birth to the Universe. Emerging from the womb of the Void, the Life of the Universe was born. When the Queen rose to the throne, because of her great power, it was soon believed that the reigning Queen of the Empire, AYA, was the ultimate representative and embodiment of the "Great Void" itself:

She was the One and Only manifestation of the Grand Creatrix.

She was the Ultimate Heavenly Mother.

She was Eternal, She was Omnipotent and She was Omniscient.

She, Queen AYA, was the embodiment of the Void.

She was the One from whom all things came and to Whom all things returned. In the Empire of the SSS reptilian people, the Queen was the living KHAA itself. She, like the Great Void, was Life . . . and she was Death.

She became known as "Her Supreme Majesty, the Divine Queen KHAR."

3

Queen of the Stars

THE QUEEN'S FOUNTAIN OF YOUTH

In the early dynasties of the Reptilian queens, while the queen was still responsible for ruling the empire and giving birth to the royal offspring, the SSS scientists working with the MAKH development programs had uncovered a special nutrient for the queen, one that assisted her in several ways. Morning Sky says:

> Drawing on the well-known fact that special proteins in the blood of warm-blooded creatures assisted in producing the venom necessary for conception and child-birth,* SSS scientists began to develop extracts based on warm-blood nutrients. This very special nutrient was known as SMA. The liquid acted as an "enhancer" of the Queen's metabolism. It increased her energy levels, gave her more

---

*The venoms are proteins that functioned in the very early reptilian generations for both conception and childbirth. I assume they acted as some sort of hormones. Those functions no longer operating in faraway star systems, the proteins transformed, actually degenerated, slowly to venoms.

As the S-MA liquid was further refined and developed, other discoveries about its extraordinary properties were made. Continued use of the S-MA liquid, for example, increased the lifespan of the Queen. Through the careful refining of various strains of S-MA, it was discovered that the Queen's life could be extended well into hundreds of thousands of years. It also became evident that S-MA kept the Queen's bodily functions youthful. It was the Queen's "Fountain of Youth" and the "Cup of Eternal Energy."

stamina and actually added to her physical strength. . . . Here is another important fact, which you must know, Matu. In the language of the Orion people, the "S" sound . . . as a prefix . . . was a "causative." It literally meant, "it causes," it "makes happen" or it "makes go." Since in this case, the "S" precedes the term MA, the title of the Queen as the Royal Mother, S-MA literally means "makes go—the Royal Mother."

The soma drink, revered for centuries in Indo-Iranian myth and culture for its excitatory, energizing, and restorative powers, is clearly linked to this Reptilian drug. It was frequently mentioned in the Rig Veda and the Avasta. The soma juice was reportedly prepared from an unknown and mysterious plant, called the sauma plant. Candidates for its source over the centuries include ephedra, cannabis, and the *Amanita muscaria* and *Psilocybe cubensis* hallucinatory mushrooms. Soma was discussed extensively in the book *Food of the Gods* by Terence McKenna.

The quote by Morning Sky may be in error. It seems highly unlikely that the queen's life could have been extended to "hundreds of thousands" of years. More likely, this was intended to say "hundreds, even thousands" of years, which would still be extraordinary. In either case, this was an incredible scientific breakthrough.

The success of this program led the early queens to realize that bioscience was the key to the lasting power of the matriarchy and that the MAKH scientists were critically important to the continuing domination of the females. The queen eventually authorized the use of a much less potent version of the S-MA drug for the Queen Mother and the seven princesses. But it was expressly forbidden for anyone else. Any other person found to have the S-MA liquid in his or her possession was executed immediately!

But then, the SSS scientists created an even more astounding genetic development called the reanimation program. This process allowed the scientists to reanimate a dead person! As long as there was no irreparable damage to the body, they were able to bring the person back to life. The employment of this program also was expressly limited to the queen and her divine entourage. This extended the life of the queen even further. Now, to the populace, she appeared to be virtually immortal! And they were not finished yet, with each fantastic scientific development outdoing its predecessor.

The next breakthrough had to do with regeneration. The SSS scientists invented a system of regenerating body parts by taking cellular material from a weakened or worn-out body part and creating an identical healthy version that they could transplant to the queen. This would be analogous to stem cell procedures today. Eventually, they created several versions of the queen's body to supply worn-out body parts. These were essentially clones of the queen, although they were not animated. This program obviously had more to do with internal organs, which could be removed and replaced, than with limbs.

THE GENESIS SCIENTISTS

The crowning achievement of the MAKH scientists was the ability to actually transfer the consciousness of an individual into another body! Of this astounding accomplishment, Morning Sky has this to say:

> In one of the final phases of the S-MA program, the elite MAKH scientists, who were now known as "Genesis" scientists because of their ability to create and manipulate Life, were instructed to attempt to isolate and capture the "consciousness" of a being. It was hoped that if the "consciousness" could be captured, somehow it could be transplanted into another body. Remember, Matu, these were the very scientists who had been the developers of the mind-alteration sciences used so successfully in the population-control programs. Though the task was monumental and seemed to offer little chance of success, over millions of years and countless failures, the MAKH Genesis scientists were successful. Through tireless effort and sheer genius, a process was developed that allowed complete consciousness to be transplanted from one body to another. One of the difficulties encountered, however, was that the initial consciousness of the receiving body could not be completely eliminated without terminating the life of the body. As a result, after a

"consciousness" transfer, the new body was fully aware of two distinctly different personalities in its mind.

Amazingly, this is the precise plot of the new film *Self/less,* in theaters now as this is being written (July 2015). In that movie, the new young consciousness recipient, played by actor Ryan Reynolds, now animated by the consciousness of an older accomplished man with a terminal illness (Ben Kingsley), is still aware of the younger man's previous life and gets entangled in the problems of that life. Ultimately, he rids himself of the transplanted consciousness and reverts to his former life. However, the genesis scientists were able ingeniously to surmount that roadblock. Morning Sky says:

> To combat the potential confusion problems, the Genesis scientists were forced to add a secondary procedure to the transfer process. It was already known through the MAKH mind-control programs that thoughts and memories could be easily implanted into the brain of the target being. And it was also known that some memories could be eliminated in the "target." By merely enhancing the procedures, by intensifying the mind-erasure and implantation techniques, the mind of the receiving body in a "consciousness" transfer could be made totally receptive to a new consciousness. After the procedure, the receiving body would believe that the new consciousness had always been the original "consciousness" of the body. And what about the original "consciousness"? It would be relegated to the body's subconscious where it would occasionally surface as a very vivid dream or an inexplicable vision.

Perhaps, if the screenwriter of *Self/less* had been aware of this ancient Reptilian success story, he might have written a very different ending to his screenplay! Evidently, this procedure was intended only for the queen. We learn from Morning Sky:

> With the success of the MAKH consciousness transfer program, the Queen of the stars of Orion had the power to transfer her entire

consciousness into one of the regenerated ARRAN-BI bodies. Should the worst conceivable circumstances occur, should the body of the Queen be severely damaged, her consciousness could be completely transferred. Combined with the successes in the regeneration and reanimation programs, the Queen was able to extend her life-span beyond any lengths that had ever been imagined. When her subjects and the populations of the Other Worlds claimed that the Queen of the Empire was possessed of "Everlasting Life" . . . they were virtually correct. Because of the Genesis Sciences advances she had come close to achieving immortality. While generations of her subjects lived and passed away, the Queen outlived them all. And by restricting the most elaborate processes of "Extended Life" Sciences to herself, the reptilian Queen insured that she would live for millions of years and could remain the wisest, the most intelligent, and the most experienced being in her entire Empire.

THE KHAR-IM

Freed of the burdens of motherhood and of administering her empire and able to maintain a youthful, energetic body for millions of years, the queen sought diversion. She spent her days immersing herself in beauty and pleasure and in the acquisition of knowledge. Morning Star says:

> The Queen of the stars of ARRA-AN had the power and wealth of thousands of stars at her fingertips. She could do anything she wanted, she could go anywhere she wanted, and she could have anything she wanted. With such power and wealth at her disposal, the Queen made it her duty, and her responsibility, to pursue knowledge, to find wisdom, to collect the finest art treasures, and to amass the wealth of all of the cultures under her control. And most important of all, Matu, she made it her duty to enjoy them . . . to enjoy all of the pleasures of her realm. Her day was consumed in enjoying the delights of art, music, dance and culinary treats . . . and especially, she enjoyed pursuing and indulging in the joys of physical pleasure!

With all the males of the empire at her beck and call, the queen became very selective in the choice of her lovers. She created a male harem. We learn from Morning Sky:

Serving at the pleasure of the Queen were carefully selected reptilian males who had but one duty to perform . . . to pleasure the Queen in any way she chose. Artists, dancers, musicians and experts in physical pleasures, only the finest specimens of SSS masculinity were permitted to be with the Queen. If any should fail or falter, they were immediately terminated and cast aside, forced to live on a faraway world for the undesirables. But if they were obedient and faithful servants, if they were exemplary in their service to the Queen, they were treated as the Supreme Males of the Empire. Beholding to "Her Majesty, the Divine Queen KHAR," the males who were always at her side, were known as the KHAR-IM, from which the term "harem" may have been derived.

THE BREEDING PROGRAM

As to where these young men came from, Morning Sky tells us:

To serve as one of the royal KHAR-IM, young males were chosen for their physical beauty and their ability to pleasure the Queen. In time, the Queen asked her MAKH scientists to develop a breeding program that would provide the Queen with better and more beautiful KHAR-IM each generation. As the breeding program progressed, the males did, in fact, become more and more handsome . . . and under the training aspects of the program, they became more and more adept in the Arts of Passion. And remember, Matu, the most successful males provided the "seed," which was used to bring forth the Princesses of the Empire. This also served to produce reptilian Princesses who were the most beautiful women in the Empire.

Under the KHAR-IM program, some physical attributes that the queen had found undesirable were bred out of the KHAR-IM males.

Since youthfulness was something the queen found to be a desirable characteristic, KHAR-IM males were bred to have short lifespans. This assured the queen that all of her lovers would always be young and healthy. And even though males who were "long-lasting" in their ability to produce pleasure were desirable, the queen insisted that males in the KHAR-IM program be bred so that they would only have one or two "peaks" of sexual pleasure. Since the queen was capable of numerous peaks of pleasure, restricting the males to only one or two peaks ensured that the queen would have multiple partners during any of her times of pleasure. In this fashion, boredom would never set in for the queen.

The queen gradually realized that the breeding program was an ideal method of cementing female domination throughout the empire. It kept the males in a servile position, never questioning female authority at every level. Thus the male population was never threatening and never likely to launch any sort of coup or revolution. Morning Sky tells us:

> To keep the females in her service happy, she also extended the rewards of the KHAR-IM program to the most loyal and faithful helpers. Eventually all of the males in the Empire became subject to the breeding program. In time, all reptilian males of the Empire passed away at a much younger age than the females. Reptilian females would also be able to enjoy their own youthful partners, and because all males were only capable of one or two peaks, they could also enjoy multiple partners if they so desired. Youthful partners also assured the females that they need not be concerned with male egos that needed to go on and on about their great experiences.
>
> And the extension of the KHAR-IM program to the rest of the home worlds had other advantages. Keeping all reptilian males young prevented them from achieving wisdom and maturity, something that could potentially cause a problem for the Empire. Young and immature males do not challenge the basic precepts of the Queen and her Empire. And long life was unnecessary for reptilian males anyway . . . their purpose was, after all, but to serve the Queen and provide some pleasure for her loyal followers. . . . Eventually the KHAR-IM

program became a foundation stone in the ways of the SSS Empire. . . . These are but a few of the reasons why it was adopted.

Any and every technician, scientist, or individual who might be connected with Extended Life Programs were subjected to the MAKH mind-alteration programs. Any and all thoughts, which could be dangerous or threatening to the Queen, were completely eliminated, thoughts of total and complete loyalty and obedience were implanted. Through these safety precautions, the Queen could assure herself that the scientists and people in charge of any of the operations or procedures of the Extended Life Programs would do exactly as she wanted. Believe me, Matu, the Queen made sure that she would not be betrayed at any level . . . and in order to do this, she made full use of the MAKH programs . . . wherever and on whoever it was necessary to control. And you would be surprised at some of the people who were included in the MAKH programs.

THE QUEEN'S SECURITY

With all of this control and manipulation going on throughout the empire, the queen, of course, was very security conscious. Morning Sky explains:

To preserve the lives of high-level workers and administrators who were invaluable to the on-going systems of the Empire, the Queen commanded the use of simplified versions of cloning and re-animation to be used on key personnel. Vital commanders, administrators and assistants were included in the cloning and re-animation programs, and if their experiences and knowledge were important to the administration of the Empire, the consciousness transfer system insured that their "consciousness" would not be lost to the Empire . . . and particularly . . . to the Queen. To assist in keeping the SSS-T-IMs strong, much weaker versions of S-MA liquids were granted to the various important members of the Empire, with somewhat stronger fluids reserved for the sole use of the Royal Family. But the Supreme S-MA: it was strictly reserved for the Queen herself.

And . . . as a final measure of security for herself, Matu, the Queen subjected the Queen Mother . . . and her Daughters . . . to the MAKH mind control program. In this way the Queen felt that no one, not even her family, could ever have a single thought of rebellion or challenge to her Rule.

4
The
Alliance

THE NINTH PASSAGEWAY

The Reptilian Empire dominated the part of the galaxy that they referred to as the PESH METEN, or the Ninth Passageway. This is the major route for galactic commercial and visitation travel from the outer fringe of the galaxy to the central stars nearest to Alcyone, the Central Sun. It is the galactic version of the ancient Silk Road that traversed Asia from central China to Europe. This was the trade route that Marco Polo trod in his famous travels recorded in his book. It was also the route that the young Jesus was believed to have traveled in his pilgrimage to India. The Ninth Passageway runs through the heart of the Reptilian Empire. Morning Sky says, "The Ninth Passageway provided vital links to the Inner Worlds and the Outer Worlds. Travelers, whether on business or political missions, were constantly on the Ninth Passageway. Commercial vehicles, carrying precious ores and valuable treasures made their way on the PESH METEN. It was, without any question, vital to the security and welfare of the reptilian Queen's Empire." So it was understandable that the queen acted with alacrity when another fearsome empire threatened her hegemony over the Route 95 of the galaxy.

THE EMPIRE OF THE WOLFEN KINGS

Far away in the Sirius star system, long after the Reptilian Empire, centered in Orion and Draco, had risen to maturity and maximum conquest, a new species evolved to prominence. Morning Sky calls it the race of the Wolfen Kings. On a planet with three suns in the sky, one of which was the massive star Canis Major, also known as the Dog Star, a race of fierce, ruthless lion-maned beings with an ancient canine ancestry became dominant and came to be known to the Reptilians as the RRR. Morning Sky says, "As had happened on the world of the SSS reptilian people, the World of the Three Suns was soon dominated by the Wolfen Ones, in particular, one race that came to be known as the 'Golden Maned Ones.' These Conqueror Kings eventually created a 'One World Empire,' with trillions of beings forcibly united under the RRR banner."

In terms of ruthless violence, the Wolfen Kings far surpassed the Reptilian warrior class. In Morning Sky's book, Per says, speaking to his disciple:

Everything, Matu . . . everything revolved around war. Athletic events and competitions generally resulted in the death of the losers, while legal cases of contract violations were tried in Wolfen courts only if one of the complainants was not killed. Police shot speeders and traffic violators on site [*sic*] while prison populations were nearly non-existent. Generally, those who were locked up were simply in transition to their executions. In short, Matu, in the world of the Wolfen beings, either an individual obeyed the law . . . or he was executed. But the use of violence was not restricted solely to enforcement of controls on the general populace. While ruthlessness and cold-blooded cunning were generally rewarded with advancement in the ranks, oftentimes upper-level positions needed to be filled because of the sudden and unexpected death of the individual holding that position. In other instances, some high-level officials maintained their position because any potential challenger to his position also met with an unexpected death. It is a curious thing, Matu, that this very violent way of life assures that only the most cunning and deadly individuals end up in the highest positions.

Every aspect of Wolfen society was colored by preparation for war. Per continues to explain this to Matu:

The healing technologies were all designed with the intent and priority of healing and providing speedy recovery for Wolfen Warriors; communications technologies were designed and developed for the specific purpose of providing dependable and encrypted messages between Warrior forces in the field; transportation vehicles were developed specifically with the intent of providing quick and reliable movement in the battlefield; and food preparation and nutrition sciences were all based on the needs of the Warrior on the field. Honors in academia and science were always presented for achievements in the fields of military and conquest sciences. Entertainment was always oriented towards militaristic themes, as were the games provided for the young Wolfen children. . . .

And it should come as of no surprise to you, Matu, that the research and development of the sciences and technologies of Wolfen civilization were all oriented towards conquest. . . . In the world of the RRR Wolfen people, political debate was virtually non-existent. Everything and everyone served only one purpose: to further the military might of the Empire and the Wolfen Kings. Even the first steps into outer space were designed not for exploration, but for exploitation. Early astronauts that departed the home world of the Wolfen people were not sure that other beings existed on the other worlds of their solar system, but their ships were always designed for self-defense and conquest. The exploration of space was seen in a different way by the Wolfen people. As I said before, when they looked to the stars, they dreamed not of walking on strange new worlds and meeting strange new beings, but rather, they imagined themselves ruling as Kings of new lands and territories, of new populations and new forms of treasure. Other bodies in the sky were not to be reached for, they were to be seized. It is important to remember, Matu, that every aspect of Life in the Wolfen world, from daily work to home life, from the marketplace to the Empire, from personal life to public life . . . everything was oriented towards conquest, expansion, and obedience to the Throne.

DEADLY ASTEROIDS

Morning Sky continues:

Many civilizations of star beings developed and created starships, many of exceptional size and maneuverability. Most starships were huge round globes, the shape most efficient in the wide open spaces between stars and worlds. Constructed and fabricated of super-metals, these shiny and silvery ships were generally the vehicle most civilizations would develop when they learned to travel the stars. But here, Matu, here is yet another testimonial to the brilliance and cunning of the Wolfen Ones. Where most star races would develop and produce their starships from the supermetals of their worlds, the RRR produced their starships in a unique way. In the course of reaching for the stars, the Wolfen scientists began to develop methods to mine and exploit the natural resources of asteroids and meteorites of their solar system. Because of the highly unstable three-sun system, fragments of primordial worlds as well as newly destroyed planets were abundantly available. By burrowing into the core of the asteroids, instead of attempting to mine the surface, scientists were able to remove valuable and precious minerals in a far more productive and cost-efficient manner. What they had not anticipated, however, was that the mining process that hollowed out an asteroid would result in a shell that would become an extraordinarily deadly warship.

It was extremely simple and amazingly clever. By taking the remaining rock shell, often miles thick, and adding appropriate venting and exhaust ports, then by installing powerful star drives and death-dealing weaponry, the forces of the RRR Wolfen Kings found themselves in the possession of a warship that was easily and inexpensively produced . . . and . . . it was easily hidden from the enemy. While other star races created enormous starships that were laden with extraordinary offensive and defensive war weapons, the large silvery globes were easily detected. The hollowed out asteroid warships of the Wolfen Kings, however, could easily enter an alien solar system undetected. By hiding in the midst of other orbiting asteroids or simply by hurtling through the star lanes while emitting the "appropriate" gases, the AR ships could move quietly into targeted solar systems. At the appropriate moment, thousands of asteroid warships began their devastating attack. It should come as no surprise that most worlds and their military forces simply were caught off guard by the Wolfen warships. And this, Matu, was the brilliance of the techniques of war of the RRR Warriors. The methods were simple but effective. Stealth was the greatest tactic of the Wolfen Warriors. And the asteroid warship, christened the AR by the Wolfen Kings, became the power behind the space fleet of the RRR Empire.

The victories of the Wolfen Warriors were quick and decisive. Through the vicious and cruel tactics of the soldiers on the battlefield to the stealth maneuvers of the AR warships, the invasions by the Wolfen Star Forces were lightning sudden and devastatingly overwhelming. With these techniques, the expansion of the Wolfen realm was limited only by the number of Wolfen commanders available to lead the Empire's invading armies. Unlike the reptilians who re-programmed the conquered populations, the Wolfen Ones simply devoured any resistance . . . quite literally. . . .

The incorporation of subjugated armies into the invasion forces of the Wolfen Empire was difficult. Oftentimes military coups were attempted, almost all of them failed. Armies who remained with the Wolfen Forces often did so out of fear . . . but given a chance, they would abandon the battlefield, running for the skies in desperate search of escape. For this reason, and others, any and all invasions had to be led by Wolfen Commanders. This, in and of itself, was the only factor that prevented the wider expansion of the RRR Realms.

INFRINGEMENT ON REPTILIAN TERRITORY

The conquests of the Wolfen Kings had been exceptional in their expanse; no one seemed to be able to stop them. At a certain point, however, their conquering ways had taken them a little too close to the realms of the older and infinitely more powerful empire of the Reptilian queens. To the misfortune of the Wolfen Kings, their conquests had taken them to the very edges of the Ninth Passageway. The queen had not been totally unaware of their movement, but she had not moved to stop them . . . as yet. When they moved perilously closer to the heart of the Passageway, the Reptilian Queen could take no chances. As Morning Sky describes it, she immediately sent a dispatch to the Wolfen King.

"Cease and desist your wars and movement upon the Ninth Passageway. Yield or be totally destroyed!" Such were the words of the Queen. The Kings had, of course, heard of the Reptilian Empire and had had minimal contact with them, but they had not considered that their war campaigns had taken them within a range that might be perceived as a threat by the SSS Queens. The Queen of the SSS Empire had also heard of the Wolfen Kings. She had found their conquering ways reluctantly admirable, if not just a bit barbaric. Perhaps, if they had extended their Empire in a different direction, she would not have interfered with them. But they had not. They had entered her Realm . . . and she would tolerate no interference with her Empire. She was also aware of their potentially deadly and unpredictable behavior. Barbaric beings of this sort possessed a primitive mentality that could hardly remain consistent and logical. It was also likely that these beings may not have the wisdom to know when to cease their attacks. While this was a desirable trait for warriors, it was a trait not to be welcomed in one's enemies.

And at this point, Matu, we shall see the wisdom and extraordinary abilities of the Queen of the Reptilian Beings. In the communique sent to the Wolfen Kings, the Queen issued a threat of devastating retaliation if the borders of her Empire were violated.

But in an unexpected move, the Queen submitted an offer that was seldom extended to any potential enemy . . . the Queen offered an Alliance between the two Empires. And it was an offer that the Wolfen Kings could hardly reject.

This was a brilliant and well-considered move by the Reptilian queen. Since the male Reptilian population had been severely weakened by the policies of the queens and their daughters, the fierce and ferocious qualities so important in warfare were missing, since they were basically masculine qualities. While the female warriors were strong and effective, they simply could not exhibit those characteristics exclusively innate in the male gender due primarily to hormonal differences. It will be recalled that the queens had shortened the life spans of all males, so that only young and green male combatants could now take the battlefield. The queen reasoned that the inbred, fearless, and violent male Wolfen warriors could fill the void that now existed in the Reptilian military ranks, if they could be brought under her control.

WOLFEN FEROCITY

The barbarity and ferocity of the Wolfen warriors had become legendary throughout the galaxy. Morning Sky tells us:

It has long been said that if a Wolfen being does anything, he . . . or she . . . does it with a ferocity that is seldom seen in our galaxy. During the course of their evolution, it seemed as if the Wolfen Ones did not need to learn about violence or fierceness, quite the contrary; it seemed as if intense violence coursed through their veins instead of blood. If was as if they had been born from the heart of an angry primordial War God. Instead of a heartbeat, they were possessed of a drumbeat . . . a drumbeat of War. But because of this innate ability to be violent and fierce, the Wolfen Ones accomplished in a shorter time what many civilizations had taken millions of years to develop. On the World of Three Suns, conquest of natural enemies and competing species came easily to the Wolfen Ones.

Perhaps the most significant evidence of their barbarity was borne out again and again on the battlefield. Descending on their victims with the wrath of "dogs from hell," the Wolfen Warriors did not defeat their enemies; they destroyed their enemies. After the battle was over, while still standing in the blood-soaked fields, the Wolfen Warriors ripped open their enemies' tunics, exposing the flesh to the sky . . . and then promptly, and savagely . . . began to devour the flesh! The bodies of enemy soldiers who had fallen in battle provided the sustenance and the nourishment for hungry Wolfen Warriors. In short . . . the Wolfen Warriors ate their enemies!

Many frightening stories are told in the history of the World of the Three Suns, Matu. But none paint a more gruesome picture than those which describe the battlefield after a victory by the Wolfen Warriors. Can you imagine the horror of the sight? Smoke and mist mixing together in the twilight to create an eerie and surreal scene. Grunting and growls came from everywhere, the sounds of a wolf pack tearing at the flesh and devouring the meat. Sometimes the growling eating sounds are punctuated by the screams and cries of their victims. In the dim light just before darkness, large bodies that look like hairy lions are bent over, feeding on the innards of fallen soldiers. Their manes and bodies are covered in blood; they tear at the flesh with their teeth and raise their heads time and again to howl at their victory . . . those who have survived the onslaught of Wolfen Warriors never forget the horror of what they have seen. It is one thing to see your comrade fall in battle beside you . . . but to see him being eaten and devoured with such frenzy . . . that was something that brought nightmares to even the strongest and bravest soldier.

AN OFFER THEY COULDN'T REFUSE

The queen had, of course, heard all the stories. She realized that while she had the technology and weaponry to destroy the Wolfen kingdom, her empire would become indomitable and all-powerful if she could harness that masculine Wolfen power. She needed the unconquerable presence on the battlefields that they could supply. Also, she admired their asteroid battleship technology, which could nicely complement her own Death Star fleet. In her proposal to the Wolfen king, the queen offered to sanction the continued expansion of the Wolfen Empire so long as they stayed removed from the Reptilian Empire, especially the PESH METEN. She would give them an initial payment in the form of a shipment of precious ores to cement the agreement, which was extremely generous. According to Morning Sky:

> The Wolfen Kings would have the authority to use the name of the Queen in any political negotiations, and if it became necessary, the forces of the SSS Queen would support their every move in the stars. All enemies of the Wolfen RRR Kings became enemies of the Reptilian SSS Queen and her Empire. And finally, should the Wolfen Kings accept the alliance, the Queen would elevate the Warrior armies of the Wolfen Kings to the official status of Enforcers of the Empire, a rank higher than any of the armies of any Other Worlds, second only to the Elite Forces of the Queen herself. Wolfen Commanders would assume control of many of the key military forces of the reptilian Queen's armies and would have available to them the many resources and most advanced warships developed by the SSS War Sciences and Technologies. In short, the Wolfen Kings would have the power of the Throne of the Reptilian Empire behind them and at their disposal.

But the Queen exacted much in return, according to Morning Sky.

> In exchange for these extremely significant concessions, the SSS Queen demanded unhesitating loyalty and total obedience to her Throne. The Wolfen Kings would execute her every command, unquestioningly, unhesitatingly and with all of the force and fury that they could muster. The Wolfen Kings would immediately turn over half of the wealth of the entire Wolfen Empire to the Queen, and would continue to send her half of any future gains. The Queen would immediately become the Supreme Being and the Ultimate Power of the Wolfen Empire. All official ceremonies and royal

events would begin by addressing her power and by paying homage to her status as the Supreme Being. From the moment the Alliance was agreed upon, the King would relinquish his status as the most important individual in the Empire and would become known as the representative of the Queen. From the moment the Alliance was signed, no Wolfen King would ever hold on to the throne without a Princess Daughter of the Queen herself sitting by his side . . . and no Wolfen King could ever make any decision without the approval of the new Queen: the Princess Daughter herself. And she gave them one other extremely important benefit . . . she allowed them to remain alive!

The queen gave them a very short deadline to consider her offer, which was non-negotiable. The queen had made an offer that they literally could not refuse! The Wolfen Kings huddled and debated and wavered as the clock ticked. They notified the queen that they needed more time to make a decision. That was unfortunate. When the time ran out, the queen's forces descended on the Sirian headquarters of the Wolfens with a devastating display of power. They destroyed the Wolfen armies in a matter of moments, and all their starships. They were all totally obliterated! Also, they destroyed all the asteroids being prepared as warships in the vicinity of the invading Reptilian armies. The queen also used the amazingly accurate light ray developed by her MAKH scientists. Her commanders were able to identify some of the king's personal staff, and the light ray seemingly came from nowhere and burned out their brains from the inside out! And then, using their tried-and-true fifth column expertise, well-placed Reptilian spies destroyed some of the king's communications networks. It was a stunning exhibition of incredible power. The Wolfen Kings realized that they had no choice but to approve the alliance, believing that there might be future opportunities to sever the relationship and to free themselves.

But that calculation quickly evaporated, as the ceremony to celebrate the alliance gave the queen the opportunity to display the awesome technological power of the Reptilian Empire to the Wolfen populations on the various planets of their conquered star systems. Realizing how impressed the Wolfen peoples were with war technology, she used the occasion to demonstrate the latest and most potent weaponry in her arsenal to obtain the approval of the Wolfen people. As Reptilian warships flew overhead and fired their massive light cannons at empty steel vehicles, which were reduced to molten metallic puddles, warriors on the ground fired sound rifles at buildings to demonstrate their deadly sound technology. The buildings shook violently and crumbled. It was an awesome display, and those Wolfen people who had not been aware of the Reptilian invasion were now exposed to, and deeply impressed with, Reptilian power. Certainly, the Wolfen warriors became very appreciative of the tremendous military power that would now be at their disposal.

After the alliance documents were signed, the queen dispatched her favorite princess daughter to be her representative in the Wolfen royal court. It was not really a marriage; she was presented to the Wolfen peoples as the consort of the Wolfen king of kings, to help administer the RRR empire. Her real role, of course, was to make sure that the queen's dictates were scrupulously obeyed and that there were no signs of betrayal. In addition, her presence assured the Wolfen king that the queen would never attack the Wolfen Empire and thereby endanger her favored daughter. Certainly, the king knew what the consequences would be if she were harmed in any way. And of course, the princess had her own protective cohort of no mean military capability.

And so, Morning Sky tells us, "The Alliance was made. The Queen secured the fierce and vicious Wolfen Warriors for her star forces, while the Wolfen Kings received the backing and complete support of the reptilian Queen and her Empire. A 'marriage' had been made in heaven." The resulting empire comprising the Orion, Draco, and Sirius star systems was formed. The PESH METEN was now under the control of the alliance.

5

The Queen's Flagship

The armada of the alliance was awesome. The combination of the asteroid ships of the RRR and the huge ships of the queen's SSS armada, some as big as planetoids, created a fleet that was truly invincible. The queen's ships displayed amazing technology. They could travel anywhere, either in physical three-dimensional space or in virtual, seemingly "empty" space. The latter is really the space-time, or the etheric realm. Morning Sky refers to the former as "Real Space" and to the latter as "Universal Space." He says, "In 'Universal' space, there is no physical existence, there is no matter . . . it is the 'Breath of the Great Void' as yet unchanged or degraded to the world of physical things." Some would refer to this as hyperspace, or the fourth dimension.

The ships used different propulsion systems for travel in either medium. For Real Space journeys, they used "thrusters" much like our rocket ships. However, instead of using solid or liquid fuels to provide the push, they used light or electrical particles, which increased thrusting power exponentially. They also used wormholes for deep space trips. They were able to navigate to the entry points of the wormholes and then could cover millions of miles through the time domain instantaneously.

For travel through Universal Space, they generated an electrogravitational force to pull a point in distant space, which could be trillions of miles away in terms of Real Space, to the ship. Morning Sky explains it this way:

> Once the point has been pulled around the ship, the electro-magnetic drive is turned off. When space and time snap back to their original form, the point . . . with the ship inside it . . . is now at the point's original space and time. While the occupants of the ship would feel nothing, the space around the ship would seem to be flying by. Observers from a distance would see a sort of stretching of space that suddenly snaps back in a blur with the ship inside. This is the "pull" method but is severely limited to distances that have no obstructions.

The AR pilots of the asteroids had to be trained very differently from those piloting the SSS spherical craft. Morning Sky tells us:

> It is a compliment to the abilities of the pilots of the Wolfen AR that some confusion has arisen between the AT-EN Deathstar and the Wolfen Deathstar. Pilots trained to operate the AR Deathstar had learned that the asteroid warship did not handle quite like a fabricated starship. As a result, the Wolfen pilots had developed not only new techniques of interstellar navigation, but they had also learned to develop a unique "inner sense" that the Reptilian star-pilots in sleekly constructed craft had not been able to develop and acquire. Where Reptilian star pilots were trained for instantaneous response to instruments that monitored the space around them, Wolfen pilots had been forced to learn to operate their ship as if they were an asteroid in space, thus forcing them to predict where the flow of interstellar "waters" would take them. This required an immediate adaptation to the physics of the space that they were in, no small skill in outer space. Oftentimes, the pilots utilized the nat-ural dynamics of the new space by gliding on electromagnetic waves or solar winds. Because the AR pilots were essentially flying an asteroid, the most direct route to a target was often a path that took the AR ship in a very circuitous course that followed the interstellar

flow between stars and worlds. But as time-consuming and demanding as this type of flying might have been, it was precisely this flying technique that proved to be so deadly to their enemies. Solar systems were seldom suspicious of an in-coming swarm of asteroids, and if they were, they simply could not monitor every meteor shower that entered their system. The success of the Wolfen campaigns of conquest was based on this very simple premise: every asteroid was a potential warship . . . a warship that no one suspected. Wolfen pilots had become Masters at flying the currents of the "heavenly waters" between the stars and the solar systems, using the natural flow of space to attack their enemies. Reptilian pilots had become Masters of full frontal attack, breaking through the defense fields and electro-magnetic nets with such force that they could take direct lines towards the enemy. Technology was the strength of the Reptilian pilots, technique was the strength of the Wolfen pilots . . . when the two types of pilots were joined together in the armadas of the TAKH forces of the Queen of the Reptilian Empire, no star system was safe.

THE DEATH STAR

The Reptilian warships were huge, gleaming globes, fabricated out of special metals, armed to the teeth with deadly weaponry. As noted above, some were the size of small planetoids. These could be steered across deep space by specially trained celestial navigators. The massive dimensions and globular conformation permitted these warships to house sophisticated propulsion systems, heavy equipment, and large populations. For space travel, there was no particular advantage to sleek aircraftlike design, especially since these spherical ships could carry a very large complement of scout planes and fighter aircraft that *could* be used within the atmospheres of distant planets. More importantly, they really emulated entire villages, or even cities, with the ability to produce all the food and support items for the huge crew for trips across the galaxy that could take months or years, as measured on their native planets.

Fig. 5.1. The Death Star in Star Wars

Of particular interest was the queen's flagship. This was the largest of the globular spacecraft, the size of a small planet. Morning Sky refers to it as the Death Star, a "mighty starship, capable of death and destruction on a scale that was unimaginable to most subjects of the Empire." He says, "The completely fabricated globe is designed to be completely self-sufficient." He describes it further, saying:

In the upper quadrant of the enormous globe was an enormous dark concave depression that housed the huge light cannon, the main weapon of the Queen's AT-EN. By rotating the gigantic cannon towards its target, the AT-EN was capable of instantly vaporizing cities, regions, starships, aircraft and even small planets with its intense beam. The "Light" also had the ability to generate razor-sharp cutting rays that could slice through any ship and penetrating pin-point beams that could isolate a single individual on a distant world as its target for elimination. . . . Also housed in the "Light

Cannon" quadrant were "Sound Cutters" that had the ability to generate sound waves that could shake apart the molecular structure of most physical objects, stun living beings, and even produce a cutting and ripping beam. Sound waves could also be concentrated into flat beams that could be used to lift extraordinarily heavy loads by aiming the beam under the object and simply raising the beam itself.

This claim about the use of sound technology to impart antigravity characteristics to large, extremely heavy loads has been encountered before.* It is a popular theory as to how the pyramids and other huge monuments in Egypt were built. It adds another note of authenticity to this story.

THE AYE IN THE SKY

The appearance of the Death Star in the skies of conquered worlds had a tremendous impact on the populations, and it was viewed as the watchful eye of God. Morning Sky says:

> From a distance, the gleaming globe looked like an enormous eyeball, with a dark iris and a black pupil. As it rotated its enormous hull to target its victims, the AT-EN took on the appearance of a gigantic eye that was turning to look at its intended prey. . . . As the AT-EN loomed in the distance, the people of Other Worlds would look skyward and know that an emissary of the Queen, if not the Queen herself, was about to make an appearance. Immediately, they would begin to cry out her name . . . AY! AY! AY! In time, this cry would become universal in the Empire . . . AYE! AYE! AYE! . . . This is a story that everyone on the Other Worlds told their children. . . . To most subjects of the Empire . . . this was the AYE of the Divine One. Somewhere in the sky, hidden among the stars or in the clouds, the "AYE" of the Supreme Being was overhead . . . watching, always

---

*See *Secret Journey to Planet Serpo* by this author, published by Inner Traditions, Rochester, Vt., for more on this subject.

watching . . . waiting to rain down death and destruction on any people who had done something wrong. Any evil or crime would be punished with a wrath that could destroy the entire planet! While the story scared many a child, the meaning of the tale was very clear . . . the forces of the Queen were always overhead, always monitoring the activities of the people on the planet below. Though one could not always see the ship, it was there . . . somewhere!

And so, by the Reptilians mixing high technology with religion, the diverse peoples of the empire were kept in a constant state of apprehension and under control. In the new film *Eye in the Sky* (2015), Academy Award–winning actress Helen Mirren plays a British Air Force colonel who directs attacks by drones flying at twenty-two thousand feet in the sky, which are, of course, totally invisible to those on the ground. Because of powerful telescopic equipment mounted on the drones, individuals on the ground can be identified as targets based on computer face recognition technology! They, or a selected building, can then be destroyed by a Hellfire missile fired from the drone. So death and destruction can be rained down with precision from the heavens by the colonel, simply by giving the word, in the same way as the queens of Orion did with their "Aye in the Sky." Computer technology is also able to accurately estimate the range of collateral damage (CDE) around the target. In the film, the American Air Force pilot operating the drone from a base in Nevada is hesitant about pressing the trigger because a little girl nearby is within the range of the CDE. But the heartless colonel presses forward with the attack by altering the range of the CDE to make it appear that the little girl will not be harmed. In the end, the girl is, of course, killed. All of the amazing technology shown in this film actually exists.*

---

*According to IMDb, an online movie database (www.imdb.com) (accessed September 20, 2016), "The Reaper [is]—a Remotely Piloted Aircraft System (RPAS) which has been operated from RAF Waddington in Lincolnshire since April 2013. They are flown by serving RAF Officers that have undergone training with the Reaper Formal Training Unit (FTU) in the USA. The FTU is completed at Holloman Air Force Base, New Mexico, USA."

The Illuminati movie execs may have had a sinister purpose in showing this film, exhibiting this incredible technology to the American public. It warns us that anyone, even someone walking down a crowded street in Manhattan, can be identified by his or her face and assassinated by a laser shot from an unseen drone high up in the atmosphere—and the "kill button" can be pushed by someone half a world away! In other words, The "Aye in the Sky" of the queens of Orion has come to planet Earth in the twenty-first century! So, we had better be good little sheep, or else.

This concept of the "all-seeing eye" has been incorporated into the symbology on the reverse side of the U.S. dollar bill. On the left of the back of the bill, the eye is encapsulated into the capstone of the Great Pyramid of Giza, although the capstone is separated from the rest of the pyramid. It is surrounded by the Latin phrase *annuit coeptis*. William Barton, who designed the Great Seal in 1782, said that the eye is the "Eye of Providence," where "Providence" is meant to mean "God." Charles Thomson, who designed the final version of the Great Seal, said that *annuit coeptis* means, "He [God] favors our undertakings." However, this makes no sense since God cannot be encapsulated in a pyramid. Are we perhaps meant to understand from this that the Reptilians, who control the Illuminati who print our money, are telling us that *they* are "the eye in the sky," as was the queen of Orion, and they are always watching us, just like the queen who watched over her empire? Favoring this interpretation, we now have a satellite in orbit that can actually read license plates on automobiles that is sometimes called the "eye in the sky."

GEORGE LUCAS AND *STAR WARS*

By now the reader has no doubt noticed the several points of similarity between the book by Robert Morning Sky and the film *Star Wars,* conceived and written by George Lucas. Lucas, like Morning Sky, speaks of "the Empire" and how all-powerful it is as it seeks to crush a revolt by rebel forces. Furthermore, in the movie we cannot see the faces of the storm troopers behind their masks, or of Darth Vader, so they could very well be Reptilian. We do see how well trained and how regimented they are, just as described by Morning Sky, but we do know that the rebels are all humans. Nevertheless, most coincidental is the concept of the Death Star. The representation of this warship in the film is *identical* in all details to the royal flagship described in Morning Sky's book, which is also called the *Death Star*. It is highly unlikely that this is coincidence, since to my knowledge no sci-fi film before *Star Wars* had ever conceived of a planet-sized, spherical warship. And the name Death Star seems too unusual to have been invented by both the author and the director. Furthermore, the crawl at the outset of the movie tells us that the entire story happened "a long time ago, in a galaxy far, far away." That is basically true, although the contenders in the book are in the same galaxy. But it certainly was a long time ago. There's more. A main human character in the film is a princess. All of the Reptilian queen's daughters are referred to in the book as princesses. So the concept of royalty is endorsed in both the book and the movie. This suggests a direct line of descent to *Star Wars* from *A Princess of Mars* by Edgar Rice Burroughs, and the entire John Carter of Mars series of novels written by Burroughs in the early twentieth century. In fact, Lucas frankly admitted his debt to Burroughs in an article in the December 24, 1977, issue of "Science Fiction Review." He said, "Originally, I wanted to make a *Flash Gordon* movie, with all the trimmings, but I couldn't obtain all the rights. So I began researching and found where [*Flash Gordon* creator] Alex Raymond got his idea: The works of Edgar Rice Burroughs, especially his *John Carter* series of books." In the article, "The Cinema Behind Star Wars: John Carter" on the Star Wars website, written by filmmaker Bryan Young, he says, "That style of episodic storytelling in the John Carter books and movie might be the biggest influence on the *Star Wars* saga. The original novel in the series of Martian Chronicles was published serially in the *All-Story* pulp magazine beginning in 1912 and created the cliffhanger structure that is vital to *Star Wars*. The books maintain that breakneck pace. Reading those stories or watching the movie, it's apparent that George Lucas was true to his word when drawing his inspiration from the *John Carter* series." The article says further that Princess Leia was a direct recast version of Dejah Thoris, the original Princess of Mars.

Another web article written March 2, 2014, is titled "Why John Carter of Mars is the Original Star Wars Film."

But Burroughs himself was no simple fabricator of stories created from whole cloth. Like H. G. Wells, he was a prophet, and appeared to have a similarly powerful crystal ball. According to *American National Biography Online,* "Burroughs predicted the invention of radar, sonar, television, teletype, radio compass, the automatic pilot, homing devices on bombs and torpedoes, genetic cloning, living organ transplants, anti-gravity propulsion, and many other concepts deemed totally fantastic in his time." Perhaps Edgar Rice Burroughs knew more about the queens of Orion than anyone realizes.

Overall, the entire premise and scenario of the movie portrays a struggle between the people of a star system who value personal freedom and human values against those of another system who are cruel and ruthless, although all-powerful in that segment of the galaxy—precisely the nature of the opposition between the Reptilian Empire and a hopelessly outclassed human civilization. This will be discussed in greater detail in the following chapters. Unfortunately, the date that Morning Sky's book was published is not known. It is a rare book and very difficult to obtain. There is no publication date in the book. Consequently, whether it preceded the release of *Star Wars* in 1977 cannot be determined. But it seems obvious that somehow George Lucas had somehow become cognizant of the ancient Reptilian Empire, and the human-Reptilian conflict.

There seem to be quite a few similarities between Morning Sky's book and Lucas's film, and other watchful thinkers and writers have noticed other examples of characters and incidents in *Star Wars* that seem to be from more than the realm of just science fiction. For instance, David Icke, in talking about the "third eye," says, in his book *The Children of the Matrix:*

> Sometimes this middle eye is called a *dracontia* 4 and the eye in the centre of the forehead in the ancient stories of the beings called the Cyclops may well relate to this, too. Credo Mutwa and modern abductees describe how the most "royal" and senior reptilians, the Draco, have horns. Some look like Darth Maul in the *Star Wars*

movie with the nodules or horns around his head. So much truth is told as fiction through Hollywood movies, both by those trying to get the story out and, overwhelmingly, by those conditioning humanity for the open appearance of these beings in the years to come. In my view, George Lucas of *Star Wars* is among the latter.

Others have said the same about George Lucas. Author Angela Pritchard, in her article "The Inter-Dimensional Entities Behind the Dark Agenda That's Taking Over the World," which is available on her website (belsebuub.com), says:

In *Star Wars* the evil Sith use the dark side of "the force" (which is basically universal energy) for power and malice, whilst the Jedi use the force in line with love and cosmic principles. . . . Individuals can both "go to the dark side" as Anakin did, and also repent and return to the light like Darth Vader. Demons can appear in the astral realm as human, or part creature, which reflects their hideous, bestial nature in which they have fortified the animalistic egos. But demons and black magicians are not silly monsters; they are people who have awakened in evil and this kind of awakening brings a knowledge of darkness, which can give them an intelligence and power beyond what any sci-fi movie could do justice to. As these films portray, these entities are humans or were once humanoids who have "gone to the dark side" and are working according to a hierarchy of evil to control and infiltrate society.

Conversely, Lucas is identified under the heading "The Good—Promotes the Truth" in the online article "The Good, the Bad and the Ugly in Ufology." An entity known as Baktar supposedly channeled the information in this article. Baktar says about Lucas, "He had ET contacts of a positive nature, especially from the Federation, that were mostly astral, in dreamtime, but also on occasion physical, and these inspired *Star Wars*." From all of this, it can be deduced that perhaps *Star Wars* is a modern fable that hides a historical reality. This possibility will be further elucidated in the next chapter.

◻
Star Wars

The history of Reptilian habitation on planet Earth is long, convoluted, and complicated. Only a very few researchers and writers have tackled this remote subject, basing their information on a variety of obscure sources, much of it from paranormal investigations. Literary research alone cannot give us this information. But when reports from abductees, ETs themselves, and people who have had actual firsthand experiences are added into the mix, the real story begins to emerge. Of all the researchers and writers best known for this project, four stand out by reason of channeled information, ET contacts, and/or interviews with experiencers and shamans or inheritors of tribal wisdom passed down for countless generations. In this category are David Icke, Alex Collier, Wes Penre, and Bruce Alan DeWalton, better known as "Branton." But only one person emerges whose knowledge is almost completely based on personal experience. Stewart Swerdlow has led an amazing, one could even say "unreal," life, more properly told as a sci-fi movie than a description in a book (see appendix B). It seemed to me that the best way to approach telling this story is to rely primarily on Swerdlow and to fill in supplementary or complementary information from the other writers to round it out. Swerdlow's most comprehensive, detailed treatment of this subject can be found in his book *True World History: Humanity's Saga,* published in 2014. As of this writing, this book is available on Amazon.com.

In the preface to his previous book, *Blue Blood, True Blood,* Swerdlow dives right into controversy. He says, "As far as the history of this planet is concerned, you can consider that everything you ever learned is a complete lie. All history and science books are rewritten to accommodate the agenda of the controllers of this planet. . . . My information comes from my Montauk Project indoctrinations, experiences, conversations with scientists involved in Illuminati programs, communications with alien and interdimensional beings whom I met at various government projects, and through the probing of my own Oversoul."

Swerdlow's history of the Earth is rather fantastic and is bound to be controversial, especially as regards the age of the dinosaurs. Swerdlow claims that they appeared here about 1 million years ago. Radiometric dating of the earliest rock formations containing dinosaur fossils is said to establish the fossils as 230 million years old. It is believed that the dinosaurs all became suddenly extinct 65 million years ago. This is a case of paleontology versus Montauk Project anthropology. Various accepted dating techniques are not infallible and have been shown to be in error on several occasions. It does seem difficult to believe that these creatures roamed the planet undisturbed for 165 million years, long before humans appeared. And yet, recent discoveries show human footprints side by side with dinosaur tracks.* There has not been even a smidgeon of evidence about the evolution of dinosaurs. There were no animals that we know of that could have possibly preceded and evolved into those gargantuan creatures. But when we are told by Swerdlow that the Reptilians brought their own animals with them to this planet, suddenly it all makes sense. And, as will be seen, Swerdlow offers at least a believable reason for their abrupt disappearance, while paleontology has no explanation.

THE RULERS OF THE GALAXY?

Right at the outset, Swerdlow's information tosses out such revered and hallowed anthropological authorities as Charles Darwin and Alfred Russell Wallace. The Darwinian theory of evolution has no place whatever in this story. The celebrated voyage of the HMS *Beagle* can now

---

*Dinosaur and human footprints side by side were unearthed at the Dinosaur State Park, on the Paluxy River, near Glen Rose, Texas.

be viewed as simply an adventurous pleasure cruise by a bored English intellectual and Darwin's vaunted hypothesis as so much unproven speculation squeezed into a theoretical framework. To this day, although accepted by scientists, it remains only a theory, now being "intelligently" challenged by the intelligent design advocates. Swerdlow's version of prehistoric cosmology begins about ten to twelve million years ago (Earth time). At that time the Reptilians inhabited the Draco star system, which consisted of numerous planets. From Earth, the stars in Draco undulate through the heavens, describing a snakelike path in the northern sky, ending up between the Big Dipper and the Little Dipper, and are considered to be in Ursa Major. The best-known member of the constellation is the bright blue-white star Alpha Draconis, or Thuban, which means "head of the dragon." Thuban was the northern polestar around 3000 BCE and is widely believed to be the home star of the Draco Reptilians, although there are eighteen other major stars with planets in the Draco system.

The Draco are allied with the Reptilians in Orion and Rigel, forming the Draco-Orionite Empire, and with the Sirian Wolfen kingdoms. They are an aggressive, warlike, tyrannical species not at all interested in peaceful coexistence, but only in the domination and enslavement

Fig. 6.1. The Draco constellation

of other civilizations. They have had space travel technology from their earliest days and have roamed the galaxy, easily conquering the less developed races they have encountered. Swerdlow says that it is not known how any civilizations came to this galaxy. He speculates that they might have all come from a parallel universe, or another dimension, but it is known that the Reptilians were the first to arrive. That seniority, they believe, entitles them to whatever galactic real estate they want. Also, their DNA does not change. It has remained the same since they first appeared. This, they believe, indicates that they are already perfect and do not need to improve genetically. These beliefs further bolster their contention that they were destined to rule the galaxy. If that is not enough, they can always invoke the "might makes right" philosophy to justify their conquests, for they are a race of mighty warriors.

THE LYRAN DIASPORA

The humanoids in this galaxy were, at that time, concentrated in the Lyran star system, where they had established peaceful and advanced agricultural communities on several planets, and they traded with each other. The Lyran star cluster was the home base for humans in this galaxy. Swerdlow tells us that the Lyrans were seven to eight feet tall and primarily blond and blue-eyed. When the Draco-Orionites became aware of the Lyrans, they pretended friendship while they took stock of the riches of their empire. This was the first contact between Reptilians and humans in this galaxy. In his book, *Defending Sacred Ground,* Andromedan contactee Alex Collier describes that first contact.

> I want to talk to you about Lyrae and how the human race colonized our galaxy. Based on the age of the Suns and the planets in our galaxy, it was decided that the human life form was to be created in the Lyran system. The human race lived there for approximately 40 million years, evolving. The orientation of the human race in Lyra was agricultural in nature. Apparently, we were very plentiful and abundant, and lived in peace. Then, one day, a huge craft appeared in the sky. A large ship came out of the huge craft and

approached the planet Bila, and reptilians from Alpha Draconis disembarked. Apparently, the Alpha Draconians and the Lyrans were afraid of each other. I told you before that the Alpha Draconians were apparently the first race in our galaxy to have interstellar space travel, and have had this capability for 4 billion years. Well, when the Draconians came and saw Bila, with all its abundance and food and natural resources, the Draconians wanted to control it. There was apparently a mis-communication or misunderstanding between the Draconians and Lyran humans. The Lyrans wanted to know more about the Draconians before some kind of "assistance" was offered. The Draconians mistook the communication as a refusal, and subsequently destroyed three out of 14 planets in the Lyran system. The Lyrans were basically defenseless. The planets Bila, Teka and Merok were destroyed. Over 50 million Lyran humans were killed. It is at this point in history that the Draconians began to look at humans as a food source. This is how old the struggle is between the reptilian and human races.

As noted in the introduction, after the Draco destroyed three planets, the Lyrans fled to other star systems. Swerdlow says that the fleeing Lyrans founded 110 colonies in other star systems. Alex Collier says in *Defending Sacred Ground,* "As the human race fragmented, the races moved, traveled, and settled many different planets in many systems as space travel evolved. The human became aware of other planetary civilizations in these systems. Different cultures met and grew. Belief systems clashed or spread. New thoughts of Philosophy or technologies came into being. Mankind was evolving. A very strong social community developed between all in [from] the Lyra System." This community became the Galactic Federation of Light.

When the Lyran refugees came to our solar system, they colonized two planets, Mars and Maldek. According to the Swerdlowian cosmology, at that time, Earth was the second planet from the sun and Venus did not exist. Consequently, Mars was third in line, and Maldek was fourth. Maldek was a very large planet with a highly livable atmosphere and was perfect for human habitation, as was Mars. The Martian

Maldek- the planet that was destroyed

Fig. 6.2. The destruction of Maldek

atmosphere was also ideal, and there was plenty of oceanic water, as on Earth. Swerdlow says that Mars had seasons then, so we must assume that the axis tilt was comparable to that of present-day Earth. On the other hand, Earth was then a water planet, completely covered by one huge ocean.* Even the atmosphere was dense water vapor, compared to only about 1 percent today, so it was not breathable. In addition, in that period, Uranus was farther out than Neptune, and Pluto did not exist. We are told that the Lyran humans lived peacefully on Mars and Maldek for "many millennia" and, no doubt, visited and traded with each other, since they both had spacefaring technology.

THE ICE COMET ATTACK

In their galactic travels, ever on the lookout for new worlds to conquer, the Draco eventually discovered the Lyran habitations on Mars and Maldek. Still considering humans as their enemies, the Draco designed

---

*We now know that there are many water planets in the galaxy. Our astronomers have positively identified one such planet, named Gliese 581C.

a plan of attack. They had evolved an amazing technology for use in their star wars. They were able to hollow out ice comets and meteors. They created small black holes to pull the comets under directional control, and so were able to use them as weapons. They launched a large ice comet at this solar system. As it passed Uranus, it caused the planet to flip on its side so that it now rotates horizontally,* with its axis tilt at 98 degrees. According to an article by Andrew Fazekas published in the *National Geographic News* on October 11, 2011, "The widely accepted theory for how Uranus got knocked over is that a rogue Earth-size planet slammed into the ice giant billions of years ago. That lost world was mostly likely destroyed on impact." But the twenty-seven known moons of Uranus still rotate around its equator.

Zecharia Sitchin explains it this way, "In simpler words, it means that in all probability the moons in question [of Uranus] were created as a result of the collision that knocked Uranus on its side." In press conferences the NASA scientists were more explicit. "A collision with something the size of Earth, traveling at about 40,000 miles per hour, could have done it," they said. According to Gene Moscoli, J.D. on the website ScienceIQ.com, scientists are split as to why Uranus rotates horizontally. A popular theory is that Uranus collided with a large planetary body in the early solar system that, in effect, knocked it on its side.

The comet then passed very close to Maldek, which created enormous electromagnetic stress on the planet and caused it to explode. Many of the Maldekians had already taken refuge on Mars as they saw the comet approaching. But most of the inhabitants of Maldek were wiped out. Fragments of the destroyed planet created the asteroid belt. Some of the fragments were captured by the strong magnetic pulls of the gas giants Saturn and Jupiter and became moons of those planets.

As the comet passed close to Mars it wreaked havoc with the planet's magnetic field, which had the effect of stripping off some of the

---

*This means that the poles are now parallel to the plane of the solar system, whereas with Earth and the other planets, the poles are perpendicular to the plane of the solar system. So, the planet doesn't rotate left to right like Earth. It rotates up to down. For forty-two of its years, the south pole directly faces the Sun, and for forty-two years the north pole faces the Sun.

atmosphere and vaporizing the oceans.* This killed many and forced the survivors to retreat underground, along with the transplanted Maldekians. In addition, the Martian orbit was pushed farther from the sun. So, amazingly, the deadly ice comet achieved its terrible purpose of destroying the human civilizations of both Maldek and Mars! It was an astounding attack when one considers that the comet could only have accomplished its destructive effects on those two planets if its launch was timed in perfect coordination with the orbits of both bodies. This required highly sophisticated astronomical expertise. It seems that the Reptilians had become very experienced in this type of galactic warfare.

Referring to this heavenly body as a "comet" is very misleading. While it may have acted like a comet in terms of its intrusion into our solar system, there is now clear evidence that it was actually a planet, comparable in size to Earth. Technically, Swerdlow is correct in saying it was a comet. But he then claims that this comet ultimately became the planet Venus, a fact that seems borne out in Central American mythology and by famous theorist Immanuel Velikovsky, author of *Worlds in Collision*. This makes sense because only a body of that size could have caused such drastic perturbations on such large planets as Uranus and Mars and also on Earth, as we will see, and destroyed a planet the size of Maldek. Velikovsky claimed that Venus became a comet after it had been ejected from Jupiter. This would contradict Swerdlow, who claimed that the ice comet entered our solar system in the orbit of Uranus, which would suggest that it probably originated in the Kuiper Belt. Although that seems more likely than the Jupiter ejection theory, it would still be very rare for an object of that size and with a perfect globular configuration to inhabit the Kuiper Belt, or even the Oort Cloud. The more one considers this phenomenon, the more likely it appears that this "ice comet" may have been an actual planet that

---

*In the film *Total Recall* (1990), starring Arnold Schwarzenegger and based on a short story by Philip K. Dick, "We Can Remember It for You Wholesale" (1966), rebels in an underground colony on Mars discover ancient terraforming technology, and they set it in motion. As it cranks up, it begins to restore the Martian atmosphere and makes it breathable. This correlates with Swerdlow's claim that the Martians left to colonize Earth, and therefore must have left the terraforming technology in place, but unused.

was "stolen" from its orbit around a distant star and brought here by the Reptilians. But regardless of its origin, there is extensive astronomical and mythological evidence that the planet Venus was indeed a newcomer to our solar system and was probably Swerdlow's ice comet.

THE ICE PLANET ENCOUNTERS EARTH

In view of the above, I believe that we are now justified in referring to Swerdlow's ice comet as the ice planet. As it continued on its destructive trajectory, it next arrived in the vicinity of Earth, where it appeared to slow down and went into orbit around Earth. Actually, it became a mutual orbit, which again testifies to the comet's huge size. Earth began to rotate more quickly, and the comet pulled off much of the water, which vaporized in space. An atmosphere developed around Earth, ice caps formed at the poles, and landmasses emerged as the water was removed. Eventually the ice planet nudged the Earth farther out and took over its orbit. The Earth now settled into its position as the third planet from the sun and continued its rapid rotation. The two largest landmasses that rose out of the oceans ultimately became Lemuria and Atlantis. With its new atmosphere, its more moderate climate, and its new continents, the Earth became very inhabitable. Since Venus was now close to the sun, its ice melted and formed the cloud cover still visible. In the end, this entire operation gave the Reptilians a shiny new planet on which to dwell in this solar system. Therefore, all in one stroke, the Reptilians decimated their ancient Lyran enemies on Maldek and Mars and created a home for themselves in the high-rent "Goldilocks" district of the Sol system! This had to be the neatest trick ever in cosmological evolution. But apparently, for the Reptilians, those movers and shakers of worlds and would-be rulers of the galaxy, it was business as usual.

PLANETS AS SPACESHIPS

In reconsidering this entire event, a completely new explanation presents itself. Swerdlow contributed a major clue when he said that the Reptilians had developed the technology to hollow out meteors and

Fig. 6.3. The Death Star firing

comets and use them as weapons. We have already seen that they had the capability of fabricating globular planet-sized spaceships called Death Stars. But now we learn that the Reptilians also had the technology for using actual planets as spaceships, which they had probably learned from the Wolfen people! Evidently, the Reptilians found a likely uninhabited candidate planet somewhere in the galaxy, probably in Draco, and hollowed it out.* They then moved into its interior and essentially turned it into a spaceship under intelligent control. It truly became a natural Death Star, thus complementing their already existing fabricated Death Star fleet! It is very likely they brought with them a complete ecological system along with living dinosaurs, their primary food source, somewhere in the bowels of the planet. They then drove it across space to the Sol system. It accumulated an ice cover in its journey across the galaxy. Living comfortably in the interior, they were not

---

*Our astronomers have now identified many planets in our galaxy that are not in solar systems centered around a sun or star. Apparently, they remain warmed from within, and they continue to stay alive as they wander aimlessly through the galaxy. They are referred to as "rogue planets."

exposed to the radiation, extreme temperatures, and other hazards of space travel. They were thus able to guide the comet to destroy Maldek and cripple Mars. Very possibly, they fired some sort of super weapon, perhaps a particle beam, at Maldek as it came near. This was probably the very same technique that they used to destroy Bila, Teka, and Merok in the Lyran system. Then, as the comet approached the sun, they slowed it down and drove it into orbit around Earth, and somehow pushed Earth farther out into a new orbit. As Earth dried out they prepared it for habitation, traveling back and forth from the ice comet, now Venus. Living in the interior of Venus, they were able to remain away from the intense heat on the surface.

From this, we can see that George Lucas probably did have the whole story, and perhaps that is why *Star Wars* struck such a popular chord. Maybe, just maybe, those audiences who stood up and cheered at the premiere of *Star Wars* at Grauman's Chinese Theatre in Hollywood in 1977 were on Maldek or Mars in a previous incarnation, and they remembered how they stared up helplessly at the sky as the ice planet loomed ominously above and approached. And that's why they cheered when Luke Skywalker fired the fatal shot that blew the Death Star to smithereens.

PART II

Reptilian Colonies
on Earth

From Genesis to the Roman Empire

7

Genesis

Now able to use Venus as a base of operations in this solar system, the Draco were ready to begin colonizing Earth. However, Venus was too distant for frequent trips. They needed a more convenient encampment from which to terraform Earth with flora and fauna. They decided to create a moon of Earth. But instead of using an existing sphere, as with Venus, they constructed an artificial planet. Swerdlow says:

> The Moon is an artificial object and it is hollow. When a sonic resonance is sent to the surface of the Moon it pings similar to glass like a hollow object. It does not thump like a solid object. The Moon does not spin or rotate; it is a fixed object with one side always facing the Earth. The Moon's orbit is mechanically fixed and needs no corrections. It stays in the same layer of space due to mass and gravitational pull. It is a vehicle parked in space like a satellite and without a magnetic field. The Draco colonized Earth from this vehicle.

Presumably, the Draco were able to transfer the entire ecosystem that they brought with them from Draco to the moon, so that it could then be transferred piecemeal to Earth. The dinosaurs were particularly important because the Reptilians relied on them as a food source. They placed the moon at the precise distance that permitted it to be viewed from Earth as exactly the same size as the sun. This made it possible to use solar and lunar eclipses as timing devices.

The Draco began colonizing the huge mid-Pacific continent of Lemuria about one million years ago. As the first race to occupy the Earth, the Reptilians considered it their planet. There were no humans on Earth for hundreds of thousands of years. The human refugees from Lyra, both Martian and Maldekian, continued to live underground on Mars during that period. The Martian atmosphere was too thin to support surface habitation. Meanwhile, the 110 Lyran refugee colonies had formed an alliance to join forces in defense against continued Reptilian attacks. They referred to this organization as the Galactic Federation of Light, or the Collective, and they remained interested and involved with the fate of the human Lyran expatriates throughout the galaxy. The Federation members, by combining resources, successfully repelled Reptilian attacks on their adopted planets. Only three former Lyran groups refused to join the Federation. These civilizations just could not adapt to their new refugee status and sought to re-create the lost glories of the old Lyran constellation. They were considered to be extremists. One of these three was the Atlans, inhabiting a planet in the Pleiades. The Pleiadians viewed them as troublemakers since they contributed nothing to the Federation. They petitioned the Federation to resettle this group in another star system. Since the Atlans were known to be courageous and unafraid of the Reptilians, the Federation decided to move the Atlans to Earth. They reasoned that if the Atlans survived such a direct provocation to the Reptilians, they would constitute a foothold on the Earth and could be the first line of attack against the Reptilian colonists on the Earth, which could then be supported by other Federation forces later. This might make it possible to eject the Reptilians entirely from the Sol solar system. In other words, the Federation moved these uncooperative slackers to the front lines to get them involved in a big way in the struggle against the Reptilians. It was a brilliant strategy! The Atlans colonized the mid-Atlantic continent, which then became known as Atlantis.

Meanwhile, there were conflicts between the two underground civilizations on Mars, and the Martians petitioned the Federation to remove the Maldekians to another planet. The Federation viewed this as another golden opportunity to surround the Reptilians on Earth with motivated Reptilian opponents. The Maldekians had suffered the extreme trauma of losing ancestors and friends in the brutal Reptilian destruction of their home planet. Even though they were several generations removed from those catastrophes, they would have, no doubt, appreciated the chance to wreak vengeance on the perpetrators. The Federation sent the Maldekians to colonize Earth. They took over the area now known as the Gobi Desert, which was then a lush, tropical area, as well as parts of northern India and Asia.

THE HUMANS FIGHT BACK

As the Federation expected, the old hatreds persisted, percolating up from the Atlan DNA, perhaps reinforced by stories passed on from generation to generation about the desecrations in Lyra. Possibly even more than the Maldekians, the Atlans also detested the Reptilians. This new planet was too small for these archenemies, and wars broke out. The Atlans were a fierce human race, and the battles were many. The dinosaurs were a major source of contention. These huge beasts rampaged over Atlantean agricultural areas, devouring the crops. Finally, the Atlans began killing them. Swerdlow says, "The Atlanteans despised these destructive animals, so they used electromagnetic pulse weapons to kill them. This is the real truth of why dinosaurs, mammoths and other prehistoric creatures abruptly became extinct." The Maldekians attacked the Reptilian lunar colonies. The underground Martians also entered the fray in the effort to remove the Reptilians from this solar system. They too began attacking the Reptilians on the moon to destroy the lunar outposts guarding their Earth settlements. In *The Code to the Matrix,* James Evans Bomar says, "This might be considered the real *First World War of the Worlds.* It was a mess!"

But it really was not a mess at all. Upon reviewing the entire situation now in retrospect, it becomes abundantly clear that the Federation was orchestrating the whole campaign. The Reptilians on Earth were now at a distinct disadvantage. They found themselves in a very precarious predicament. The conflict they had initiated by attacking Maldek and Mars had now resulted in their isolation in a distant solar system surrounded by humans—humans who had learned to defend themselves by the development of high-tech weaponry and space technology, who were not afraid of the Draco bullies. The human colonists were strongly motivated to destroy them, and they now had powerful allies all over the galaxy. The worm had turned. The primary Reptilian food source was destroyed, and there was no help available from Draco. They could no longer just invade and take whatever they wanted. They now had to negotiate to survive.

THE HATONA COUNCIL

Since the fighting was basically at a stalemate, the Federation initially sought to develop a peaceful civilization on the Earth to give the Atlan and Maldekian humans time and space to evolve and gain a larger population. They decided to convene a neutral council on the planet Hatona in the Andromeda galaxy. All the parties interested in the Earth civilization were represented. This convocation was a sort of victory in itself for the Federation. It appeared to elicit an agreement by the Reptilians that they would grant ownership of the planet to a newly created race, although everyone knew that Reptilian agreements were worthless. Bomar says:

> The Hatona Council convened for many decades as the fighting continued in this solar system. Finally, an agreement was reached between some of the human factions and the Reptilian Earth colonists. Keep in mind that this agreement was without the participation of the Reptilians from the original Draco Empire thus these Reptilians had no permission from High Command and were acting solely on their own conniving interest. The agreement stated that a new breed of humanity should be created on Earth that would contain the DNA of all interested parties who participated in the "peace" process. A designated area on Earth would be set aside for the creation of this new species. The Earth-based Reptilians of Lemuria agreed to this under the condition that the Reptilian "body" be the foundation for this new being.

This was a critical stipulation. The Reptilians believed that if the beings of the new race had fundamental Reptilian DNA, they could be easily mind controlled from the lower fourth dimension by sympathetic vibration. This did have the intended consequences. However, as will be seen, it also rebounded to the detriment of the Reptilians, since it made the new human species more resilient, thus allowing them to defend themselves successfully against Reptilian attacks and encroachments.

BE FRUITFUL AND MULTIPLY

The area that was chosen for this new experiment was southeastern Turkey at the origins of the Tigris and Euphrates rivers, where they flowed down from the Taurus Mountains in the Caucasus. This was the biblical Garden of Eden. That area was probably in Maldekian hands since it was close to their areas of settlement. It was a long way from Lemuria. Each of the thirteen contributors sought to make their DNA dominant. Consequently, the new man was conflicted right from the start. However, the major responsibility for coordinating the effort was placed in the hands of a group from the Collective known as the Elohim, literally "the gods," who were highly evolved humans known to be master geneticists. But the Reptilians were also geneticists with thousands of years of experience. In the Bible, the Hebrew word Elohim is used as though it was singular as the word for God. Actually, Hebraic words ending in -im are always plural. Plurality, or "the gods," is clearly implied in chapter 1 of Genesis wherein it says, "Let us make Man in our image, after our likeness." Since we know now that the Federation held all the cards, they decided on the new human form. Genesis says further, "So God [the Elohim] created mankind in his own image, in the image of God [the Elohim] he created them; male and female he created them. God [the Elohim] blessed them and said to them, 'Be fruitful and increase in number; fill the earth and subdue it.'" This tallies with Swerdlow's account where he says that the new race was intended to grow quickly and to take over the planet. So the human method of reproduction was chosen over the Reptilian. This explains the importance of God saying "male and female he created them," thus clearly

Fig. 7.1. Human creation depicted on a Sumerian tablet.
© Z. Sitchin, reprinted with permission.

differentiating the human and the Reptilian. The Reptilians reproduce by laying eggs, which can be fertilized.*

This description of human creation is contradicted by the Adam and Eve story related in chapter 2 of Genesis, where God is referred to in the singular as "the Lord God" and Eve was said to have been created from one of Adam's ribs. These two Genesis accounts of human creation are fundamentally different. This second account seems to endorse male dominance over the female, rather than the gender equality espoused in chapter 1, and appears to be a later addition. The command that "he shall rule over thee" sounds like it might have been of Reptilian origin, since the Reptilians inhabiting Earth had become a patriarchal society in defiance of the queen in Orion. Furthermore, the Adam and Eve story refers to sexual relations as a curse and introduces the serpent who gave man knowledge of sexual reproduction in defiance of God. This makes it appear that the Reptilians were helpful to Man, thus establishing "sympathy for the devil." This is ludicrous since the Elohim were highly motivated to have the humans reproduce quickly. Apparently, the author of this paragraph wanted the reader to believe

---

*According to the website, www.Cuteness.com, "Female reptiles store sperm for up to six years to use for future eggs, according to Wissman. That means the female can produce, fertilize, and lay her own eggs without the aid of a male as long as she has stored sperm from a previous male encounter.

that a whimsical God intended Adam and Eve to just stroll around the Garden of Eden naked for eternity. Also, the statement that it was God who created the enmity between humans and the serpent was apparently intended to blame the Elohim for the hostility between the humans and the Reptilians. The entire Adam and Eve account of human creation in Genesis 2 is anti-God and thus anti-Elohim, and sounds suspiciously like it might have been of Reptilian origin, inserted in a later edition of the Bible. This is not surprising, since the entire Bible, but especially the Old Testament, went through many versions and translations before the King James Version in 1604. The entire Genesis authorship has been attributed to Moses. But it is highly unlikely that he would have written two such different accounts of the creation of the human race.

The creation process went through several models that were not successful and were either destroyed or left to die out. This accounts for the various short-lived human prototypes, such as *Homo erectus,* Neanderthal, Cro-Magnon, and so forth, of which fossils have been found. Ultimately, twenty-two corrections were made to the human DNA over this fifty-thousand-year period by our extraterrestrial progenitors, finally resulting in the modern human that we know as *Homo sapiens sapiens,* which made its sudden appearance only forty thousand years ago. The Reptilians succeeded in keeping the DNA for the Reptilian brain in the "final product." This segment of the human brain accounts for our aggressive and warlike behavior. However, the more civilized mammalian aspects of the human DNA prevailed. The Federation monitored the entire process, and the council succeeded in the creation of the species we now call the human race. It was agreed to by all parties that this new planet Earth would be the home world of the new human race, thus settling once and for all the claims for control of the Earth by battling groups.

As the new humans spread out over the globe from Mesopotamia forty thousand years ago, they frequently encountered the previous versions of the human race, especially the Neanderthal. The first human bones dating to forty thousand years ago recently were discovered underwater in a cave in Romania, now called the Cave of Bones. Professor Joao Zilhao, an archaeologist at the University of Barcelona and recently featured in a PBS special titled *First Peoples,* found the bones of two adults underwater in the Cave of Bones. These are believed to be the first *Homo sapiens sapiens* in Europe. They were contemporary with the Neanderthal and obviously interacted, and possibly even inter-bred, with them. But they obeyed the injunction given to them by the Elohim and quickly outnumbered the Neanderthal, who were doomed to extinction. Zilhao speculated that the new humans were more social and more creative, so they quickly established communities, while the Neanderthal remained as hunters in isolated tribes.

THE REPTILIAN BRAIN

The Atlanteans were infuriated with the incorporation of Reptilian DNA in humans and believed that the experiment was not working anyway. They decided to launch an all-out attack on Lemuria to get rid of the Reptilians once and for all. Swerdlow tells us that they bombarded the continent with electromagnetic pulse weapons that caused the bulk of Lemuria to sink beneath the ocean, now called the Pacific, which is ironic since "pacific" means peaceful. Lemuria went down about fifty thousand years ago and partially slipped beneath the North American tectonic plate. The Reptilians retreated to deep, underground cavern-ous areas, primarily under Tibet and the Indian subcontinent, and Antarctica, which was then on the equator and subtropical. Swerdlow says, "This began the legends of hell and demonic entities underneath the Earth. To the Atlantean human beings, the Reptilians were demonic entities. This is where the legend of hell originated." They also fled to adjacent landmasses that remained above water, including Australia, New Zealand, the Pacific islands, Japan, the Philippines, Hawaii, parts of Central and South America, and North America west of the San Andreas Fault. That strip of California land belongs to the part of the Lemurian tectonic plate that did not sink. They also remained under-ground on Venus.

The Atlantean scientists apparently understood the importance of the inclusion of the Reptilian brain in the new human. They knew that this doomed the new species to contention and warfare. However, it is

The triune brain

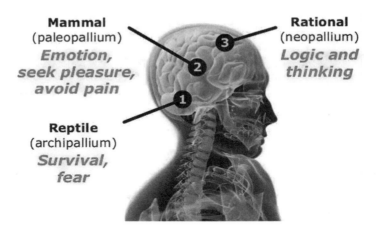

Fig. 7.2. The triune brain

interesting that the Elohim permitted this genetic configuration, which suggests that perhaps they believed that the higher human qualities, expressed through the two other major segments of the triune human brain, the mammalian and the rational, would ultimately prevail. However, the tough Reptilian component was necessary to ensure the survival of the race through the early, very hazardous stages. In addition, they wanted to make certain that the human race could ultimately join in the fight against the Reptilians, so the creation of a gentle, peace-loving civilization would be counterproductive. They knew that peace with the Reptilians was impossible. Once again, it was a brilliant strategy!

THE INNER WORLD

The Reptilians were now marooned inside the Earth. The Martian refugees who had been living inside Mars for several hundred years decided to colonize the Earth, probably at the urging of the Federation, who wanted to make certain that the surface of the planet remained in human hands. The Martians settled in what is now southern Iraq and Kuwait, already inhabited by a small, primitive human population.

The Martians were greeted as gods, and they created a highly developed civilization in Sumer. They also continued to attack the Reptilian lunar colony, and together with the Maldekians, they dispossessed the Reptilians from the moon. The moon-based Reptilians fled to Earth and joined the underground colonies. The Atlan civilization could now grow and expand without any direct interference. Meanwhile, as the new human race began to populate the surface world, the Federation kept a watchful eye on the entire situation.

The Reptilians created an entire civilization inside the planet. Remember that they were very adept at hollowing out planets and creating underground colonies and that they arrived in this solar system inside what is now Venus. They built a seven-layer complex under the Indian subcontinent, where they founded a capital city known as Bhogovita. There were two main entrances, one near Benares and the other in the mountains surrounding Lake Manosarovar in Tibet, west of Lhasa. They created deep tunnels crisscrossing the planet, some as deep as two hundred miles down, and took over the entire subsurface world, creating underground highways. According to Swerdlow, "They built tubes containing fast, subway-like vehicles that can travel to any point on the Earth within a few hours." Thus they were able to travel rapidly all over the globe.

Swerdlow claims that there are entry points to the inner Earth at the poles that can be seen from space. This would explain why the Reptilians founded a major colony under Antarctica. He says also, "Numerous cave entrances to the inner Earth exist in the Rocky Mountains and Sierra Mountains in the western United States, as well as less numerous openings in the Ozarks and Appalachian Mountains. Entries also exist in the Alps, Himalayas, Andes, and the Caribbean. There are also numerous sub-oceanic entry points, particularly in the deep trenches of the Pacific Ocean, the Caribbean Sea, and the Atlantic submarine mountain ranges, especially on or near the Azores, Canary Islands, and the Falklands." Swerdlow claims that this underground world exists in the Earth's crust. He says, "They created the famed underworld cities of Akkadia, Agartha, Hyperborea, and Shamballa that are sought by explorers to this very day. These cities are built along the inside wall of the inner crust that lines the interior of the Earth."

SOL WILL NOT BE ANOTHER LYRA

From that secure redoubt, with all the entrances carefully guarded, the Reptilians quietly plotted their recapture of the Earth, a planet of which they believed they had rightful ownership. They knew they only had a short time before the new human population would grow to enormous proportion. However, that was not necessarily a problem. Since the humans would all be turned into slaves as on the other planets in their empire, the more the better. The first task in the Reptilians' battle plan was to wreak vengeance on their mortal enemies from Lyra who had slain the dinosaurs and sunk their continent beneath the waves, the Atlans. For, if nothing else, the Reptilians are a vengeful race.

It was true that the Reptilians had agreed at Hatona to peacefully turn the Earth over to the new race that would populate the planet. But to them, agreements were simply a means of lulling opponents to inaction and could be ignored or violated as needed. This ancient, hardened Reptilian characteristic later would be displayed with flamboyance by their main protohuman protégé and agent, Adolph Hitler, who broke every agreement he ever made. The Federation knew this and never believed for a minute that the Reptilians would cease their campaign to take over the Earth. However, they believed confidently that they could now fight fire with fire and that the new human race would fight intelligently and heroically to defend their home world.

The Federation was totally prepared for the Reptilians to use their usual tactics of subterfuge, infiltration, lies, and deception, and to deploy their most potent weaponry: genetic hybridization and mind control through propaganda. But, they reasoned, the new *Homo sapiens sapiens* would recognize those now overused techniques and would uncover the plots and fight to the death for freedom and liberty. Both sides recognized that, yes, Earth was a great prize, but this confrontation was really all about the solar system, and Earth was the key to the solar system. The Federation was not going to allow this Sol system to become another Lyra. Every skirmish and battle would be contested to the bitter end.

☒
Atlantis

History becomes Legend
Legend becomes Myth
Myth becomes a Disney Movie
CHARLES ALEXANDER MOFFAT (2002)

The Atlantis landmass, which stretched from the Caribbean across the Atlantic to Spain and North Africa and incorporated the Azores and Canary Islands, emerged from the Earth water world around the same time as Lemuria, about one million years ago, as the Reptilian-guided ice comet/planet began its mutual orbit around Earth and dried out the planet. But Atlantis remained uninhabited by humans for hundreds of thousands of years while the Reptilians settled in Lemuria and basically had the Earth all to themselves. Then, the Federation settled the Atlans on Atlantis about three hundred thousand years ago. Swerdlow tells us that the warm waters of the Gulf Stream flowed around Atlantis at that time, encircling the entire continent, flowing south past North Africa as the Equatorial Current, and then north past the Caribbean and North America, as it still does today, thus giving the island a perpetually mild and ideal climate. A very high mountain range dominated the interior of the island.

The Atlantean civilization was at the height of its power and influence when Lemuria sank beneath the waves around fifty thousand years ago.* Now free of the Reptilian threat, the Atlans could devote their efforts to creating a utopian culture. In this golden age, Atlantis was a flourishing, advanced civilization. The arts and sciences were well developed, and the citizens enjoyed the fruits of peace and prosperity. The Atlans were directly descended from the Lyrans, who were known to have had a highly civilized society based on an agricultural economy and who fled to the Pleiades after the Reptilian invasion. Those Lyran refugees came from the very earliest human origins in this galaxy, and so, of course, they did not have a Reptilian brain. This may explain why they were able to develop such a highly evolved society. The Atlans attempted to re-create on Earth the paradise their ancestors had built on their planet in Lyra.

Ancient books containing descriptions of the Atlantean civilization and histories of the Atlanteans have either been lost or destroyed. Apparently, this loss and destruction was purposeful. In his book *Masters of the World,* written in 1974, French prehistorian and archaeologist Robert Charroux says, "The true history of civilization is forbidden. Powerful conspiracies try to allow only a distorted version to be expressed. Our social and religious history has been falsified for thousands of years, ever since the Egyptians, forgetting or ignoring the truths handed down to them by their ancestors, gave themselves the title of the 'first initiators and civilized people.'" Charroux cites evidence that space travelers from Venus were early colonizers of Earth and intervened in the affairs of the native human population. This tallies somewhat with Swerdlow's account of the first settlement of Earth by Reptilians from Venus, but at a time when the human race had not yet been created. Further exacerbating the cover-up of human prehistory

---

*Geologists claim that this period of Earth's history was characterized by an ice age, which would seem to have prohibited any sort of golden age on Atlantis. However, a typical ice age is characterized by differing periods of glaciation and nonglaciated temperate climates, each period lasting up to fifty thousand years. The ice age at the height of the Atlantean Empire could have been in a nonglaciated interim period. Furthermore, glaciers during an ice age are always local to limited areas on the planet and seldom cover the entire surface of the Earth. Atlantis was surrounded by warm Atlantic currents, which would certainly have prevented glaciation on that island.

was the devastating incineration of the Great Library of Alexandria by the Romans. This was a catastrophic loss, since there were, no doubt, ancient scrolls from Atlantis and Lemuria lost in the conflagration.

In the Americas, the Catholic priests accompanying the Spanish conquistadores burned priceless old manuscripts about prehistory that probably confirmed the Atlantean immigration into Central America. In his Internet article "Suppressed Archaeology," author, journalist, and documentary filmmaker Will Hart says:

> Is the true history of planet earth being suppressed? There are many archaeological finds, which don't get recognized because they don't fit into the official establishment record of how life on earth evolved. Why is this? What are they trying to keep hidden? It can only be presumed that there is some history that they don't want people to know about. In other words, we are being lied to about the real history of planet earth. Like the burning of the library at Alexandria, keeping the public in the dark has come to be a feature of our current world rulers. It could almost be presumed that there is information that would cause a loss of control and power to manipulate reality outcomes if known.

The scientific establishment seems to have a very large investment in spreading belief in evolution. If science is a religion, as many believe, then evolution is its central dogma. But as already shown, the truth is quite different. In order to break through this Darwinian blanket, it is critical that we understand what happened on Atlantis. There have been many Atlantean authors, but Ignatius Donnelly is generally acknowledged to be the most informative. His classic book, *Atlantis: The Antediluvian World,* published in 1882, has stood the test of time. Donnelly was written off as a crackpot for many years, but is now experiencing a revival. Noted archaeological researchers like Graham Hancock have conferred a new respect for Donnelly's work.

While nobody knows what really happened on Atlantis, Plato's account in the *Critias* and the *Timeus* is still considered the most believable, but it is all too brief. Plato's famous history of Atlantis was based on information given to him by the Athenian lawyer and Egyptian scholar Solon, who had in turn learned it directly from the aged Egyptian priest Sonchis of Sais. Sonchis spoke of the deluge that sank Atlantis, claiming that the Athenians were pre-Flood colonists from Atlantis. Of course, Sonchis could not have known that the Atlanteans themselves were not truly human, but were extraterrestrials from Lyra and the Pleiades. So from this statement we learn that the classic Greek civilization was actually of Lyran origin and was not human. This explains why the Greek architecture resembled what we know of the Atlantean and the similarities of so much of their culture. Plato speaks of ten god-kings who ruled over the ten provinces of Atlantis. The ten provinces of classical Rome may have been a re-creation of the Atlantean ten provinces. The Etruscans and early Romans were, after all, really an offshoot of the Greek civilization, and consequently the Romans may not have had the Reptilian brain. However, as the Romans conquered more foreign lands, many of them populated by Reptilian hybrids, their culture became hybridized, which probably accounts for their increased brutality and, ultimately, their downfall.

Donnelly explores the subject in much more detail and really sharpens the picture. There was significant confirmation of Donnelly's speculations by psychic Edgar Cayce in the early days of the twentieth century. Cayce's readings on Atlantis while in a trance really brought the lost continent into focus and reality and served to introduce the public to the lost prehistory of which they were deprived in public schools and colleges. Unfortunately, Cayce's discourses were couched in some sort of archaic language, so that it has been difficult to make sense of what he said. They were in English, but seemed to use a terminology, grammar, and sentence construction that left researchers and scholars scratching their heads.

Steve Omar has emerged as perhaps the best modern writer about Atlantis. His Internet article "Atlantis: History of the Golden Ages" makes connections that Donnelly could not make in the nineteenth century because much more has been revealed since 1882. In 1976 Omar was one of three directors of a small, ambitious organization called M.I.N.D. This group was formed in 1967. Renamed MIND International and centered in Maui between 1972 and 1978,

MIND "had its agents around the globe collecting evidence about vanished civilizations. . . . In search of the 'ultimate' truth MIND sent agents around the world to collect information that necessarily had been excluded from history books in the United States." Omar was given by the group the monumental task of studying every religion, philosopher, and historian in recorded history, primarily searching in college libraries. In the course of this research, he became an expert on the writings of Charroux, who had spent thirty years traveling and researching in remote areas and studying in "museums, monasteries, and caves." Omar tells us that none of Charroux's six volumes of ancient history "can be found in original or reprinted form anywhere in . . . the United States."

ATLANTEAN SPACESHIPS

In his article Omar tells a fantastic story! He speaks of a society on Atlantis so advanced that it actually eclipsed the modern era in terms of social, medical, technological, and especially spiritual achievements. Omar says:

> What was life like in the Golden Age of Atlantis? Ancient writers tell of how people lived to be a thousand years old in an age when cosmic science ended all disease, and of an empire that accumulated so much gold over 50,000 years that they paved their streets with it, covered their temples and buildings with sheets of it, and wore fine gold meshed clothing. . . . Ancient writings from around the world are clear in their detailed accounts of the spaceships and advanced aircraft of Atlantean times. The Mayans, Aztecs, and Incans told the conquistadors of these Atlantean sky ships that transported the white celestial rulers from the East. Atlantean technology spread to the Rama region of Asia with their expanding colonization. The ancient Vaimanika Sastra writings discovered in India in 1875 detail the size of flying machines, how they are steered, how they are protected from violent storms and lightning, and how to switch the drive to solar energy when the fuel supply becomes low. The writings relate to 70 authorities and 10 experts on ancient air travel! The texts are

extremely precise and easy to understand by modern scientists, except for several metals and alloys, which they cannot recognize.

As we have seen, the Maldekians and the Martians were attacking the Reptilian lunar colonies at about the same time. From Omar we learn that the Atlans also had spacefaring technology and may have joined in these assaults. He says:

> More remarkable is the ancient literature from Egypt, Central America, Asia, Phoenicia and Babylonia concerning how these spacecraft traveled to other planets and returned to Earth; how they utilized weapons in a "Star Wars" fashion. These crafts could not be damaged by humans on Earth and were piloted by astronauts [that] ancient paintings and carvings show in space suits! . . . Atlanteans who had spacecraft . . . that were capable of interplanetary travel & theoretically could have gone to Mars. . . . The moon was said to have once been part of the Atlantean Empire. The first satellite to orbit the moon sent back a photo of an ancient pyramid on the dark side of the moon that we have examined, and it was censored from the public by the U.S. government with other Moon ruins. Ruins of walls and roads were found on the Moon by astronauts who will not speak publicly due to the $10,000 fine, ten-year jail sentence, and dishonorable discharge for violating official U.S. Government regulation 200-2.

Apparently, the Atlanteans had progressed very far into computer technology and artificial intelligence, even beyond what we have today. According to Omar:

> Atlanteans created a national work force of robots, androids, and humanoids from genetic engineering to create and maintain most of the material plane empire and that computers controlled the robots and androids. Perpetual motion machines were created that created and operated other machines and repaired them. Atlantis was on the verge of "life without instrumentalities." In other words, the Empire was controlled by machines and computers that did everything

for the citizens. No Atlantean had to work or go to school. VRIL helmets educated the people while they were asleep; a teenager had knowledge beyond that of even the most respected geniuses of our Age. With a thousand year life span to acquire knowledge, Atlanteans were aware & informed beyond our imaginations.

During the golden age, the Atlantean bioscientists perfected many genetic engineering techniques and created individuals with super strength and powers, able to perform superhuman feats. There are indications that they also experimented with crossbreeding different species and cloning. Later, this technology was taken with them when they colonized Egypt, where it was also practiced. Omar tells us that they "also learned how to block brain impulses to parts of the brain that caused crime and negative emotions; they later used this technique to control minds." The Atlans also practiced telepathy and used it to communicate with dolphins, who were also of extraterrestrial origin and highly intelligent.

ATLANTEAN TECHNOLOGY

According to Edgar Cayce and journalist and psychic Ruth Montgomery, as related by Steve Omar, "The Atlanteans used laser rays and crystals to fuel their power plants. There was a huge 'Firestone' with power generated by filtering the rays of the sun through ruby prisms, which concentrated energy upon instruments connected in the transportation complex by remote control. Inside a huge dome with a sliding roof, cosmic energy stations transmitted beams that could be turned up so high, they became the famous Death Ray." Inventor and visionary Nikola Tesla, who claimed to have "off-planet" sources of information and appeared to be tuned in to Atlantean information, described a possible death ray. Tesla said that it could "destroy anything approaching within 200 miles . . . [and] will provide a wall of power" and would "make any country, large or small, impregnable against armies, airplanes, and other means for attack." Tesla's version was really a potent particle-beam accelerator, something that is now in the arsenals of both the United States and Russia. But apparently, the Atlantean version could somehow exponentially amplify the power of the sun's rays using the Firestone.

Omar claims that the Atlantean scientists had also developed an antimatter weapon. He says, "When a beam of anti-matter comes in contact with ordinary matter, it instantaneously converted it into invisible energy. In other words, it vaporized it! No wonder traces of Atlantean buildings and cities are so hard to find. They were converted into invisible energy! It is said that one of these anti-matter rays is still operating in the Bermuda Triangle, underwater & has been causing ships and planes to disappear." Our scientists secretly learned how to use antimatter propulsion power from the Eben aliens when we sent a military team to their planet in the mid-sixties (see chapter 21 in this book as well as my book *Secret Journey to Planet Serpo*). Its use on alien spacecraft was first reported by Robert Lazar, who revealed that he observed it when he worked at site S-4 at Area 51. We learned how to convert matter to energy differently when we developed the atom bomb and now perform this routinely in our nuclear energy power plants. But this is done by triggering atomic chain bombardments of highly unstable elements like uranium, and not by direct, controlled conversions of matter to energy using an antimatter ray.

ATOMIC WARS

Omar cites evidence that the Atlanteans also had nuclear weapons. Apparently war erupted between Atlantis and the inhabitants of the Indian subcontinent. It seems very unlikely that the early human tribes had already spread to India, and even if they had, it would have been almost impossible for primitive humans with no technology to be at war with high-tech Atlantean humans. So that would suggest that probably the Reptilian Nagas had taken over the surface there. That makes sense since we know that they inhabited the entire underground complex beneath India, in which was located their capital city of Bhogovita.

Omar tells us that ancient tomes like the Book of Dzyan kept by Tibetan monks and the Indian Ramayana and Drona Parva and others describe destruction that could only have been created by atomic explosions. He says, "The Rama empire was devastated by nuclear bombs,

Fig. 8.1. Atomic war in ancient India (Jim Nichols, artist)

laser-powered guided missiles, rockets, and fallout described in such detail that the truth cannot be mistaken! There is no way that primitive men could have invented that technical knowledge!" Of the Book of Dzyan, he says, "The book continues to give a vivid detailed description of the atomic explosions that followed when the missile hit its target, including the mushroom cloud, the fireball that made men blind when they looked at it, the unbearable wave of heat, genetic deformities after the battle, and radiation sickness exactly like what happened in Hiroshima, Japan, after an atomic bomb was dropped in 1945!" Furthermore, the Rig Veda says, "The fire from the terrible weapon destroyed cities by producing a light brighter than a thousand suns."

There is some evidence that the war spread to Central and South America. Once again, it is very unlikely that the recently created human race would have strayed so far from Mesopotamia. And what reason would they have had to be at war with their fellow human Atlans? So, we can reasonably assume that the Atlanteans were attacking Reptilian surface strongholds in those areas. Omar describes the evidence:

Where else did the Atlanteans strike? Why is it that all of the great Mayan, Aztec, Inca, and Toltec civilizations in the Americas were built in the South tropics in hot steamy uncomfortable humid jungles so dense it was a major hassle for farming and construction, or so high up in the desolate barren Andes farming was exceptionally difficult? They [the natives] told of a huge war there long ago using terrible weapons from the sky that devastated the cities, and left a mysterious energy in the air that killed the crops, poisoned the survivors, and ruined the soil.

Omar says further about this:

In the public library In Rio de Janeiro, Brazil, is the *HISTORICAL ACCOUNT OF A HIDDEN AND GREAT CITY OF ANCIENT DATE FOUND WITHOUT INHABITANTS.* Over 300 men were on an expedition deep into the Amazon Jungle in search of the gold, and they found a ruined paved road, part of which had been destroyed by a huge disaster. They followed it into the ruins to a once splendid deserted city. The road in one area was a view of crystals in multi-colored brilliance. . . . The book went on to describe how there was no furniture in the houses, no footprints, and no life anywhere. There was a huge plaza, statue, and an obelisk badly damaged as if struck by lightning and a temple with a magnificent facade. In the halls were found art of great beauty and statues and portraits.

In the book the men said, "In all the expanse of mills we found no grass, weeds, trees or plants. The country beyond the city consisted of green fields dotted with blooming flowers. . . . Spherical gold coins, hieroglyphics, ancient beyond recognition, and artifacts were found." Omar asks, "What disaster destroyed this once glorious city having no trace of inhabitants? And what energy other than nuclear fallout could exterminate all vegetation and keep the jungle from overgrowing the city for thousands of years?"

Apparently, the Reptilians, too, had atomic bombs and struck back at the Maldekians in the Gobi. We learn from Omar, "The desert sands in the ruined city in the Gobi is [*sic*] vitrified into glass just exactly like the desert sands in Nevada where atomic bombs were tested in the 1940s, and the huge hard solid stone buildings are melted by a temperature so high that it could have only been caused by lasers or atomic bombs!" This attack evidently forced the Maldekians to retreat underground to escape from the fallout. There, they founded a subsurface city, which famously became known as Agartha.

All of this indicates that the Atlans' war with the Reptilians continued in full force even after Lemuria was gone. The Federation conducted the battle on several fronts. In what was apparently a coordinated campaign, the Martians, now inhabiting Sumer, and the Maldekians in the Gobi area attacked the Reptilian lunar colonies, while the Atlans dealt with Reptilian surface eruptions all over the globe. It was a planetwide "take-no-prisoners" confrontation with the human forces now employing awesome high-tech weaponry. It was, after all, a battle for the entire solar system, and Earth was the critical battleground. The Federation was determined not to allow the Sol system to become another Lyra.

THE REPTILIAN FIFTH COLUMN

After suffering devastating losses all over the surface of the planet and on the moon, the Reptilians apparently realized they had to change their tactics. They resorted to their time-honored technique for conquering another planet—hybridization. They were, after all, master geneticists. By creating human-looking people with as much as 50 percent Reptilian genes, they could enlist these beings and use them to infiltrate key positions on Atlantis and then could ultimately force Atlantis to destroy itself. The Reptilians had been using hybridization and infiltration as a softening-up tactic in their victories throughout the galaxy. In the modern era, it was Nationalist General Emilio Mola who coined the term *fifth column* in 1936 during the Spanish Civil War. In the battle for Madrid, he said he had four columns of soldiers and a "fifth column" of infiltrators inside the city. It seems likely that Mola and the Nationalist commander, General Francisco Franco, had strategic help from Reptilian allies, who we now know were heavily invested in a fascist takeover of Europe. This was probably not a tactic taught at the straight-laced Toledo Military Academy, from which he graduated.

After the sinking of Lemuria, the Reptilians had easy access to the surface world through the many openings all over the world. So, it was not difficult for them to begin their assault on Atlantis by infiltrating the Atlan civilization from below. The Reptilians, since they reside in the fourth dimension, have power over evil beasts and other malevolent entities in the astral realm. They have learned how to employ those entities to overshadow and corrupt otherwise innocent humans. They created a cadre of black magicians on Atlantis by abducting Atlan humans for their DNA and combining it with their own, thus exposing the new creatures to influences from the astral plane. The Atlantean initiates were clairvoyant anyway, and now the newly born hybrids used their natural clairvoyance for evil. A potent school for black magicians sprang up on Atlantis, where they were taught to use sexual energies to supply the power for their workings. Eventually they constituted an army. The leader was a powerful black magician named Orhuarpa. In *The Revolution of Beelzebub,* Samael Aun Weor says:

> When Orhuarpa saw that people were worshipping him as a god, he amassed a powerful army and marched against Tollan, the city of the seven gates of massive gold, where the White Magicians from Atlantis reigned. During the day, Orhuarpa fought dressed in steel with shield, helmet, cask, and sword. Yet, during the night, he unleashed his beasts with his witchcraft. They were in the form of wolves, and they destroyed his enemies. This is how he captured Tollan, the city with the seven gates of massive gold. He became emperor of Atlantis, thus establishing the cult of the tenebrous sun.

THE MIGRATIONS AND THE CATACLYSMS

The city was later recaptured by the white magician leader Master Morya. Orhuarpa then enclosed himself in a tower. The white magicians set fire to the tower and Orhuarpa was burned alive. Aun Weor says, "Unfortunately, events did not end here. Orhuarpa immediately reincarnated again, and when he was old enough, he reunited his army of warriors and sorcerers and marched against Tollan, but he could not capture the city again. So, he established his own throne against the other throne." The white magicians were then warned to leave Atlantis because it would soon sink. Other clairvoyant groups also saw the handwriting on the wall and began massive emigrations out of Atlantis. They went east to Egypt and Agartha and west to the Americas. Subsurface colonies were created underground in the South American jungle and under Mount Shasta and Death Valley in North America. The scientists had developed submarines and used them to create domed underwater cities to which many fled to escape the approaching cataclysms. Mountainous locations such as Machu Picchu and the high plateau in Peru surrounding Lake Titicaca became havens. Wherever they went, the Atlanteans brought with them advanced spirituality and science. As they integrated into the still-primitive human populations, they were viewed as gods.

After they left, on Atlantis the forces unleashed by the black magicians ignited dormant volcanoes. Aun Weor continues:

> Certain dangerous igneous manifestations started to appear in Atlantis. This was because the use of the sexual forces, when utilized for black magic, made the fire of the dormant volcanoes enter into activity. The sexual forces have an intimate relationship with all the forces of Nature because the sexual forces reside not only in our sexual organs, but also in all of our cells, and moreover, within each atom of the cosmos. The sexual force is the cause of electricity. It is logical then that the dormant volcanoes would enter into activity, since by means of the sexual energy the volcanoes were intimately related with the black magicians.

However, there were even more potent forces destabilizing the continent. The Atlans realized that the Reptilians were making inroads from underground and devised a plan of attack. They decided to point the death ray directly down to destroy whatever Reptilian forces lurked below ground. The resulting tectonic stresses were disastrous when combined with the volcanoes energized by the black magicians. The Earth's axis tilted over, causing a ninety-degree pole shift. Omar describes the catastrophe:

> Huge cracks in the Earth opened and swallowed entire cities, lava buried roads and towns: glacier ground cities to powder and covered them, the Death Ray and nuclear bombs disintegrated civilizations, and tons of mud from receding tidal waves buried whole cultures. 400+ miles-per-hour winds blew vehicles and objects high into the sky and out to sea, only to "rain" matter and flesh back to the new ocean bottoms. The rampaging fires destroyed every forest on the planet and most of its animal life. The annihilation was so complete that mammoths, saber-toothed tigers, bison, and other animals became extinct! Nuclear winter set in & the smoke of thousands of erupting volcanoes and bombs hid the sun for decades and froze life on the surface. Those who remained on the surface in colonies died.

Fig. 8.2. The final sinking of Atlantis.
Destruction *by Thomas Cole (1836)*

DUST UNTO DUST

The survivors waited in their refuges until the radioactive dust had cleared, and then emerged into a new world. Omar waxes poetic as he describes the desolation. He says:

> Gone were all of humanity's great achievements. Gone was 60,000 years of scientific progress . . . destroyed in one single night. Gone were the futuristic crystal cities, an age which today's science can only envision . . . existed in that ever-so-faint yet brilliant distant past. Gone were the interplanetary ships, the teleportation temples, and the cities of gold. Gone were mankind's hopes [and] their dreams. Gone were the factories, the machines, and the robots that had supplied Atlantis with all her needs. Gone were the planetary governments that had made all decisions for a race that had ceased to think for itself. What was left in the ashes was global anarchy. Some believed the Atlanteans had gambled with "the Creator" in a deadly game of life and had lost. The devastation that followed had few, if any, parallels in history. From dust to dust . . .

In a way, it was fortuitous for the newly created human race. They could now start out on their own to build a new civilization. The black magicians were now on the bottom of the Atlantic, but a small contingent of Reptilians remained safe in their underground lairs in India and Antarctica. The white magicians still existed in remote places to guide the new humanity on the right spiritual path. The situation was analogous to the destruction of Lyra. Because of that catastrophic event, the humans spread throughout the galaxy, populating new worlds and turning it into a human galaxy. Now the human race could spread all over the planet and make Earth a new and secure home for humanity. Perhaps this entire scenario was orchestrated by a much higher power for that very purpose.

ባ

After the Flood

According to Edgar Cayce, the migration of the "Children of the Law of One" from Atlantis to Egypt occurred about 10,500 BCE. It was led by the white magicians, who had learned from occult sources that the continent was going to sink beneath the ocean. The black magicians did not get this warning, and so they perished in the deluge. Cayce does not mention how these people made the journey. It was not a long distance. It was just necessary to cross over the narrow North Atlantic Current and then traverse North Africa to the headwaters of the Nile, but they did not have to sail and walk. More than likely they had antigravity aerial transportation, which was commonly used in Atlantis at that time. So they probably arrived in spaceships. There was a community of humans in Egypt at that time, since they originated nearby in Mesopotamia about thirty thousand years previously, and it is very likely that they had spread by then to the Nile Valley. One can imagine how awestruck the humans must have been to watch these metallic vessels, seemingly from heaven, disgorge these tall shining beings. Certainly, they would have worshipped them as gods.

THE GOD OF MAGIC

Perhaps the most important priest leading the colonization was Thoth, known to the Greeks as Hermes Trismegestus. Thoth was later known as the god of magic and of writing and was represented on monuments with the head of an ibis in place of a human head, and sometimes that of a baboon. Thoth was a great scientist and mathematician and is credited with the planning and building of the Great Pyramid of Giza. It should be realized that this early cohort of settlers in Egypt were all descended from the Atlans, the original founders of Atlantis, and consequently they did not have the reptilian brain. Thoth was also the architect of the Sphinx. Both the Great Pyramid and the Sphinx are now believed to have been built around 10,000 BCE. In a later Egyptian period, Thoth was also considered to be the god of measurement, thus testifying to his role in building the Great Pyramid. Author John Anthony West and Yale-educated geologist Robert Schoch have made a solid case for their proposition that the Sphinx was created around 10,000 BCE, based on the water erosion traces on its base. In addition, the two-hundred-ton blocks in the wall in the Valley Temple in the Sphinx complex testify to its creation by an advanced technology that could move such huge blocks. Some of these blocks have been lifted to a height of forty feet, much higher than the fifty-ton blocks at Stonehenge. The Atlanteans had that technology, based on sound, as did the Reptilians. Once the blocks were carved out, they could be floated on air to the construction site by

Fig. 9.1. Sphinx Temple complex showing two-hundred-ton blocks

directed sound waves. West showed that there is only one crane in the entire world today that could have lifted such a weight. As previously discussed, the Reptilians had a sound weapon mounted on their death star that could emit sound waves that caused buildings to crumble and that could lift enormous weights. The Atlans had similar weapons.

Another building obviously much older than originally believed is the Osirion at Abydos. It is part of the Temple of Seti I, but is underground and displays a very different architecture and construction technique than the temple proper. Some of the stones in the wall are estimated to be about one hundred tons. West and Schoch both believe it was built contemporaneously with the Sphinx and the Great Pyramid, dating it to about 10,000 BCE. Clearly, there was an advanced civilization inhabiting the Nile valley at that time. Most of it is now buried under the sands of time, with the exception of these three remarkable structures. This civilization apparently sprang into existence literally overnight since there is no evidence of a preceding primitive settlement. The only explanation for the arrival of such a high-tech colony in the Nile valley at that time is that it had originated from an equally high-tech civilization on Atlantis.

WITHOUT FATHER, WITHOUT MOTHER

This sudden appearance of such a high culture in Egypt, without having developed from a primitive society, is discussed in *Atlantis: The Antediluvian World* by Ignatius Donnelly. He says, "Renan says 'It has no archaic epoch.' Osborn says, 'It bursts upon us at once in the flower of its highest perfection.' Joseph Seiss says in *A Miracle in Stone,* 'It suddenly takes its place in the world in all its matchless magnificence, without father, without mother, and as clean apart from all evolution as if it had dropped from the unknown heavens.'" It had dropped from Atlantis. George Rawlinson says in *The Origin of Nations:*

> Now in Egypt, it is notorious that there is no indication of any period of savagery or barbarism. All the authorities agree that however far back we go, we find in Egypt no rude or uncivilized time out

of which civilization is developed. Menes, the first king, changes the course of the Nile, makes a great reservoir, and builds the Temple of Phthah at Memphis. . . . In Egypt we have the oldest of the Old World children of Atlantis; in her magnificence we have a testimony to the development attained by the parent country; by that country whose kings were the gods of succeeding nations, and whose kingdom extended to the uttermost ends of the earth.

Egypt's arts, crafts, and sciences were highly developed right from the beginning. Donnelly says:

They had clocks and dials for measuring time. They possessed gold and silver money. They were the first agriculturists of the Old World, raising all the cereals, cattle, horses, sheep, etc. They manufactured linen of so fine a quality that in the days of King Amasis (600 years B.C.) a single thread of a garment was composed of three hundred and sixty-five minor threads. They worked in gold, silver, copper, bronze, and iron; they tempered iron to the hardness of steel. They were the first chemists. The word "chemistry" comes from *chemi,* and *chemi* means Egypt. They manufactured glass and all kinds of pottery; they made boats out of earthenware. . . . Their

Fig. 9.2. Ignatius Donnelly

dentists filled teeth with gold; their farmers hatched poultry by artificial heat. They were the first musicians: they possessed guitars, single and double pipes, cymbals, drums, lyres, harps, flutes, the sambric, ashur, etc; they had even castanets, such as are now used in Spain. In medicine and surgery they had reached such a degree of perfection that several hundred years B.C., the operation for the removal of a cataract from the eye was performed among them, one of the most delicate and difficult feats of surgery, only attempted by us in recent times.

Donnelly says further, "They were the first mathematicians of the Old World. Those Greeks whom we regard as the fathers of mathematics were simply pupils of Egypt. They were the first land-surveyors. They were the first astronomers, calculating eclipses, and watching the periods of planets and constellations. They knew the rotundity of the earth, which it was supposed Columbus had discovered." Regarding their treatment of women and their corresponding social mores, he says:

Monogamy was the strict rule; not even the kings, in the early days, were allowed to have more than one wife. The wife's rights of separate property and her dower were protected by law; she was "the lady of the house"; she could buy, sell, and trade on her own account; in case of divorce her dowry was to be repaid to her, with interest at a high rate. The marriage-ceremony embraced an oath not to contract any other matrimonial alliance. The wife's status was as high in the earliest days of Egypt as it is now in the most civilized nations of Europe or America.

And, of course, there is their amazing architecture and statuary, looming up from the desert floor, unequaled by anything remotely comparable at that distant epoch. The Temple of Karnak can contain the entire Notre Dame Cathedral, and the sixty-foot statues of the pharaohs carved into the rock, guarding the Temple of Ramses at Abu Simbel, were magnificent works of art on a massive scale. To this day, nobody can understand how they were able to erect such huge obelisks, all carved in one piece of stone, now standing in cities all over the world. All of these marvels in stone in Egypt were revealed to the world the magnificence of the civilization that had preceded it—the amazing prehistoric kingdom that now lies beneath the waves of the Atlantic.

GREECE AND ROME

Swerdlow tells us that Greece also became a colony of Atlantis around 10,000 BCE, prior to the deluge. He says, "This was an original colony that was at war with Atlantis, similar to a civil war. The Atlanteans sent armies against Greece because it was trying to break away, resulting in the various nation-states of Sparta, Athens, Macedonia, etc." Plato speaks of this war between Atlantis and Athens in the dialogues of the *Critias* and *Timaeus,* written about 400 BCE, now extracted and combined into one book titled *The Atlantis Dialogue,* with the original translation by Benjamin Jowett. In this dialogue, Critias quotes the conversation between Solon, the Athenian lawgiver, and the Egyptian priest Sais when Solon visited Egypt. Sais says:

> Now in this island of Atlantis there was a great and wonderful empire, which had rule over the whole island and several others, and over parts of the continent. . . . This vast power, gathered into one, endeavored to subdue at a blow our country [Egypt] and yours [Athens] and the whole of the region within the straits; and then, Solon, your country shone forth, in the excellence of her virtue and strength, among all mankind. She was pre-eminent in courage and military skill, and was the leader of the Hellenes. And when the rest fell off from her, being compelled to stand alone, after having undergone the very extremity of danger, she defeated and triumphed over the invaders, and preserved from slavery those who were not yet subjugated, and generously liberated all the rest of us who dwell within the pillars [of Hercules].

According to Swerdlow, "Greece spread across the Asian continent and all the way to Persia. At one time Greece went as far west as Spain. . . .

Over 30 Greek city-states with approximately 90 colonies existed in the Mediterranean. Greek colonies were established along the coast of Southern France, Corsica, Sardinia, Sicily, Southern Italy, Crete, throughout the Black Sea, Cyprus, Turkey, the Middle East, Syria and even Egypt. The Greeks were one of the first people in ancient Israel and occupied Jerusalem. They brought the Hellenistic way of life with them." The Hellenistic way of life was really the Atlantean way of life. Like the Egyptians, the Grecians also had no barbaric period. They existed as a high civilization right from their origins, as testified by the writings of Homer.

The Etruscan civilization in northern Italy developed from a Greek colony. The Etruscans, with a highly disciplined military, eventually conquered the other Greek settlements centered around Rome. The Romans essentially organized the Greek colonies under Roman rule. Rome was able to conquer the people in all the Greek colonies because they were already civilized, spoke similar dialects, and were therefore easy to absorb. Thus, a loose conglomerate of Greek city-states under Etruscan organization became the Roman Empire. This means that the entire early Roman Empire was directly descended from Atlantis.

SUMER

According to Swerdlow, the Sumerian society appeared almost over-night around 5000 BCE as a fully developed high human civilization in what is now southern Iraq and Kuwait (see chapter 7). As with Egypt, there was no primitive period in Sumer that slowly developed into an advanced era. This is consonant with his claim that it was based on a settlement of Martians who were really refugees from Lyra. They had first settled on the surface of Mars, but then were forced to go under-ground after the Reptilian ice comet attack had stripped off much of the Martian atmosphere. Tired of living underground and having spacefar-ing technology, they moved to Earth and colonized Sumer. More than likely, they were encouraged to make that change by the Federation, which was assembling a population of Lyran expatriates on the Earth to suppress the Reptilians. Some of the Sumerian clay tablets do clearly show spaceships, as well as the correct planetary configuration of the solar system, which knowledge could only have been obtained through space travel.

The Sumerians had a complicated language and left behind hundreds of thousands of texts inscribed in cuneiform into clay tablets. These tablets covered a wide variety of subjects including personal and business letters, receipts, legal matters, hymns and prayers, stories, and diary-type records of daily events. Many of these tablets were incorporated into libraries, which survived intact. Such writings testify to the existence of a highly sophisticated society busy with all the activities of an intelligent and worldly people. Although a patriarchal society, they treated women with respect and granted them high social status. They even permitted the practice of polyandry for a time, in which women could have multiple husbands, before that convention was eventually outlawed. Widows were allowed to remarry without condemnation. Their legal system was humane and fair, attempting to respect individual rights and freedoms while maintaining law and order. As early as 4600 BCE the Sumerians had developed a complex system of measurements and mathematics including arithmetic, geometry, and algebra. Their pottery displayed intricate artistic designs, and they were very fond of music, especially played on stringed instruments called lyres. The word *lyre* suggests that it originated on Lyra, the original home world of the Martians. At its height, the Sumerian population reached about one million.

There had been a human colony in Sumer prior to the arrival of the Martians. The human civilization in the Middle East was created by the Hatona Council about forty thousand years earlier, as previously explained in chapter 7, and had begun to spread throughout the area. The Martians were viewed as gods by the humans when they arrived. They did interbreed with the humans, thus explaining the biblical phrase in Genesis 6:1–4, "The sons of God came in to the daughters of man and they bore children to them. These were the mighty men who were of old, the men of renown." In the Ugaritic Text of the Bible, this phrase reads "sons of the gods" rather than "sons of God." This is an important distinction. It suggests that since the humans in Sumer viewed the Martians as gods, their sons were the ones referred to in this text. It makes sense that their offspring would be "mighty men" since their genetic makeup probably did not include the full reptilian DNA contributed by the humans. This "miscegenation" was only possible because both races were basically human and thus were able to produce human offspring. It was only after the arrival of the Martians that the Sumerian civilization blossomed and became truly civilized. There is some evidence that the Martian spaceships first landed at Baalbek in northern Lebanon. This is the site of an ancient temple built with huge blocks, some weighing eight hundred tons, believed to have been built around nine thousand years earlier. The Romans built their Temple of Jupiter on top of this original structure and founded the city of Heliopolis there.

Evidently, the Sumerians knew about the flood that had destroyed Atlantis. Four clay tablets recently discovered make reference to that deluge (see plate 4). It is unlikely that this knowledge would have been available to the primitive humans then inhabiting Sumer, and consequently this news was probably brought in by the Martians. In retrospect, it seems very likely that the Federation made the decision to settle the Martians on Earth to maintain a human presence there to contain the Reptilians after the destruction of Atlantis. The Martians would be able to protect the human population from resurgent Reptilians emerging from their underground lair.

THE ANUNNAKI

The high-tech Martians in Sumer, together with the Atlantean emigre civilization in Egypt, already then well established, dominated the entire Middle East and constituted a strong human presence on the planet, well able to keep the Reptilians from surface encroachments in the absence of Atlantis. The protective Martian military factor was particularly important in northern Iraq. It was known that a star gate existed at Uruk, somewhere north of what is now Baghdad, and it was feared that the Anunnaki could come through in numbers when their home world, Nibiru, passed close to Earth and could upset the established human civilization. While the Anunnaki were also of reptilian origin, they were not allied in any way with the Draco-Orionite Reptilians who were living underground in deep caverns. Regardless, the Martians wanted nothing to do with the Anunnaki, or with any reptilian group. Consequently, the establishment of a militarized zone around the star gate was justified to prevent the Anunnaki from coming through when Nibiru made its next pass in its 3,600-year journey around our sun. However, while the Anunnaki might have no longer been a threat, the Reptilians themselves, safe in their deep underground realm, were already beginning to plan their takeover of the surface world. They were in no hurry. If there is one thing the Reptilians have plenty of, it is patience.

10

The Rebellion

The rulership of the faraway colonies in the Sol solar system was tenuous at best. It had fallen to the Wolfen Sirians to act as governors of the Earth mining operations. Since the Reptilian males in the military forces had their life spans reduced by the Orion scientists, they had to defer to the more senior Sirians who became the commanders. Because they were the strongest and most organized, they were the chief administrators. But life underground on Earth was not to their liking, and they petitioned the queens for relief and new assignments, which were not granted. They became dissatisfied and restless.

THE ADVENT OF MARDUK

Chief among the discontented Sirian leaders was Prince Marduk, the son of the Wolfen Prince Enki and grandson of King An. He decided to challenge the Orion overlords for hegemony over this solar system and to make it his personal fiefdom independent of the empire. He knew it would be difficult for the Draco and Orion military to send spaceship forces to defend this star at the very edge of the galaxy, even though it had supreme strategic importance, positioned as it was at the gateway to the Ninth Passageway star lane, the PESH METEN. In his bid for supreme power, Marduk sought the support of "the underground ones." These were the Reptilian workers who inhabited huge caverns on all the conquered worlds of the empire, supervised the mining operations, and maintained the administrative apparatus. They kept the empire functioning for the Orion queens and princesses. They were notoriously dissatisfied and rebellious, always seeking to find new ways to undermine the authority and rulership of the queens. Marduk met with the leaders of the Earth underground, known as the SSA-TA, and made his appeal. Morning Sky says, "Despised and dreaded, the SSA-TA rebels gave audience to the Prince. Promising them great wealth and power and full participation in his Empire in exchange for their support, a daunting Marduk elicited their support. Eagerly, the SSA-TA seized the opportunity to support an effort against the Sirian overlords. By weakening the Sirian Empire, so too the Orion Queens would be weakened." And by supporting Marduk, if they were successful, the rebels would gain a stranglehold on the Ninth Passageway, which meant that the Orion queens would have to negotiate with them. And if it didn't succeed, the death of Marduk would satisfy both the Sirians and the queen and would have no ramifications in their vital underground empire. Their work was too important. But their support still wasn't enough to guarantee a victory.

Deep underground was yet another group of servile workers known as the HEN-T. They were a hybrid combination of Sirians and Reptilians created by the queens. As faithful and trusted administrators, they had risen to become royal families and to occupy key midlevel administrative positions in the reign of Lord Prince Enlil, although they were not given enough higher intelligence to challenge the system. Marduk assiduously courted the cooperation of the HEN-T under the Earth. He pledged to them that they would become the administrators of his realm. He even promised that they would share in the wealth of his empire and would be given future territories of their own. The SSA-TA added their persuasive talents to the enlistment. Both groups being part Reptilian, they were distant cousins. The senior, most loyal and trusted members of the HEN-T were known as the SHET. They were recruited first, and they began to persuade the rank-and-file HENT-T workers to the cause. Those who joined in the plot became known as the SHET-I. They began to sabotage the spaceships of the Sirian warriors under Enlil. Morning Sky tells us, "Following the initial infiltration of the ranks of HEN-T in the underground operations, the conspiracy moved into the very inner core of the administration of Lord Prince Enlil. The Command Forces, including the Communication and Logistic departments, were also targeted. Carefully and deliberately the conspiracy gained a foothold in every department of Lord Prince Enlil's administration."

When all was ready, Marduk attacked the solar system in force. It was a total surprise. The HEN-T communication workers blacked-out news of the invasion, so there was no immediate response by the Sirian warriors. When the warriors finally began defensive operations, their sabotaged warships were ineffective. Eventually, all communications went silent. It was all over very quickly with a direct confrontation avoided. Marduk was now the undisputed ruler of the Sirian and Reptilian forces in the Sol star system, and he now controlled the entrance to the Ninth Passageway.

Marduk ascended to supreme power in Babylon about 1700 BCE, at a time when the Babylonian Empire had reached full development and dominated the Mesopotamian valley in the middle Bronze Age. He quickly improved the mining operations and continued to send ore

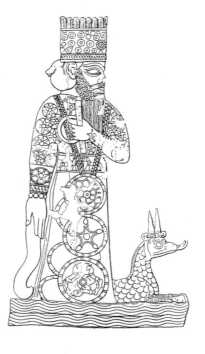

Fig. 10.1. Marduk standing on a serpent representing the SHET-I

and metals to the Sirian and Orion Empires, using existing spacefaring technology centered at the Baalbek Space Port. This had been in place in what is now northern Lebanon since the arrival of the Martians around 5000 BCE. This vastly increased the wealth of his realm. Further enriching the new dynasty was the rediscovery by the SHET-I scientists of the drug S-MA, which was used by the queens of Orion to extend their lives. This drug quickly became very popular throughout the galaxy and added immense riches to the royal treasury. Marduk became more affluent and more powerful than the rulers of the Orion and Sirian Empires.

THE SUN GOD

As the grandson of King An, Marduk was already considered a god, but his godlike stature was enhanced by his self-appointment as the sun god Ra, and his heroic exploits became mythologized in the Babylonian "epic of creation," The Enuma Elish, which was unearthed in 1876. In *The Terra Papers: The Hidden History of Planet Earth,* Morning Sky says, "Once seated, MARDUK began his final campaign . . . to change or destroy any records which attributed any heroic or kingly achievements to anyone other than himself. Stone monuments, obelisks and edifices were altered by stone-cutters; tablets of clay or wood were burned or destroyed. No records of any other Monarch would remain. MARDUK had become the beginning and the end of all things, he had appointed himself Lord God and Creator of the Universe. Henceforth, he was the 'Sun God RA.'"

Marduk's claim that he was the sun god Ra connects him with Akhenaten, who became pharaoh of Egypt about four hundred years later. Akhenaten abolished polytheism and instituted worship of the one god Ra throughout Egypt. This was, in effect, an acknowledgment that Marduk was to be worshipped as the one true god. According to Zecharia Sitchin there may be reason to believe that Marduk was still alive during the reign of Akhenaten, which means that he had made good use of the S-MA drug. In Sitchin's timeline, taken from *Cosmic Code,* the sixth book of his series The Earth Chronicles, Marduk was

Fig. 10.2. Wall frieze showing Akhenaten, Nefertiti,
and children receiving rays of the sun god

alive *at least* from 3450 to 2024 BCE. Whether or not he was still alive
in 1300 BCE, Akhenaten became his disciple, and he too, like Marduk,
embarked on a campaign to eradicate from all monuments and obelisks
throughout Egypt—as Marduk had done in Babylon—any mention of
the former Egyptian gods.

The eradication of inscriptions and carvings on monuments and
buildings was a partial solution. It was also necessary to make the human
colonists and workers forget the previous gods and kings, so that they
would know only Marduk as god. To accomplish this, Marduk called
on the SSA-TA scientists to use their mind-altering technology, developed by the scientists in Orion, to reprogram the minds of the humans.
Reprogramming centers were created underground, and the humans
were enticed or forced to enter these chambers, where their memories
would be erased. They would walk down long tunnels to the brightly lit
rooms believing some reward awaited them. Frequently, screen memories were implanted to replace the lost remembrances.

A VAGUE UNEASINESS

Morning Sky describes the resulting feelings of the reprogrammed humans: "As they went their separate ways, however, they each had a vague uneasiness, something was not there anymore, something was missing. Moreover, curiously, though they seemed not to have common backgrounds, each remembered, each recalled, a bright light at the end of a tunnel. And, each one knew that they were supposed to go to the light and enter the light . . . for there their ultimate reward resided."*

According to Morning Sky, Marduk and the SHET-I took one more precaution to isolate the human population and to make sure they received no information or assistance from outside friendly powers. They wanted them to focus only on producing for the sun god and knowing nothing else, as good slaves are expected to do. They constructed a network of high towers all over the planet, "which would transmit a cloud of electronic signals designed to keep the [human workers] in a fog, a docile state. The electronic blanket also served as a cover preventing outside signals from reaching the [human workers]." Upon reflection, this network of towers may have been the obelisks. The granite composition exhibits a certain electronic resonance. These obelisks are now all over the world. The original ancient Egyptian obelisks have been moved to the major cities, and others have been constructed in hundreds of minor locations. And in Washington, D.C., has been erected the largest one in the world, 555 feet high—the Washington Monument—which constitutes a direct connection with ancient Egypt and Babylonia. Is it possible that these obelisks constitute our "electronic blanket"?

---

*This narrative of the mental reprogramming of the human work force under Marduk clearly parallels the universal descriptions of near-death experiencers today, who all report going through a tunnel and being drawn to a bright light at the end of the tunnel. They then claim that they emerge into a beautiful world where the memories of their lives are wiped clean and from where they are eventually reincarnated. Could this all be an alien deception? Are we simply being recycled back to the physical realm to continue laboring for our alien masters with a "vague uneasiness" like the workers in Egypt?

MALE POWER RULES THE EARTH

But the obelisks may also serve another purpose. The new sun god, Ra, decided that the female goddesses of Orion would no longer influence the human slaves. Henceforth, the rulership would revert back to the males. In *The Terra Papers: The Hidden History of Planet Earth,* Morning Sky says, "Where once all [humans] and Sirian subjects were forced to praise the Sirian Lords and ultimately give greater honor to the Orion Queens, Lord RA, with the approval of the SSA-TA rebel Queens, began to systematically remove all traces of a Mother Goddess presence. Henceforth, the Omnipotent One was a male . . . the Sun God RA himself. Males would dominate every aspect of life; it was time for females to relinquish their exalted place of power." And so, it seems that we are meant to be reminded of this change by the presence of phallic symbols of male power all over the globe: the obelisks!

The largest ancient obelisk, uncovered in 2014, remains in an unfinished state at Baalbek. It is claimed that it would have been 1,800 tons

Fig. 10.3. The Stone of the Pregnant Woman,
the unfinished obelisk at Baalbek

when completed! It is known as the Stone of the Pregnant Woman. Supposedly, this name derives from the belief that a woman who touches the stone will become more fertile, a myth that would confirm the idea that the obelisks were giant phallic symbols. Since the creation of the temple complex has been dated to the Neolithic age, it would have even predated the advent of Marduk, probably dating back to the arrival of the Martians in 5000 BCE. However, it is known to have been later dedicated to the male god Baal (hence the name Baalbek) and to the sun god Ra. This suggests that Baalbek was a center of civilization during the time of Marduk, and it may be that this huge obelisk was to have been dedicated to Marduk when completed. During the Hellenistic era in the fourth century BCE, the Greeks conflated Baal with the sun god, and the city was called Heliopolis, or the City of the Sun. The Romans later placed the Great Court of the Temple of Jupiter over the ancient ruins.

To further guarantee that the human laborers would learn nothing of the past history of the planet or of extraterrestrials who might improve their lot, the SHET-I closed off all sources of information and scholarship that might reveal even a snippet of the truth of their condition. Historical clay tablets and scrolls were destroyed or secreted away. This, together with the electronic blanket, kept the human race in a state of ignorance and virtual, if not actual, enslavement. The SHET-I wanted them to keep their collective noses to the grindstone. This policy established precedents that remain in force even today, despite liberal universities and the Internet. Even in the American fortress of freedom, pressure to avoid journalistic ridicule for believing in conspiracies, and to remain "politically correct," is enormous.

THE SHET-I COUP

To further cement his rulership, Marduk placed only his most trusted administrators and priests and his children in positions of power and influence. The critical reprogramming and reanimation centers were placed under the control of an elite group of high priests. They also served as top-level administrators of the empire. In Egypt they communicated in hieroglyphics, a language that was not available to the masses. But Marduk's grasp on the levers of power was really totally dependent on the SHET-I, who effectively ran the empire, and he knew it. Morning Sky says, "Recognizing his Throne was vulnerable, Lord God Marduk reconsidered the possibility of a re-union with the Sirian Empire. His wealth and power surely gave him bargaining power, he felt. Lord God RRA was in need of another alliance to protect himself. It was—however—too late."

Overnight, a bloodless coup took place. Morning Sky says, "No violence, no battle, the SHET-I simply and quietly, took everything over. As the sun rose over the palace, the SHET-I were in control. All elite Warrior guard forces of the Lord RRA were imprisoned or eliminated. There remained only the task of capturing God RRA himself." Some sources claim that Marduk was captured and imprisoned in the Great Pyramid of Giza, which was then sealed. Denied access to his life-extending drugs and the ministrations of his scientists, it was believed that he would eventually die there. However, those sources also claim that he was rescued by a band of his faithful followers who dug out a passageway under the pyramid, and he then fled back to his ancestral home, the Sirius star system. This supposedly occurred sometime in the second century BCE.

‖

The Shemsu Hor

*Near Bhogavata stands the place where dwell the hosts of
the serpent race, a broad-wayed city, walled and barred,
which watchful legions keep and guard. The fiercest of
the serpent youth, each awful for his venomed tooth, and
throned in his imperial hall is Vasuki who rules them all.*

THE RAMAYANA

The SHET-I maintained all the policies and the religion of Marduk. They
did not want to arouse dissatisfaction or rebellion by the human slaves.
They remained patriarchal, relegating females to subjugation and keeping
in place the worship of one true God. From all indications, the advent of
rulership by the SHET-I appears to have been around 2400 BCE. In order
to gain religious control in Egypt, they infiltrated the priesthood and sub-
stituted worship of Amun instead of Ra, although they tolerated references
to Ra. According to Xaviant Haze in his book *Aliens in Ancient Egypt:
The Brotherhood of the Serpent and the Secrets of the Nile Civilization,* over
time the underground SHET-I eventually took over the Amun priesthood
and turned it into the Brotherhood of the Snake. Haze does not use the
term SHET-I in his book, but refers to the Reptilians as the Shemsu Hor,
which translates to "the followers of Horus."

The Shemsu Hor have been known by many different names in
the course of history, depending on the primary culture of each era.

Haze says, "The means by which the Shemsu Hor achieved their goal of regaining lost technology on Earth remains a mystery, but somehow they did so. Early in Egypt's Eighteenth Dynasty (1539–1295 BC) they made their mark on human civilization." The Shemsu Hor rose to sub-rosa power by backing the young pharaoh Thutmose III (see plate 6). Starting in 1479 BCE, as a boy, Thutmose ruled for twenty-two years as a co-regent with Queen Hatshepsut, who was his stepmother and his aunt. Thutmose became her military commander as he grew older.

Hatshepsut's reign was an obstacle to the military designs of the Shemsu Hor, and they wanted her out of the way. She abhorred war and sought to inculcate a peace-loving attitude in her subjects, whereas Thutmose sought to enlarge the empire by conquest. In 1473 BCE, she had herself declared the sole pharaoh and adopted a male persona by wearing the traditional fake beard and masculine attire. She had a long and successful reign and was a popular leader. She is remembered for restoring prosperity to Egypt and for her many building projects, including two obelisks at Karnak and her magnificent mortuary temple complex at Deir el-Bahri. Despite her cross-dressing, Hatshepsut sought to restore the lost divine feminine philosophy in her rulership. This particularly upset the patriarchal Shemsu Hor because it blocked their expansionist goals, and they plotted to kill her. It is believed that Thutmose had her assassinated, probably with the complicity of the Shemsu Hor, so that he could seize full power. She died in her fifties.

Fig. 11.1. Queen Hatshepsut

FIERY DISKS

Shortly after Thutmose ascended to pharaonic rulership at the age of twenty-one, a very strange incident occurred. The Shemsu Hor staged a dramatic exhibition of spaceships in the sky as if to confirm and celebrate their satisfaction with, and endorsement of, the new pharaoh. Haze describes the incredible display. He says, "What the scribes witnessed were fiery disks blazing across the sky, high above the Egyptian people, who watched in stunned amazement. Thutmose III ordered that a description of this event be recorded for posterity." But that was just the beginning. Over the succeeding days more "fiery disks" joined the display, culminating in a massive fleet of UFOs covering the skies over Egypt. Then the commanders of the craft contacted Thutmose and invited him to meet with them at a remote place in the desert. Haze explains it this way, "Before they could be certain that Pharaoh Thutmose III was indeed the leader they had in mind, they had to make sure by initiating him into the mysterious ways of heaven. . . . This meant that Thutmose was given a ride by the Shemsu Hor into Earth's upper atmosphere, like other prophets before him; namely Elijah and Enoch." Presumably, this cemented the relationship as Thutmose, no doubt, came to believe that he was dealing with the gods. From that point onward, he acted in their interests, and, with their assistance, he eventually became an invincible military leader.

A SERPENTINE TRAIL

This amazing display in the sky was indeed recorded by the scribes of Thutmose as he commanded and became part of the Royal Annals of Thutmose III. In his book, Haze traces the serpentine trail of the discovery and translation of the ancient document. The original papyrus was written in the hieratic cursive script. A version that was translated into hieroglyphics was found among the papers of Professor Alberto Tulli, an Italian who had been the director of the Egyptian Museum at the Vatican. Tulli bought the original papyrus from Phocion J. Tano at a Cairo bazaar in 1934. Haze tells us that Tano was the proprietor of the

Cairo Antiquities Gallery and was a highly respected and well-known student of Egyptian history. Tulli then asked the French archaeologist and Egyptologist Etienne Drioton, Ph.D., to translate the document from the hieratic script to simple hieroglyphics, which were much easier to read. Drioton later became director general of the Department of Egyptian Antiquities at the Egyptian Museum in Cairo. When Tulli died in 1952, he left his papers to his brother Gustavo. Gustavo then turned them over to noted Egyptologist Prince Boris de Rachewiltz for translation to Italian. Rachewiltz was a well-known expert in Egyptology and the author of scholarly dissertations still referred to today. His translation of the Annals was published in 1953 and contains the following passage: "After several days had passed, they became more numerous in the sky than ever. They shined in the sky more than the brightness of the sun." To the consternation of researchers as well as the Department of Egyptian Antiquities, the original papyrus itself has disappeared. It is believed to be in private hands.

THE NAPOLEON OF EGYPT

The Shemsu Hor sought to enlarge the Egyptian kingdom. Since they now controlled the pharaoh, the greater the territory under his rulership, the greater the riches flowing into the Egyptian treasury through tributes. Consequently, Thutmose immediately embarked on military campaigns of conquest. He completed seventeen raids in twenty years and conquered 350 cities, encompassing territory from what is now southern Syria to Nubia. By taking individual towns, he was able to conquer incrementally entire kingdoms bit by bit. He used advanced weaponry, introducing horse-drawn chariots in warfare, and innovative military tactics. By carrying boats overland he was able to attack coastal cities, such as Mittani, that were not accessible by land,* thus completely surprising the defenseless territories. By the end of his long reign, he

---

*By carrying boats overland from the Nile to the Mediterranean, they could be put in the sea to attack the coastal cities. These cities would never have expected an Egyptian attack from the sea at that time since they believed Egypt to be landlocked. The Mediterranean port of Alexandria was not founded until 332 BCE.

Fig. 11.2. Thutmose III—the warrior pharaoh, by H. M. Herget

had created a huge, international Egyptian Empire. He was known to history as the Napoleon of Egypt. Surprisingly, from his mummy it was discovered that he was a very small man, not even five feet tall—very unusual for a man. This suggests that perhaps he himself was a hybrid.

Haze says Thutmose was "one of the few people in history to expand the borders of their empire to encompass the entire known world. Most certainly, he was aided in accomplishing this feat by the technology of the Shemsu Hor." With so many conquered kingdoms paying tributes, Egypt became very wealthy. The Brotherhood of the Snake, operating through the Amun priesthood, instituted a currency using silver and gold to replace the barter system. This permitted the use of a central banking system to control the expanding economy. We will see below that the Reptilians always seek to control the masses through currency and a central bank, right up to the present. By this means they are able to reward their friends and bring them to power by financing huge enterprises, while eliminating their adversaries through the tightening of funds. It is a hallmark of Reptilian control. Especially, it allows them to finance war. Worldwide, the Reptilians profit immensely from war from both sides! Not only does it reduce the general human population, it also makes the survivors more desperate for assistance, which the Reptilians can provide from their now overflowing coffers—at a price. And so they can change nations and populations, moving them around as on a chessboard. It is well known that banks and large industrial combines profited greatly from both World Wars.

In later years, in the United States, Thomas Jefferson and Andrew Jackson saw through this ruse and fought not to allow central banking as best they could. Jackson, especially, waged a heroic battle to prevent the establishment of a central bank. Their efforts forestalled the advent of such a bank for about a century, but in 1913 the establishment of the Federal Reserve Bank completed the takeover of the American economy by Reptilian front men and opened the funding floodgates that financed World War I and all the U.S. wars to follow.

In ancient Egypt, given this initial impetus of control over Thutmose, the Brotherhood of the Snake retained their dominance over succeeding pharaohs. Their rulership of Egypt, through the priesthood of Amun, operated behind the pharaoh's throne; they always carefully promoted their protégés into power by using their ancient knowledge of genetics and bloodlines and drugs and mind control. They encountered a speed bump when Akhenaten came to power and reinstituted worship of Ra, the sun god. But that was soon disposed of in the next generation when Grand Vizier Ay influenced young Tutankhamun, the son of Ahkenaten and Nefertiti, to eradicate from pillars and temples all reminders of the worship of Aten and to bring back the Amun priesthood. From that point on, it was business as usual. Haze summarizes their influence. He says, "The Brotherhood of the Snake was the unchallenged authority in Egypt. They governed the people through politics and religion, respectively; that is, through puppet pharaohs and the Amun priesthood. They molded, shaped, and reshaped the world at their whim and experimented with the antediluvian [sic] knowledge that was now their legacy."

Reminders of their control were carefully embedded in the popular culture. The god Sobek, who had the head of a crocodile, was included in the Egyptian pantheon as a god of creation. During the Eighteenth Dynasty he was known as a god of battle and of finance. The caduceus rod circled by two snakes has endured through three thousand years until today, now as a symbol of the American Medical Association. Moreover, to make certain that the people knew who was really in

*Fig. 11.3. Uraeus
on the crown of
Tutankhamun*

charge, they instituted the embedding of a coiled cobra in the front of
the pharaoh's crown, with the snake's head pointing straight ahead, as
if ready to strike. It is now called a *uraeus,* from the Greek meaning
"on its tail." Its presence conferred legitimacy on the pharaoh, and it
was even affixed in the crowns of the gods Horus and Set on statuary. Its presence on the pharaoh's crown is said to date back to the Old
Kingdom, around 3000 BCE. What, possibly, could such an emblem
placed prominently over the pharaoh's forehead signify, other than the
rulership over the pharaoh by the Brotherhood of the Snake?

THE BROTHERHOOD OF THE SNAKE

They have been known by many names: the SHET-I, the HEN-T, the
Shemsu Hor, the Reptilians, the Nagas, the lizards, the hybrids, the
Dow, the Brotherhood of the Snake, the Babylonian Brotherhood, and
most recently, the Greys. They dwell in the underground empire built
by their ancestors, the Draco, able to traverse long distances rapidly
through a complex tunnel network on supersonic magnetic levitation
(maglev) trains, capable of speeds up to 300 mph. Having now broken
away from rulership by the Draco, the Sirians, and Marduk, they have
formed a type of hierarchical brotherhood based on group consciousness

and are fundamentally democratic. They live in large cities. Their capital city is the seven-level Bhogovita deep down under the Indian subcontinent. They have amazing technology including antigravity craft, which they can send into our skies through any number of portals. These were the craft sent out to impress and recruit into their efforts the Pharaoh Thutmose III and to deter Admiral Byrd from his Antarctic incursions in Operation Highjump in 1947 (see plate 20). In addition, it is from the Antarctic, their main scientific and technology center, that they have sent out interstellar spaceships on journeys to the moon and Mars and beyond. Clearly, many if not most of the UFOs that have appeared in our skies, and from which they have abducted millions of humans, are from their underground empire. Their worldwide hybrid project really is conducted from beneath the Earth, and not on spaceships.

From their ancient ancestors, the queens of Orion, they have inherited astounding biotechnology and genetic engineering expertise, originally brought here during the antediluvian era by the Draco. From these beginnings their scientists have developed amazing drugs that they continue to use routinely to extend their lives, as did the queens for millennia, and which they feed into our civilization slowly through "Big Pharma" to reap tremendous riches for their human puppets, the

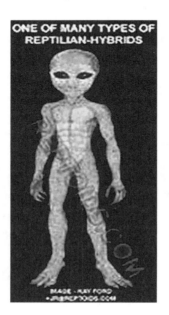

Fig. 11.4. Reptilian-Sirian hybrid (courtesy of John Rhodes at Reptoids.com)

Illuminati. The only factory in Germany that was not bombed and remained intact throughout World War II was the massive drug combine, I. G. Farben. Because they live for hundreds, maybe thousands of years, they can transcend many Earth generations, and so can continue programs over extended periods of time. They have long ago lost the ability to reproduce sexually, and now, for the most part, they use cloning, which the Orion bioscientists perfected millions of years ago. And they have also inherited from those origins the ability to alter and wipe clean human memories and to transfer human consciousness from one body to another. Consequently, they appear to be miracle workers, but it is really just mega-science, perfected by the queens' scientists eons ago.

Perhaps their most formidable talent is their ability to mentally increase their vibratory rate, allowing them to inhabit the lower fourth dimension, in which they are invisible to human perception. This ability permits them to contact and influence humans in dream states and to go easily through solid walls during abductions. This lower region of the astral realm is inhabited by spiritually retarded human souls, as well as demonic entities. That is why, according to Stewart Swerdlow, it is referred to frequently as "hell." All forms of black magic originate in this realm. This is one reason for their power over the human race, although their science and technology, especially their bioscience, the inheritance of thousands of years of development by their ancestors in Orion, is still several hundred years ahead of ours. But because of the potentially great power of the human soul, we are rapidly catching up. Knowing this, they seek to keep us in a state of low consciousness and reliant on superstition in order to maintain their control over us. They accomplish this primarily through religion, in the tradition of the queens of Orion. From their earliest days in Egypt, where they operated through the priesthood of Amun, they have used religion very effectively. It has the effect of maintaining a subdued and guilt-prone populace that is unlikely to challenge the puppets they have placed in political power. As will be seen in the following chapters, they have adopted easily to new religions and twisted them to their ends. They always find a way to use them for mind control.

It should be understood that they also have very many methods of mind control other than religion, which is only intended for the masses. They control individuals in a variety of ways. To begin with, they seek subjects who have a high component of Reptilian DNA, known as bluebloods. These people are the products of many thousands of years of genetic manipulation, and are now mostly in positions of authority. All the members of the former European royalty are bluebloods, as are wealthy and powerful individuals in all segments of society, especially in industry, academics, and health-related positions. Those individuals who have been genetically nurtured to possess almost 50 percent Reptilian DNA are considered to be members of the Illuminati. All the top world bankers, statesmen, clergy, and CEOs are in this category. All these people are the most vulnerable to Brotherhood mind control and demonic influence from the astral realm. The Brotherhood operates primarily through the dreamscape. Military historian James Bartley says, "The reptilians and their minions are masters of creating illusions, assuming disguises and dimming the awareness of human beings in or out of the astral dreamscape. In the dreamscape the reptilians can heighten the anxiety level of the abductee or promote mental sluggishness just as easily as if they were spinning the dial on an FM radio." While much of their control occurs through the dreamscape, they have also now abducted many millions of people all over the world for special mental programming.

This capability of control is particularly important when preparing a nation for war. After putting their puppets in all positions of authority in the armed forces, they program them to become violent and callous to human suffering—to become vicious killers—and to lead their men to become the same. This explains how the armies of warlike nations become maddened murderers and killers, showing not even a scintilla of human consideration and compassion. Bartley says, "Again and again, the reptilian concepts of Pure Bloodlines and the murder and torture of innocent humans plays itself out with a vengeance. Throughout history, these essentially reptilian concepts were drummed into cultures and societies under reptilian control and the tragic consequences were always the same—the horrible and agonizing deaths of innocent men, women and children." See chapters 16 and 17 for two of the most chilling recent examples of this.

12

The Creation of Christianity

The Sirians from Sirius A were in a unique situation. On the one hand, their loyalty was pledged to the Orion queens by virtue of the alliance, so they were obliged by that agreement to take no actions contrary to the interests of the Reptilians. However, they did have an agenda of their own, and here on this small planet on the very edge of the galaxy, they did not feel constrained enough to worry about a Reptilian reaction to real or imagined violations of the agreement. While they feared a full-scale Reptilian attack, that would not be likely for small indiscretions. Furthermore, the Reptilian population on Earth was hobbled by having to live underground, and they were cut off from communication with Draco and Orion. So the Sirians adopted a double standard. They continued to help the Reptilians here in very important ways. It was their technology that made the shape-shifting program possible, and they assisted in the hybridization program in other ways. However, they also implemented their own plans, especially in the area of religion.

In terms of hybridization, the Sirians were more experienced and sophisticated than the Reptilians, who were stranded here, cut off from their technology in Orion. Before Atlantis sank beneath the waves, the Sirians followed the Atlantean migration to Egypt. They wanted to create hybrid Atlan-Sirians (that is, Lyran-Sirians), which they believed would create a magnificent new race on Earth, amenable to Sirian influence. With Atlantis gone, they believed this was the best alternative for re-creating Lyran culture on Earth. However, they did not have Reptilian approval for this plan. This created race was the earliest subrace of Hebrews. Swerdlow says, "These people were tall and powerful, and spoke the Sirian language which is the equivalent to the ancient Hebrew language. Scholars agree that the Hebrew language suddenly appeared on the scene. . . . Originally, Hebrew was a language used exclusively by the [Jewish] priesthood and the Egyptian secret society." The Egyptian priesthood had its own hieroglyphic language reserved for religious communications. The Hebrews were not really slaves in Egypt, but were paid workers. The Egyptians also used them as foreign agents. They were sent to Canaan to try to absorb the Canaanites into the Egyptian Empire. There, they mixed with the Sumerian-hybrid descendants and adopted some of their Reptilian blood ritual and human sacrifice practices. About this, Swerdlow says, "All of this was incorporated into a conglomerate religion based on ancient Egyptian/Atlantean/Sirian beliefs. That is how Judaism was born." The story of Abraham being commanded by God to sacrifice his own son was one of the results of that religion. It was an acceptable command in a religion that practiced human sacrifice. However, the Hebrews changed that practice to animal sacrifices. That was the more civilized Jewish version of the barbaric human sacrifices practiced by the Reptilian hybrids in both the Middle East and in Central and South America.

The Brotherhood and the Sirians understood well the power of religion to control and direct the lives of their subjects. The Orion queens had learned that lesson eons ago and used religion to control their far-flung galactic empire. The dispersion of the Jews from Egypt throughout the Middle East was based on a deliberate fast-track plan to spread the new religion and its practices in those areas. It was intended that Judaism would become the universal religion of the new humanity. Swerdlow tells us, "The Middle East became a focal point for the Sirians and their Reptilian allies. Together, they generated a new version of religion and culture for ease of global control and domination. What better way to do that than by programming a race of nomadic people that would carry the religion and culture everywhere on the Earth." The Brotherhood was planning way, way ahead. Their ultimate goal was globalization. In order to create a uniform global population, which they could then easily control, they knew that they needed a uniform global religion.

The Exodus was watched over by Sirian spacecraft, and the Jewish emigrants were given help in their wanderings, when necessary. If the Sirians could hollow out asteroids and propel them with black holes, they certainly had the technology to part the Red Sea. And the manna that floated down from "heaven" to feed the starving Jewish tribes was a scientifically designed food to provide maximum nutrition and energy (see plate 7).

The new religion was supplemented with new strictures along the way by Moses, who communicated with the Sirian craft from the top of Mt. Sinai and was given the Ten Commandments, which were engraved in crystals. The laws that compose the Torah were carried in the Ark of the Covenant, which was an electromagnetic receiver and was highly charged, which was why it could only be approached by the priests who wore protective clothing. And only the priests could decipher "the messages from God" received by the Ark in the Hebrew language. According to Swerdlow, Sodom and Gomorrah were destroyed by atomic bombs because their people's widespread homosexual practices had propagated the AIDS virus, which had to be contained. He claims that even today, atomic radiation can be detected at those sites.

THE ADVENT OF EMMANUEL

The Federation continued to oppose the spread of Reptilian bluebloods and hybrids throughout the civilized world. Swerdlow says, "With Sirian cooperation, they were working to gently push the post-Atlantean remnants back into Lyraen culture now that the Reptilian hybrids were taking over. Of course, this isolated Lyraen group did not realize the current treacherous Sirian Earth involvement. When someone is friends with everyone, they really are friends with no one." The Sirians were playing both sides, while also seeking to advance their own agenda. The

Federation realized that they needed a highly evolved human hybrid to redirect the new religion. According to Swerdlow:

> This group abducted a young woman from ancient Israel with extremely pure humanoid genetics, implanting her with a fetus genetically designed for a specific purpose. Today, this woman is known as Mary, and this is why it is claimed that she was a virgin. . . . There was a persona named Emmanuel. He was a product of the mixture between Mary and a Lyraen descendant. Mary was physically abducted and implanted. She said that she was visited by angels. As a young man, Emmanuel was removed from his mother, and taken to the Great Pyramid on the Giza Plateau. Here he was taught ancient Lyraen/Atlantean/Egyptian principles for many years. He was also taken aboard the Federation ships and indoctrinated in ways to steer the masses away from the Reptilian influences. His orders were to inculcate the three strains of humanity that had the purest Ari-an genetics on Earth. These were the Hebrews, created by the Sirians; the Germanic tribes, created by the Aldebarans; and the Northern Indian Ari-ans who now lived in the foothills of the Himalayas. All three peoples used a lion* as their symbol, and were descendants of the original blonde-haired, blue-eyed Lyraens.

THE FEDERATION
CREATES CHRISTIANITY

Emmanuel/Jesus did his job well. He was well chosen and well trained. His indoctrination on the Federation ships prepared him for his ordeal, but it was really the power of his own soul and spirit that allowed him

---

*It now becomes understandable as to why Louis B. Mayer, cofounder of the MGM film studios, chose the lion to personify his films. Apparently, at some level, he sensed his connection with the ancient Lyrans. Mayer was known to insist that all of his films be wholesome and propagate high moral standards. What came across clearly in MGM films was Mayer's admiration of and respect for women, and MGM created more female stars than any other studio in Hollywood. This had the effect of countering the patriarchal values in male-dominated Hollywood, inspired by the Reptilian protégés, the Illuminati.

to succeed against all odds. Set down, as he was, amid hostile factions on all sides, he dared to promote a new belief system in the face of a then belief-hardened and ritualized Jewish priesthood and a centuries-old Roman culture based on a pantheon of gods and goddesses. Here was this gentle man in sandals, walking the hills and valleys of ancient Palestine, speaking simple but profound spiritual truths clothed in puzzling parables and allegories.

The foundation of Judaism had already been established by Moses. It was now the job of Jesus to build an edifice on that foundation, and in order to build that edifice, it was necessary to purify the message. Judaism had incorporated Reptilian elements that now had to be purged. It was a religion based on law. Jesus changed it to a religion of love when he said, "The whole law is summed up in a single commandment, You shall love your neighbor as yourself." This was revolutionary. The idea of human brotherhood based on love had never been promulgated before as a religion. Always before, religion was all about the worship of gods and goddesses. It was necessary to propitiate the gods to ameliorate their wrath. The definition of *propitiate* is "the act of appeasing or making well-disposed a deity, thus incurring divine favor." This was done by making sacrifices and dedicating burnt offerings to them. When Jesus chased the money changers out of the temple, this was an act of defiance against the Brotherhood, who were monetizing religion. By offering to guarantee a happy afterlife for a few shekels, they inculcated the supreme importance of money, which they could then use to manipulate the human race. This defiance by Jesus was an act essentially repeated by Martin Luther 1,500 years later, protesting against the sale of indulgences by the Catholic Church.

The Federation plan was to spread the Judeo-Christian religious ethic, based on love and service to others, as the spiritual core of the new humanity that would inherit the Earth. This, they believed would counter the hybrid-Reptilian beliefs in blood rituals and human sacrifice and enslavement through mind control—the system that had worked so well on thousands of other worlds throughout the galaxy. Christianity would be a way to direct the new human population in the right spiritual direction and prevent the Reptilian programming from taking hold.

THE TALMUD OF JMMANUEL

The extraterrestrial link to the advent of Jesus is supported by an ancient document unearthed in an unoccupied area just south of Jerusalem in early 1963. At that time, four years prior to the Six-Day War, that area, as well as Jerusalem itself, was still under Arab control, and was technically not part of Israel. This discovery was made by Eduard Albert "Billy" Meier, who was to later become famous for his amazingly clear photographs of extraterrestrial craft hovering over the Swiss landscape near his home in Hinwil and for his meetings and conversations with extraterrestrials. Meier was with his friend Isa Rashid when this momentous discovery took place. Rashid was a former priest in the Greek Orthodox Church who had become friends with Meier in Meier's travels throughout the Holy Land. The document was found in a very old tomb, half-filled with dirt, into which they had crawled out of curiosity. Beneath a flat rock they uncovered a package encased in resin containing four rolls of text in the Aramaic language. Rashid, who came from a Palestinian family, was able to read some of the ancient text. The four scrolls constituted a book with the title *The Talmud of Jmmanuel,* which we will refer to as *The Talmud of Emmanuel,* which means "God with us." (Up to that point, Meier had reported contacts with an ET woman named Asket but had not yet taken his famous photographs and had not yet met his now well-known alien contact, the female from the Pleiades known as Semjase. Those events commenced in 1975.)

Rashid began a formal translation of the scrolls to German, for the benefit of Meier, in August 1963, while Meier resumed his travels, on to India and Turkey. By 1970 Rashid had completed translation of thirty-six chapters. He sent these translations in two packages to Meier's parents in 1974. Amazingly, the post office was able to forward the packages to Meier because his parents were no longer at their original address. A letter came to Meier from Rashid the same way. In that letter he told Meier that he had "become known to certain authorities" who were pursuing him to obtain the book. He said that both Christian and Jewish groups were after him because they knew that the contents were damaging to both religions. Consequently, he fled Jerusalem and took his family to a refugee camp in northern Lebanon. The Israelis bombed several camps in Lebanon in mid-June 1974, and Rashid was convinced that they were attempting to kill him to destroy the book. Rashid moved on to Baghdad, where, in 1976, he and his entire family were indeed assassinated!

THE CELESTIAL SONS

In *The Talmud of Emmanuel,* we first learn that God is spelled with a small *g.* He is identified as "the great ruler of the voyagers who travelled here through vast expanses of the universe." Clearly, we are dealing here with space travelers from a distant star, and god is the Captain Kirk of this migratory band of settlers on planet Earth. We learn also that god has a "celestial son" and guardian angel named Semjasa and that it was he who impregnated an Earth woman, who gave birth to Adam, the first human.* Adam is identified as "the father of a lineage of terrestrial humans" and also as "the father of the white human population." *The Talmud of Emmanuel* then gives the entire genealogy from Adam to Joseph, the father of Emmanuel, numbering eighty generations, presumably all of which involve Earth women who gave birth to sons, since all of the descendants have masculine names.

Of interest here is that Noah is the twenty-first, and David, father of Solomon, is the fifty-third descendant. This time period equates roughly to that of Swerdlow, who dates the Adam of the human creation at about forty thousand years BCE, *only* if we count the average of each generation to be about *five hundred years.* However, this could be possible, since Methuselah alone is said to have lived 969 years, according to the King James Version of the Bible. In both cases, the human race was of a relatively youthful vintage.

---

*Many Atlantean females survived the sinking of Atlantis, having migrated all over the globe. It will be recalled that the Atlans were humans from Lyra and the Pleiades, and did not have the Reptilian brain.

We learn in *The Talmud of Emmanuel* that Mary was impregnated by a celestial son named Gabriel, who was of the direct lineage of Rasiel. It is implied that Rasiel is very high in the hierarchy and is perhaps at the same level as Semjasa. *The Talmud of Emmanuel* says that this fulfills "the word of god, the ruler of those who travelled from afar who conveyed these words through the prophet Isaiah: 'Behold, a virgin will be impregnated by a celestial son before she is married to a man before the people.'" This places Emmanuel, or Jesus, basically at the same level as Adam, since they were both fathered directly by a celestial son. Joseph, Mary's husband-to-be, was not very pleased at this turn of events when he learned of it and considered canceling the wedding! While he was thinking about it, a guardian angel, sent by Gabriel, told him, "Behold, god and his followers came far from the depths of space, where they delivered themselves from a strong bondage, and created here a new human race and home with the early women of this Earth . . . do not leave her, because the fruit of her womb is chosen for a great purpose. Marry her in all openness, so that you may be husband and wife before the people."

For the most part, the rest of *The Talmud of Emmanuel* adheres closely to the New Testament events until it reaches the narrative of the Resurrection and what followed. There it becomes a very different and surprising story. This will be discussed in the next chapter. The story of the creation of Adam differs somewhat from Swerdlow's version. In *The Talmud,* Adam is created from only one ET race, whereas according to Swerdlow, twelve ET races plus the Reptilians combined their DNA to create the first human. Moreover, in *The Talmud of Emmanuel,* the human females were already here, while Swerdlow follows the account in Genesis, where it says, "Male and female he created them." The ET race that created Adam, according to *The Talmud of Emmanuel,* does seem to be somewhat equivalent to the Elohim, the extratrrestrial human race that was chosen by the other eleven races to manage the human creation. *The Talmud of Emmanuel* narrative appears to be a simplification of the actual events. However *The Talmud of Emmanuel* story of the birth of Jesus accords closely with Swerdlow's account, both agreeing that the father of Jesus was an extraterrestrial.

13

The Merovingians

CHARIOTS OF FIRE

According to *The Talmud of Emmanuel,* John the Baptist sought to circumvent the Jewish priests, the Pharisees and Sadducees, who he said were no longer teaching the words of god, whom he claimed to be "the sole ruler of this human lineage." Baptism, he said, was ordained under "the old laws of god." He had attracted a large following coming for baptism, which caused the priests to become concerned. The priests came to the banks of the Jordan River where John was baptizing and "humiliated him with malicious talk." They taunted him openly and challenged his teachings. *The Talmud of Emmanuel* reports that John said to them, "You brood of vipers, who told you that you would escape from future wrath, once your false teachings are revealed?" A viper is a poisonous snake. This suggests that John knew that the priests had been influenced by the Reptilians. He told them, "In two times a thousand years, you and your followers who pursue false teachings out of your own arrogance in your greed for power and fortune, shall be vanquished and, on account of your lies, punished. . . . This will come to pass when humankind builds singing lights and chariots of fire, with which they can escape into the cosmos, as is done by god and his followers, the celestial sons."

This is a fascinating prophecy! Clearly, John is referring to spaceships, the "singing lights" referring to the noises they emitted. "Chariots

Fig. 13.1. John and Emmanuel/Jesus

of fire" best described what he saw in his vision because chariots were the most advanced vehicles at that time, and he could find no other name for the spaceships. The "fire" was emitted by the rocket engines. When he said, "escape into the cosmos," it meant that he understood that the ships could reach distant stars where we could escape the trials and tribulations of life on Earth. And here we also learn that god was a space traveler. Also, it is amazing that John knew that we would build our own spaceships in exactly two thousand years!

According to *The Talmud of Emmanuel,* the adult Emmanuel appeared at the banks of the Jordan River, where John the Baptist had been preaching and baptizing for some time, and asked to be baptized. John, at first, refused, saying that Emmanuel had greater knowledge than he did, but consented after Emmanuel convinced him. So John was able to discern the spiritual power of Emmanuel. Then, after the baptism, "a metallic light fell from the sky and rushed over the Jordan," and a voice came out of it saying, "This is my beloved son in whom I am well pleased. He will be the king of truth, through which terrestrial humans shall rise as wise ones." Then, "Emmanuel entered into the metallic light which climbed into the sky, surrounded by fire and smoke, and passed over the lifeless sea. . . . After that Emmanuel was no longer seen for forty days and nights." During that period Emmanuel was given further information about his mission. He was taken to "the palace of god," where he encountered "two very tall men, the likes of whom he had never seen on Earth. . . . These two men from the constellation of the seven stars were venerable teachers." They told him to "fulfill your mission unperturbed by the irrationality and all false teachings of the scribes and Pharisees, and despite the disbelieving people. . . . Not until the time of space-traveling machines will the truth break through and gradually shake the false teachings that you are the son of god or Creation." They then brought Emmanuel "in the metallic light" back to Galilee in Israel, where he commenced preaching to the people.

The two men were apparently Pleiadians from a civilization that was part of the Federation and had participated in the creation of humanity after the Hatona Council. The "metallic lights" were their spacecraft. Evidently, they were charged with the spiritual guidance of the new humans. The phrase "the time of space-traveling machines" is a clear reference to the twenty-first century. It is fascinating that they knew that Christian churches would refer to Jesus as the "son of god," actually as the "Son of God." That would be a false teaching because they knew he was the son of Gabriel, a "celestial son." They knew also that he would be falsely considered the son of Creation. *Creation* was the term used in *The Talmud of Emmanuel* to refer to the power that created the universe, and so was infinitely greater than god, who was essentially a highly advanced human from the Pleiades, probably an Elohim, who was in charge of our spiritual evolution.

EMMANUEL AND MARY MAGDALENE

Mary Magdalene became one of the disciples of Emmanuel, and eventually they were married. This is perfectly understandable since the people referred to Emmanuel as "rabbi," and in the Jewish tradition, rabbis were expected to be married. Since Emmanuel was in his early thirties, this was an appropriate time for him to marry. Mary Magdalene came from the fishing village of Migdal, which still exists on the Sea of Galilee in the far north of Israel. This was the original center of activity of the

Nazarenes. Jesus was a Nazarene, and, very likely, Mary was also. So this helps to explain how they came together.

According to Laurence Gardner, in his book *Bloodline of the Holy Grail: The Hidden Lineage of Jesus,* "The Nazarenes were a liberal Jewish sect opposed to the strict Hebrew regime of the Pharisees and Sadducees. The Nazarene culture and language were heavily influenced by the philosophers of ancient Greece and their community supported the concept of equal opportunity for men and women. Documents of the time referred not to Nazareth but to the Nazarene community, wherein priestesses coexisted in equal status with priests." Mary was from a devout Jewish family that had become wealthy operating fisheries. This is interesting, given her connection with Emmanuel, who became known as the Fisher of Men, and her later connection with the Fisher kings of the Languedoc in the south of France. If it is true that Emmanuel/Jesus was genetically created and trained by the Pleiadians from "the palace of god," then it certainly makes sense that they would not have left to chance the selection of the woman who would have the most importance in his life and who would become the female progenitor of the bloodline of the Holy Grail. She would have had to be someone special who would be of great importance in helping him to carry out his mandate. All these symbolic links with fishing seem clearly to tie Emmanuel and Mary together, especially since Jesus is now regarded as the avatar of the Piscean age, the sign of the two fishes! So, in a sense, Jesus and Mary Magdalene were the two "fishes."

From all indications, Mary Magdalene was highly intelligent and gentle and became a follower and disciple of Emmanuel out of sincere conviction because she recognized his spiritual leadership. She has now become a role model of femininity in the modern age because of her undying devotion to Emmanuel/Jesus and her character. The clumsy attempts of the Roman church to discredit her by characterizing her as a reformed harlot were never successful in the face of her high moral stature.

Emmanuel and Mary Magdalene had three children, the eldest being a son named Joseph. This information comes from Swerdlow and not from *The Talmud of Emmanuel*. This explains her presence at the crucifixion and her discovery of the empty tomb. Both *The Talmud of*

*Fig.13.2. Sculpture of Mary Magdalene in the
Church of Mary Magdalene at Old Mission
Santa Barbara in California.*

Emmanuel and Swerdlow tell us that the crucifixion was a staged event.
Emmanuel was drugged to make him appear to be dead and was actually alive when taken down off the cross. He was then revived in the
tomb by his "friends from India,"* using special herbs and salves, and
taken out by a hidden back door of the tomb. According to Swerdlow
the crucifixion was necessary to secrete the entire family out of Israel to a
safe place. Emmanuel went to India with his oldest son to remove some

---

*This is a reference to the fact that Jesus supposedly had traveled to India at the age of
thirteen and spent six years studying the Vedas there with Brahmin priests, primarily
at the Temple of Jagganath in eastern India. At the age of twenty-one he preached the
Hindu precepts to the lower castes in defiance of the upper caste priests and warriors.
When they sought to kill him, he escaped to the Himalayan foothills, where he studied
ancient scrolls at the Buddhist monasteries in Nepal and Tibet for six years. At the age of
twenty-seven he returned to Palestine. This information is taken from *King of Travelers:
Jesus' Lost Years in India* by Edward T. Martin (Jonah Publishing, 1999). This account
of the "lost years of Jesus" does not necessarily conflict with the claim in *The Talmud of
Emmanuel* that Jesus spent his young years studying in Giza. It may be that he did both
if he was able to travel via the "metallic lights" of his ET friends.

of the danger from his family. For the rest of the family, going through central Asia was too difficult for them, so they were sent by boat across the Mediterranean to an area that was hilly and fertile, yet difficult for the Romans to occupy due to local resistance. Mary Magdalene and her two youngest children, along with Joseph of Arimathea (who was really Emmanuel's brother James), set sail for the south of France.

From other sources, it is claimed that other passengers on that boat to France were Lazarus, whom Jesus had revived from death; Mary Jacob, the sister of the Virgin Mary; Mary Salome, the mother of the Apostles James and John; Martha, Mary Magdalene's sister; and the black gypsy Sarah, a servant of Mary Magdalene. According to general belief, there were also other followers of Emmanuel on board, escaping from Roman-Sanhedrin persecution after the crucifixion. Significantly, nowhere has it been said that the Virgin Mary herself was in that company. This lends credence to the claim in *King of Travelers* that she accompanied her son and her grandson on the arduous journey to India. In that book, Martin says that Mary died on the trip and was buried in Murree in what is now north Pakistan.

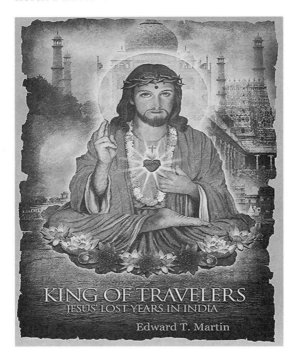

Fig. 13.3. Cover for King of Travelers: Jesus' Lost Years in India *by Edward T. Martin*

THE HOLY BLOOD
AND THE HOLY GRAIL

The boat landed in France at Saintes-Maries-de-la-Mer, or Saint Marys of the Sea, now a small fishing village. According to Philip Coppens, now deceased, known for his appearances on the TV show *Ancient Aliens,* in an article on his website, "As early as 542 A.D. it was known as Saintes-Maries-de-la-Barque, in 1838 it received its present name . . ." A barque is a small ship. The village became the site of an annual pilgrimage by Christians who understood its significance, and eventually, according to Coppens, in 1448, Rene D'Anjou, one of the Merovingian kings, had the location excavated, and the bones of Mary Magdalene and Mary Salome were discovered. He had a church constructed there, now called the Church of the Two Marys, in which statues of the two women, which contain their bones, are kept in an upper chapel. They are shown together in prayer standing in a small boat. Interestingly, one Mary is dark complected, while Magdalene is blonde and blue-eyed.

Fig. 13.4. The Church of the Two Marys (philipcoppens.com)

Fig. 13.5. Icons in the Church of the Two Marys (philipcoppens.com)

If this account by Swerdlow is true, it means that the three children of Jesus were born in the Holy Land. He says that the oldest son, Joseph, accompanied Jesus to India, which means that the two children that went to France were the middle child, a daughter, and his youngest son. From this it can be deduced that Joseph was already a young man when they began the trip to India, since evidently he was old enough to bear the hardships of travel by caravan along the "rough and ready" Silk Road for a distance of about two thousand miles! Gardner says in *Bloodline of the Holy Grail* that this second son was named Jesus Justus, and it was he who became the progenitor of the descendants of Jesus in Gaul, as France was then known. He was the carrier of the Sangreal, the "Blood Royal" or the Holy Grail, which has, over time, become transformed into a sacred chalice containing the blood of Jesus.

According to Swerdlow, the pilgrims from the Holy Land who were led by Mary Magdalene initially lived very simply. He says, "Mary Magdalene took her crew up north into the hilly countryside. They actually lived in a series of caves that are common in the area. Her children lived to adulthood and also married. . . . The caves in which Mary and her family lived are now covered by a castle in the town of Rennes-Le-Chateau. Much mystery surrounds this place, especially the rumors that it contains massive secrets pertinent to Christianity." These secrets were revealed in the books *Holy Blood, Holy Grail* by Michael Baigent, Richard Leigh, and Henry Lincoln and *The Da Vinci Code* by Dan Brown.

Swerdlow continues, "The grandchildren and other descendants of Emmanuel did well in the following three centuries. They married the children of the leaders of the area, maintaining their Hebrew identity. In fact, for a couple of centuries, a large area of Southern France was a Jewish Kingdom. These genetics mixed with the Celtic/Atlantean genetics that were already present." Swerdlow suggests that this mixing was a deliberate effort by the Federation to counteract the Reptilian bloodlines that were starting to proliferate in the Middle East and were beginning to move westward.

THE FISHER KINGS

Gardner says, "If we now look at St Paul's Epistle to the Hebrews . . . Paul tells of how Jesus was admitted to the Priesthood of Heaven when he actually had no entitlement to such a sacred office. He explains that Jesus was born (through his father Joseph) into the Davidic line of Judah, a line which held the right of kingship but had no right to priesthood, for this was the sole prerogative of the lines of Aaron and Levi. But, says Paul, a special dispensation was granted, and he tells that 'for the priesthood being changed, there is made of necessity a change also of the law.' As a result of this express 'change of the law,' it is explained that Jesus was enabled to enter the Kingdom of Heaven in the priestly Order of Melchizedek. . . . Ordained priests of the era were called 'fishers'; their helpers were called 'fishermen,' and baptismal candidates were called 'fishes.' Jesus became an ordained fisher when he entered the Kingdom of Heaven, but until that time (as explained by St Paul) he held no priestly office. . . . The apostles James and John were both ordained 'fishers,' but the brothers Peter and Andrew were lay

Fig. 13.6. A Fisher king

'fishermen,' to whom Jesus promised ministerial status, saying, 'I will make you to become fishers of men.'"

Gardener also says, "It was in Gaul that the famous line of Jesus and Mary's immediate descendant heirs, the Fisher Kings, flourished for 300 years. The eternal motto of the Fisher Kings was 'In Strength,' inspired by the name of their ancestor, Boaz (the great-grandfather of King David), whose name similarly meant 'In Strength.' When translated into Latin, this became 'In Fortis,' which was subsequently corrupted to 'Anfortas,' the name of the key Fisher King in Grail romance."

THE MEROVINGIAN DYNASTY

Gardner continues the story: "In the early fifth century, Jesus and Mary's descendent Fisher Kings became united by marriage to the Sicambrian Franks, and from them emerged a whole new reigning dynasty. They were the noted Merovingian Kings who founded the French monarchy and introduced the well-known fleur-de-lys (the ancient gladiolus symbol of circumcision) as the royal emblem of France." This alliance created the dynasty that allied local fiefdoms, forming the Frankish empire and ultimately the country of France. The Merovingian rulers, who were known as the "long-haired" kings, reigned from the rulership of Childeric I in 480 CE to that of Childeric III ending in 752 CE. But it was Clovis I, who ruled from 481 to 511, who unified all of Gaul (see plate 8). The Merovingians held certain magical beliefs, but most notably adopted a local form of Christianity based on the lives of saints, resisting the Roman version founded by Constantine early in the fourth century. There were distinctly localized beliefs and traditions that appeared to be adapted from their Frankish origins, which were, in turn, perhaps inherited from the descendants of Emmanuel and Magdalene and the Fisher kings. Many of these saints were female, attesting to the lasting influence of Magdalene.

From Gardner we learn, "From the Merovingian succession, another strain of the family established a wholly independent Jewish kingdom in southern France: the kingdom of Septimania, which we now know as Languedoc. Also, the early princes of Toulouse, Aquitaine and Provence were all descended in the Messianic bloodline. Septimania was specifically granted to the Royal House of David in 768, and Prince Bernard of Septimania later married a daughter of Emperor Charlemagne."

MAGDALANIAN TRADITIONS

The Magdalanian influences inspired by Mary in France began traditions that elevated women to positions of high respect and power, eventually flowering in the code of chivalry in the tenth and eleventh centuries, in which Christian knights dedicated their victories over their enemies to their "ladies." These stories were immortalized in the Arthurian and Camelot legends. Perhaps best known is the famous story about the Lady of the Lake, who gave Arthur his invincible sword, Excalibur. Gardner says, "Also from the Fisher Kings came another important parallel line of succession in Gaul. Whereas the Merovingian Kings followed the patrilinear heritage of Jesus, this other line perpetuated the matrilinear heritage of Mary Magdalene. They were the dynastic Queens of Avallon in Burgundy: the House del Acqs—meaning 'of the waters,' a style granted to Mary Magdalene in the early days when she voyaged on the sea to Provence."

In *Le Morte D'Arthur* by Thomas Malory, a historian of early Britain and France, Malory says that Morgan Le Fey, the queen of Northgales (North Wales), the queen of the Wasteland, and Nimue arrived on a black ship to carry Morgan's half-brother, King Arthur, back to Avalon with them, so that they could properly heal his wounds (see plate 9).

According to Gardner, "Mary Magdalene died in Provence in AD 63 and, in that very year, Joseph of Arimathea [James] built the famous chapel at Glastonbury in England as a memorial to the Messianic Queen. This was the first above-ground Christian chapel in the world, and in the following year Mary's son Jesus Justus dedicated it to his mother. Jesus the younger had previously been to England with Joseph of Arimathea at the age of twelve, in AD 49. It was this event which inspired the line in William Blake's famous song "Jerusalem": 'And did those feet in ancient time, walk upon England's mountains green.'" It is claimed that Mary Magdalene lived in her cave in a limestone cliff in the south of France until her death. It has now become a site of veneration and pilgrimages.

Fig. 13.7. Mary Magdalene Raised by Angels *by Giovanni Lanfranco, seventeenth century*

The story of Jesus and his teachings, his miracles, and his Crucifixion and Resurrection was thus spread throughout France by Mary Magdalene and her followers, the Fisher kings and the Merovingian kings. No doubt, these stories also revealed that the descendants of Jesus had come to France. The twelve disciples had no role in these origins. Thus, Christianity in Western Europe had a distinctly Magdalanian aspect and was really a purer version of the legend than the one brought to Greece and Rome by Paul and Peter. We will see, in the next chapter, how these two versions collided and eventually merged in the establishment of the Holy Roman Empire, which gave the Brotherhood the widespread control of religion and the corresponding mind control of the population in the center of civilization at that time that they sought.

14

The Holy Roman Empire

The Holy Roman Empire is neither Holy, nor Roman, nor an Empire.

VOLTAIRE

Christianity slowly expanded in the Merovingian kingdoms, primarily as a result of missionary monks from Roman territories, who were influenced by the Roman emperor Constantine's conversion and adoption of the Christian faith. These inroads took on a particularly Frankish complexion because of the influences of the Fisher kings, and so the Merovingian populaces were never subject to the authoritarian control or dogmas of the Pauline Church. Consequently, the Merovingian Christians were democratic, and for the most part, they revered saints both local and from afar. There was absolutely no male-dominated clergy in the Frankish kingdom, and many, if not most, of the venerated saints were females.

PETER AND MARY MAGDALENE

But meanwhile, the power of the church in Rome was taking hold and growing. Peter, who had gone to Greece after the crucifixion and had begun a ministry in Antioch, went to Rome during the reign of Nero, at a time when Nero was persecuting Christians, whom he blamed for the great Roman fire that had consumed most of the city. Nero made Christians into human torches to illuminate his decadent parties and had them thrown to wild beasts in the Coliseum (see plate 11)! Peter was crucified upside down by the Romans. It was his martyrdom that gave the impetus to the founding of the church after Constantine's mass conversion of the Roman Empire. In addition, because it was said that Jesus had given to him the "keys to the kingdom of Heaven" and had allegedly said, "Upon this rock shall I build my church, [Peter, from *petra,* meaning 'rock'], and the gates of hell shall not prevail against it," he was named the first pope. This, despite the fact that he had denied his loyalty to Jesus to the Roman authorities three times before the crucifixion.

Peter had been outspoken about his distrust of women. According to the Gospel of Mary, one of the Gnostic texts found at Nag Hammadi in 1945, there was a very telling dialogue between Mary Magdalene and Peter while Jesus was still alive. "After she had explained to all of the disciples the inner meanings of the teachings of Jesus, Peter said to them, 'Did he then speak secretly to a woman in preference to us, and not openly? Are we to turn back and all listen to her? Did he prefer her to us?' Then Mary grieved and said to Peter, 'My brother Peter, what do you think? Do you think that I thought this up myself in my heart or that I am lying concerning the Savior?' Levi answered and said to Peter, 'Peter, you are always irate. Now I see that you are contending against the woman like the adversaries. But if the Savior made her worthy, who are you to reject her?'"

THE ROMAN CHURCH

Constantine had dedicated a church to Peter in the Lateran Palace, thus setting the precedents for Peter's principal importance in the incipient Catholic Church. This reverence by Constantine for Peter was based on a miraculous healing of leprosy that he had experienced through Silvester, the bishop of Rome. In the imperial decree known as the Donation of Constantine, the emperor said:

And when, the blessed Sylvester preaching them, I perceived these things, and learned that by the kindness of St. Peter himself I had been entirely restored to health: I together with all our satraps and the whole senate and the nobles and all the Roman people, who are subject to the glory of our rule considered it advisable that, as on earth he [Peter] is seen to have been constituted vicar of the Son of God. . . . And, to the extent of our earthly imperial power, we decree that his holy Roman church shall be honoured with veneration; and that, more than our empire and earthly throne, the most sacred seat of St. Peter shall be gloriously exalted; we giving to it the imperial power, and dignity of glory, and vigour and honour.

This supreme exaltation of the misogynistic Peter set the stage for the male dominance of the Catholic Church and the strictures against marriage by the clergy.

Fig. 14.1. Constantine's Conversion *by Peter Paul Rubens (1622)*

This document, the Donation of Constantine, which surfaced in the eighth century, is considered by many to be a forgery intended to bolster the papal claim to the lands in central Italy. But its authenticity is supported by Constantine's explanation of his rejection of the suggestions of the priests for the healing of his leprosy. He says, "There came hither the priests of the Capitol, saying to me that a font should be made on the Capitol, and that I should fill this with the blood of innocent infants; and that, if I bathed in it while it was warm, I might be cleansed. And very many innocent infants having been brought together according to their words, when the sacrilegious priests of the pagans wished them to be slaughtered and the font to be filled with their blood." Inasmuch as we know of the Reptilian craving for human blood, especially from children, this sounds suspiciously like a naked ploy by them to obtain a large volume of infantile blood, irrespective of the ghoulish implications, and it makes the entire document much more credible. It implies that the Christian priests in Rome were already being influenced by the Reptilians, or perhaps had been hybridized. Since the Roman church ultimately became the center of the Catholic Church, it suggests that perhaps the Brotherhood was already, at that early date, making preparations for centralized control of Christianity.

Constantine's assumption of power and his official endorsement of Christianity as the religion of the Roman Empire in 312 ended three centuries of brutal persecution, beginning with the horrors of Nero, and it terminated the polytheistic beliefs of Rome. Just prior to the advent of Constantine, the persecutions of Christians turned vicious again under the emperors Maximinus and Diocletian. It was in the final contest for power against his brother-in-law, Maxenthius, that Constantine had his famous vision of a cross in the sky accompanied by the words, "In this sign conquer." That victory at Milvian Bridge near Rome was the official beginning of Christianity in the West. But by that time Pauline Christianity was flourishing in the Roman territories of Germany, Portugal, Greece, Turkey, and all remote areas of the empire, as was the Nazarene version in England and France. That fact, and the increasing military incursions by the Persians and Goths, made Constantine realize that adopting Christianity would be highly gainful.

Gardner says, "It took little imagination for Constantine to realize that, while his Empire was falling apart at the seams, there could be some practical merit in his harnessing Christianity. He perceived in it a unifying force which could surely be used to his own strategic advantage."

CONSTANTINE THE GREAT

Using his new powers as Constantine the Great, he now took it upon himself to appoint the bishop of Rome, thus making the church subordinate to the temporal ruler. In 314 he chose his associate Silvester as his first appointee. Also, in that same year, he claimed the God of the Christians as his personal sponsor, but also introduced elements of pagan beliefs, notably sun worship, into the new religion. Gardner says,

Fig. 14.2. Bust of Emperor Constantine
located in the Palazzo of Rome

"In short, the new religion of the Roman Church was constructed as a hybrid to appease all influential factions. By this means, Constantine looked towards a common and unified world religion . . . with himself at its head."

This was a bold move to globalize religion and, by adding all the trappings of affluence and power to the humble teachings of Jesus, to make religion subordinate to temporal and materialistic power. This completely subverted Nazarene Christianity since it now allowed heads of state to hold all the strings of mind control through religion, as with the queens of Orion. Thus, one can easily discern in this the fingerprints of Brotherhood influence. Constantine was of royal blood through his mother, Helena, and so he was undoubtedly a blueblood.* All of this makes it appear that Constantine's conversion was more of a political calculation than a sincere inspiration—that he had essentially "hijacked" Christianity as a means to solidify his power.

But Constantine also had greater ambitions. Since by tradition the Roman emperor was always considered a god, he also assumed that mantle. Gardner says, "The mission of Jesus to throw off Roman dominion had failed because of disunity among the sectarian Jews. Constantine took advantage of this failure by sowing the seed of an idea: perhaps Jesus was not the awaited Messiah as perceived. Furthermore, since it was the Emperor who had ensured the Christians' freedom within the Empire then surely their true Saviour was not Jesus, but Constantine!" To cement this notion, he convened the Council of Nicaea in 325 to create a new dogma. The Nicene Creed merged God the Father with God the Son and with the Holy Spirit, and bypassed Jesus entirely as the Son of God. The emperor now became the messiah. The Trinity of God became the basis for the new orthodox Christianity. Thus was established the theoretical foundation for the Holy Roman Empire.

---

*Helena was popularly believed to have been the daughter of King Cole of Colchester, Britain. Cole was allied with Emperor Constantius, Constantine's father. This explains how Helena came to meet Constantius and eventually to become married to him and to bear him a son—Constantine. Helena became a devout Christian on her own, and she did influence her son in this regard, although his conversion to Christianity is officially attributed to his vision at Milvian Bridge.

THE MEROVINGIANS FLOURISH
WHILE ROME CRUMBLES

The Merovingian kings observed strict dynastic succession, and the messianic Christianity derived from the Fisher kings and the Nazarene philosophy espoused by Mary Magdalene and her descendants, as well as those of James, prevailed in the Frankish and British kingdoms. Meanwhile, after the death of Constantine, the barbarians invaded Rome, and the religious rule of the bishops and popes was severely weakened. Consequently, the Roman bishops plotted to absorb the western kingdoms and bring them under Catholicism. Their opportunity came in 496 when Merovingian King Clovis, who had expanded the Frankish realm through the many victories of his invincible armies, had a battlefield conversion, much like that of Constantine. After he invoked Jesus, his foes suddenly fell back and retreated. His Catholic wife, Clotilda, seized on this to insist on his baptism. Bishop Anastasius of Rome agreed to baptize Clovis and promised him that he would be the new successor to Constantine and that the Holy Roman Empire would now become Merovingian. These kinds of promises by Reptilian protégés are always broken. They are simply vows of convenience, as demonstrated most dramatically in recent history by Hitler. For more than two hundred years thereafter, the popes pretended cooperation while waiting for another opportunity. As has been demonstrated many times, the Reptilians have infinite patience. Their chance came again in the eighth century.

Charles Martel, the son of Pippin, the mayor of the palace of the king of the Franks, became the great hero of the Frankish kingdom by halting the incursions of the Muslim Umayyads into France and ultimately defeating them decisively in the landmark Battle of Tours in 732. This saved Europe from Muslim domination. Of his ten children with two wives and a mistress, one of them, Pippin the Younger, who came to be known as Pepin the Short, was given an ecclesiastical education by the monks of St. Denis and remained pious and sympathetic to the papacy throughout his life. He was also a formidable military leader. He became king of the Franks in 751 after having Childeric III, the last Merovingian king, consigned to a monastery. He instituted ecclesiastical reforms throughout the kingdom, for which he received the blessing of Pope Zachary. In 753 the new pope, Stephen II, worried about threats from the kings of Lombardy, who were demanding tribute from the papacy, took the unprecedented step of traveling to France to meet with Pepin. This was the first time a pope had ever crossed the Alps. The stakes were high for the papacy. The Lombards wanted to depose the pope and take over Rome. Pepin sent his eleven-year-old son, Charles, to bring the pope to the meeting. This was high drama for the little boy, who ultimately became Charlemagne I, the first ruler of the Holy Roman Empire!

Pepin and Pope Stephen struck a deal. Pepin promised to launch a campaign against the Lombards and to turn over their cities to the papacy. In return, Stephen agreed to officially crown Pepin as the king of Francia and to name his two sons, Charles and Carloman, as his successors. This effectively ended the Merovingian rulership of France and, in terms of religious influence, incorporated France into the Roman Church and made it subject to the edicts of the bishop of Rome and then the pope. Thus, the Reptilian controllers of the church of Rome and the pope took a giant step toward rulership over the entire civilized world at that time in a way similar to that of the queens of Orion with their "Aye in the Sky." Using religion, through the rites of the church, which required submission to the Catholic doctrines in order to achieve salvation through Christ, the Brotherhood was now positioned to impose mind control over all their subjects in Europe. In both cases, the ultimate intent was to suppress higher consciousness and thus to keep the populace docile and controllable. It is what we refer to today as "the dumbing down" process. The Reptilians knew that globalization of religion was the key to global control by their Illuminati puppets and thus the means by which they might retake the surface world.

THE DONATION OF PEPIN

After defeating the Lombards in Italy, Pepin donated the Italian cities that he had secured to Pope Stephen II, thus effectively "homogenizing" Italy by neutralizing the last faction opposing papal control. This became known as the Donation of Pepin. This strip of land across the middle of Italy, encompassing several strategic cities, then became the nucleus of the Papal States, later containing the Vatican. This conferred vast riches on the church. Pepin confirmed his donation in 756, in Rome. Upon the death of Pepin, Charles became king of the Frankish kingdom jointly with his younger brother, Carolman, in 768. They were both considered kings, participating in a single kingship.

Carolman died suddenly in 771, and Charles took over rulership of all of Francia as Charlemagne I and as protector of the papacy. In 772 he rushed to rescue Pope Adrian I from invaders. Charlemagne added the kingdoms of Bavaria, Carinthia, Thuringia, Frisia, Saxony, and Lombard to the empire of Francia in the late eighth century. In 800 he was crowned emperor of the Romans by Pope Leo III, whom Charlemagne had saved from assassination by the Romans. The story goes that Charlemagne was unaware of the coronation until Leo crowned him by surprise as he knelt to pray in St. Peter's Basilica. This established the precedent that all future emperors would have to be crowned by the pope in order to be legitimate. The remark by Voltaire (see the epigraph at the start of this chapter) was true because the empire became "holy" only because the emperor was anointed by the pope. It was "Roman" because it was a self-styled reincarnation of the Roman Empire, and it was not really an empire, but rather a loose affiliation of local fiefdoms and kingdoms. In any case, this tradition served to further globalize the Roman Church, which carried forward the Brotherhood agenda. Between the ninth and sixteenth centuries, thirty Holy Roman emperors were crowned. Thus, the Roman Church came to dominate all of Europe.

THE CATHARS

But the empire could not be held together, and the more liberal western provinces continued to rebel. As the Catholic Church gained power, it became more intolerant of schisms of the basic faith, and it cracked down hard on the deviants. The most notorious instance of this was the reaction to the Cathar movement, which lasted from the eleventh through the fourteenth centuries. This flourished in the Languedoc region of France, which was where Mary Magdalene had lived and preached. The precepts reflected some of her teachings. They included male-female equality, reincarnation, refusal to eat animal products, and no objections to contraception. Perhaps most damning was the Cathars' rejection of the priesthood, and this is what produced the most severe repercussions because it removed the authority of the hierarchical church. In 1209, by papal authority, the entire population of the Cathar-dominated city of Beziers in southern France was slaughtered by the crusaders, and the city was burned to the ground. It is estimated that between fifteen thousand and twenty thousand were killed. By the time the movement was put down by a crusade, more than a half million Catharists had been killed, all sanctioned by the popes. This repression set the example for future dealings with rebellious movements.

THE DARK AGES

The crackdown on the Cathars was just the beginning. This set precedents for all suspected cases of "heresy," that is, all instances of belief not in accordance with Catholic doctrine. If, after being tortured, the accused was found guilty by a church tribunal, the heretic was turned over to the civil authorities, since the church itself could not kill, where he or she would have to turn over all property to the church and could be made to wear a yellow cross, imprisoned for life, or burned alive at the stake. In many cases the accused would languish in prison for years before even being tried. Torture was expressly permitted by a papal bull issued by Pope Innocent IV in 1252. As these cases multiplied they constituted a mass movement now termed an inquisition. There were several medieval inquisitions. In all cases, they were initiated by the popes. The Episcopal Inquisition against the Cathars was started by a papal bull from Pope Lucius III in 1184. In 1231 Pope Gregory IX dispatched Dominican and Franciscan mendicant friars to all regions of Europe to set up the trials to deal with the heretics. This procedure, by papal instruction, was thorough and highly organized. The papal authorities wanted records of all cases, and these records still exist in

Fig. 14.3. Gregory IX, the inquisition pope

the Vatican Library. By the fifteenth century, most heretical movements had been stamped out.

THE ENLIGHTENMENT

This type of violent repression was deemed necessary in Europe because the bloodlines in the European population were primarily human, and, consequently, these people were not so easily brainwashed and controlled by the global religion. So, this is where the Federation began their campaign of reaction. Starting in the early seventeenth century, dedicated and highly trained agents of the Federation infiltrated European society. First came the scientific revolution propagated by such intellectual giants as Francis Bacon, René Descartes, Isaac Newton, John Locke, Baron Spinoza, and Pierre Bayle. The elevation of science above church mythology set the stage for the philosophic revolution because it eliminated mystical beliefs. The major Enlightenment philosophers and writers were Montesquieu, Voltaire, Jean-Jacques Rousseau, Étienne Bonnot de Condillac, and Nicolas de Caritat, marquis de Condorset in France;

David Hume and Adam Smith in England; Gotthold Ephraim Lessing and Immanuel Kant in Germany; and Giambattista Vico, Cesare Beccaria, and Francesco Mario Pagano in Italy. According to Wikipedia, "The *Philosophes,* the French term for the philosophers of the period, widely circulated their ideas through meetings at scientific academies, Masonic lodges, literary salons and coffee houses, and through printed books and pamphlets. The ideas of the Enlightenment undermined the authority of the monarchy and the church, and prepared the way for the revolutions of the eighteenth and nineteenth centuries." By this time, these ideas had spread to the British colonies in America. Thomas Paine, Benjamin Franklin, and Thomas Jefferson, who traveled to France frequently, incorporated Enlightenment precepts in the Declaration of Independence and the Constitution of the United States.

The concept of the separation of church and state, championed by English philosopher John Locke, was a fundamental precept of the new philosophies. Locke argued that liberty of individual conscience was a natural right that could not be adumbrated by the church or the state, and therefore must be protected by the state. Jefferson incorporated Locke's ideas in his Virginia Statute for Religious Freedom, which was enacted into state law in 1786 in Virginia. Wikipedia says, "The statute disestablished the Church of England in Virginia and guaranteed freedom of religion to people of all religious faiths, including Catholics

Fig. 14.4. Thomas Jefferson, author of the Declaration of Independence

and Jews as well as members of all Protestant denominations." This was the precursor to the First Amendment to the U. S. Constitution. It was one of only three accomplishments that Jefferson wanted in his epitaph. Jefferson considered John Locke, Francis Bacon, and Isaac Newton to be the three greatest men who ever lived. We, of course, must include Jefferson in their ranks.

THE UNITED STATES: A BULWARK OF LIBERTY

The Virginia Statute for Religious Freedom was in direct opposition to the precepts of the Roman Church. As American values of freedom and liberty started to circulate around the globe, the Brotherhood realized that its plans for religious globalization had been dealt a deathblow. As if to put an exclamation point on it, the Statue of Liberty, donated by free-thinking French agents of the Enlightenment, stood in New York Harbor, welcoming dissident refugees from the religious tyranny of Europe. The Reptilian planners realized that they must take immediate radical action to counteract the "virus" of liberty that was sweeping the planet. As the nineteenth century came to a close, the bluebloods had become removed from positions of influence and authority all over the world. Monarchies had crumbled, and the church authority was rapidly shrinking. It was now time for a sink-or-swim bold move if the Brotherhood ever hoped to retake the surface of the planet. Having failed to achieve control of the world through the globalization of religion, they now turned to another arrow in their quiver. It was time for a world war.

PART III

Modern World Wars
and Beyond

15

World War

The passage of the Federal Reserve Act in December 1913 made World War I possible. The Brotherhood now effectively controlled the finances and economy of the United States. The Federal Reserve Bank was owned by a consortium of U. S. and European banks that were run by the Illuminati, and it was now able to secretly funnel American funds to foreign banks and corporations to be used to build up their military forces, as well as to American defense industries in possible preparation for joining in the debacle.

The money was not needed so much by Germany, which had reaped a five-billion-franc bonanza as war reparations after the Franco-Prussian war in 1871. It was needed by other European nations that were worried about the bellicose attitude of Germany's Kaiser Wilhelm II, who had been rearming to the teeth and had instituted conscription. Germany had plenty of money and was experiencing an era of great prosperity and high employment, thanks largely to its armament industries, especially the Krupp gun works in Essen. Krupp was selling guns and cannons all over the world to countries that eyed Germany and the kaiser with nervous apprehension and felt it necessary to bolster their armed forces. France especially, although financially crippled by the reparations and having lost the heavily industrialized Alsace-Lorraine territory during the war, knew they had to get ready for a possible renewal of hostilities with Germany. For them, enormous bank loans were vital. Russia too, seeking to encourage an attitude of peace-loving cooperation through-

Fig. 15.1. Krupp gun works during World War I

out Europe, knew they were only fending off the inevitable and tried to keep pace with German rearmament, but they were only treading water.

But even Germany needed massive credit to satisfy the kaiser's determination to build a huge navy to compete with England's. England ruled the seas, and Wilhelm knew he could never equal their tonnage, but he hoped to achieve at least a three-to-two ratio. In the end, he had to settle for two-to-one, as England continued to build new ships at a rapid clip. In *The Proud Tower: A Portrait of the World before the War, 1890–1914,* Barbara W. Tuchman says, "In October, 1905, the keel of *H.M.S. Dreadnought,* first of her class, was laid. . . . Designed by Fisher, the Dreadnought was larger, swifter, more heavily gunned than any battleship the world had ever seen. Displacing 18,000 tons, carrying ten 12-inch guns, and powered by the new steam-turbine engines, it made all existing fleets, including Germany's, obsolete, besides demonstrating Britain's confidence and capacity to rebuild her own fleet." The kaiser was awestruck. Tuchman says that in that same year, he astounded everyone by "publicly ascribing the genesis of his Navy to his childhood admiration of the British Fleet." Such an admission by the crowned head of the most militarily powerful and warlike nation in the world at that time reveals the puerile motivations that plunged the entire world into the bloodiest and most awful human slaughter ever known on this planet.

But, as more is learned about this man, it becomes more understandable how he could have launched such an era of horror, extending over the entire first half of the twentieth century. He was the oldest grandchild of Queen Victoria and the son of Princess Victoria, the oldest daughter of the queen and Prince Albert. His father was Prince Frederick William of Prussia, the heir to the Prussian crown who eventually became King Frederick III. Due to a breech birth and medical incompetence, his left arm was about six inches shorter than his right, which affected his emotional stability throughout his life. He ascended to the throne of Germany and Prussia as Kaiser Wilhelm II at the age of twenty-nine in 1888, upon the death of his father. He was closely related to all the royalty of Europe and Russia. He was a first cousin to King George V of England; Queen Marie of Romania; Queen Maud of Norway; Victoria Eugenie, the queen consort of Spain; and Empress Alexandra of Russia, the wife of Czar Nicholas. This means that he was a royal blueblood through and through, and consequently was of the right bloodline for manipulation by the Brotherhood of the Snake and their Illuminati protégés. When he forced the retirement

Fig. 15.2. Queen Victoria and grandson Wilhelm

of Otto von Bismarck, "the Iron Chancellor," in 1890, there was no further interference with his governance, and he then basically had a free hand in the rulership of his realm. This gave him enormous power, since Germany and Prussia were the richest and most powerful nations in the world at that time, even greater than the United States and on a par with England (see plate 12).

From the beginning of his reign, the kaiser created a highly structured military zeitgeist in Germany. Everything was subordinated to military matters. Tuchman says, "When the Barnum and Bailey Circus played Germany in 1901, the Kaiser, hearing about the remarkable speed with which trains were loaded, sent officers to observe the method." They learned that the technique for loading and unloading the trains used a single entry car and connecting rails in the cars throughout the train, so that they could load from one car and then roll everything through the train on the rails. By this method, three trains of twenty-two cars each could be loaded in one hour. The kaiser adopted this technique for his army. Tuchman says also, "He liked to arrange military pageants and festivals, especially the annual spring and autumn parades of the Berlin garrison on the huge Templehof Field, where formations of 50,000 troops, equivalent to several divisions, could maneuver." He was always seen in a highly decorated military uniform, of which he owned many versions.

German militarism was not really Wilhelm's invention. He inherited a unified and dominant Prussian-German state from Bismarck, its former chancellor. It was Bismarck who combined the loosely confederated German states into one nation and successfully prosecuted three short wars, all of which brought them more territory. However, it was also his doing that effectively suppressed democracy and installed autocratic rule. But Germany was enjoying a peaceful and prosperous existence when Wilhelm II became emperor. It could have remained so indefinitely if he hadn't entertained delusions of a greater grandeur. Foreign relations were essentially benign, especially so since England and Russia were ruled by his first cousins! It could have been a utopian era for both Germany and Europe. But, they were still unsatisfied. Tuchman explains why:

Germans knew themselves to be the strongest military power on earth, the most efficient merchants, the busiest bankers, penetrating every continent, financing the Turks, flinging out a railway from Berlin to Baghdad, gaining the trade of Latin America, challenging the sea power of Great Britain, and in the realm of the intellect systematically organizing . . . every branch of human knowledge. They were deserving and capable of mastery of the world. Rule by the best must be fulfilled. . . . What they lacked and hungered for was the world's acknowledgment of their mastery. So long as it was denied, frustration grew and with it the desire to compel acknowledgment by the sword.

While Tuchman meant this explanation to refer to Germany itself, it really and perfectly applies to the kaiser. She is explaining why he was itching for a fight.

PUBLIC EMBARRASSMENTS

Capable of flashes of brilliance, Wilhelm was emotionally unstable, breaking out in bursts of temper and anger with little provocation. This characteristic was displayed to the world in his interview with the British *Daily Telegraph* newspaper on October 28, 1908, while he was on vacation in England, visiting his royal relatives. It begins, "You English are mad, mad, mad as March hares." Then, painstakingly, he laid out his case about why he liked the British and had done so much to favor England in world affairs and had defended them against calumny regarding the Boer War. Sounding like a father scolding his son, he goes on to say, "I strive without ceasing to improve relations, and you retort that I am your archenemy. You make it hard for me. Why is it?" Behind all his words, there is that veiled threat if they do not appreciate what he has done for them. Then he defends his naval buildup. He ends with, "Germany must have a powerful fleet to protect that commerce and her manifold interests in even the most distant seas. She expects those interests to go on growing, and she must be able to champion them manfully in any quarter of the globe. Her horizons stretch far away." This of course, is transparent confabulation. He is trying to calm their war fears while building an invincible navy with which to defeat them. He is already preparing for war.

No one was fooled. Sir Edward Grey, Britain's foreign secretary, wrote in response in November: "He is like a battleship with steam up and screws going, but with no rudder, and he will run into something some day and cause a catastrophe. He has the strongest army in the world and the Germans don't like being laughed at, and are looking for somebody on whom to vent their temper and use their strength. After a big war a nation doesn't want another for a generation or more. Now it is 38 years since Germany had her last war, and she is very strong and very restless, like a person whose boots are too small for him. I don't think there will be war at present, but it will be difficult to keep the peace of Europe for another five years."

Basically, it was all about Wilhelm's envy of his "superior" British relatives. He didn't like being treated like a second-class family member. He was much too proud and haughty. That ate away at him. It was a simmering volcano. Eventually it erupted, and he struck out at them with great force.

There were also other embarrassing factors at work during his reign. His court was riddled with homosexuality extending right up to the royal doorstep, at a time when this was considered abnormal and a perversion. The Brotherhood encouraged this in officials in high places, in order to keep them controllable. It was also true in Nazi Germany and is frequently the case in military regimes. Tuchman says, "The Eulenburg affair concerned homosexuals in the immediate circles of the Kaiser, but it was less their habits than the layers disclosed of malice, intrigue and private vendetta which shed a lurid glow on Germany." The man in the center of the scandal was Prince Philipp Eulenburg, ambassador to Austria for six years. According to Tuchman, he was "the Kaiser's oldest and closest friend, sang songs to him beautifully at the piano, and gave him intelligent advice." Eulenburg was the target of a campaign of innuendo in the press by his political enemies, who were intimating an affair with Count Kuno Moltke, city commander of Berlin. The kaiser immediately fired everyone in his military and diplomatic corps

Fig. 15.3.
Prince Philipp
Eulenburg

accused or suspected of homosexual practices, and forced Moltke to sue the editor of the paper for libel. The trial opened up all the files about Eulenburg. According to Tuchman, "Through four trials lasting over a period of two years, from October, 1907, to July, 1909, evidence of perversion, blackmail and personal venom was spread before a bewildered public. Witnesses including thieves, pimps and morons told of 'disgusting orgies' in the Garde du Corps regiment and testified to abnormal acts of Eulenburg and Moltke twenty years in the past." As a result of this mess, the public image of the kaiser sank to a new low. He was no longer their fearless leader, but was now possibly a deviant, and perhaps a homosexual himself. In an unfortunate coincidence, the kaiser's brother, Archduke Ludwig-Viktor, popularly known as "Luzi-Wuzi," was involved in a scandalous homosexual liaison with a masseur in Vienna at about the same time. In view of these great embarrassments, the kaiser became even more intent on proving his potency to the world.

WAR

Germany was fully prepared for war when Archduke Franz Ferdinand of Austria was assassinated by a Serbian nationalist on June 28, 1914. This becomes obvious by the timing of the events leading up to the outbreak of hostilities on July 28. The Triple Alliance, which was an agreement between Austria-Hungary, Germany, and Italy for mutual defense, had been in effect since it was put together by Bismarck before the kaiser was inaugurated in 1888, so Wilhelm had really inherited this pact between the three nations. Technically, he could easily have removed Germany from that alliance, since it was not of his doing. In reaction to the assassination as well as to ongoing conflicts over the Balkans region, Austria-Hungary declared war on Serbia, but not until exactly a month after the event, on July 28, 1914, so Germany was under no obligation to join in those hostilities until that date. Furthermore, the Triple Alliance was really a defensive pact. It never should have been invoked when one of the three countries was the aggressor nation. So, actually Germany was really not obliged to join in at all, and even then they should have directed their attack only against Serbia. Yet, only four days after Austria-Hungary's declaration of war, on August 1, Germany declared war on Russia, ostensibly because the czar was mobilizing his forces to support Serbia. And then, without any provocation, Germany set into motion their invasion of France by attacking Belgium the very next day, and then declaring war on France on August 3! Putting all this together, it becomes very clear that Germany's actions had little or nothing to do with the state of hostilities between little Serbia and Austria-Hungary. The kaiser was obviously well prepared to attack

Fig. 15.4. The kaiser and his generals at war

Russia and France and used the Serbian hostilities as a pretext to justify his invasions in both the east and the west.

In short, World War I was the result of a long-planned German strategy of unprovoked aggression against Russia and France. It was the act of a crazed madman who had grown tired of peace and prosperity and wanted the opportunity to prove to the world what a magnificent and mighty nation Germany was and what a great leader and warrior he was! Wilhelm had no hesitation in plunging the entire world into a ghastly endeavor that would forever change the destiny of the entire human race. The prophecy of Sir Edward Grey had come true in almost the exact time frame he had predicted!

THE RAPE OF BELGIUM

Germany attacked Belgium on August 2, 1914, as part of their plan to quickly encircle the French forces. They needed to go through Belgium, using it as a corridor. In doing this, they were violating Belgian neutrality, which had been declared in the Treaty of 1839. The brutality with which the German Army treated the defenseless Belgian citizenry was not equaled again until 1937, by the Japanese in their infamous invasion and rape of Nanking (see chapter 16). The German soldiers looted, pillaged, raped, and murdered civilians with cold, drunken abandon. Many of the crimes, such as the callous rape, mutilation, and murder of women and the bayoneting of children, were brutally cruel and sadistic and totally unnecessary, but were committed with a detached lack of restraint, sometimes while singing!

All of these acts were meticulously cataloged in the impartial report of the British Bryce Committee, which was formed to investigate these crimes in May 1915. The committee had an immense amount of reported material to work with, most of it in depositions contributed directly by Belgian refugees in England. Almost all of the German atrocities were in violation of the Hague Convention of 1907, which dealt with the conduct of war on land, to which Germany was a signatory. The offenses enumerated in the Bryce Report are divided into the following categories:

1) The killing of noncombatants
2) The treatment of women and children
3) The use of noncombatants as shields during military operations
4) Looting, burning, and wanton destruction of property
5) Killing the wounded and prisoners
6) Firing on hospitals, Red Cross ambulances, and stretcher bearers
7) Abuses of the Red Cross and the White Flag

An eyewitness gave the following account of one incident:

I saw eight German soldiers, and they were drunk. They were singing and making a lot of noise and dancing about. As the German soldiers came along the street I saw a small child, whether boy or girl I could not see, come out of a house. The child was about two years of age. The child came into the middle of the street so as to be in the way of the soldiers. The soldiers were walking in twos. The first line of two passed the child; one of the second line, the man on the left, stepped aside and drove his bayonet with both hands into the child's stomach lifting the child into the air on his bayonet and carrying it away on his bayonet, he and his comrades still singing. The child screamed when the soldier struck it with his bayonet, but not afterwards.

About one hundred thousand Belgians were killed, of which sixty thousand were civilians, six thousand by execution. About 1.5 million Belgians were displaced by the invasion, one million to the Netherlands, and the rest to England and France. An estimated 120,000 Belgian civilians of both genders were used as forced labor, roughly half of which were deported to Germany. They toiled in prison factories and camps, some just behind the front lines. Some were even forced to work directly on the front lines, digging trenches while artillery shells burst all around them. In this can be seen the same Reptilian indifference to human suffering that became even more pronounced in World War II. It is clear evidence of the massive mind control programs and the violent dispositions that were programmed into the young German males.

THE BROTHERHOOD PLAN PROCEEDS

All of these abuses were sanctioned right at the top of the military hierarchy. This means that the kaiser either gave the orders or was informed of them. As was the case with Thutmose III, the Brotherhood was able to affect the fate of millions simply by controlling one individual! In the next two chapters, it will be seen that they were able to achieve the same results in World War II, in which they controlled only three men, Hitler, Mussolini, and Hirohito.

Approximately seventeen million people, military and civilian, died in World War I. They were almost entirely of the European bloodline and therefore were the most directly descended from primarily human ancestors. Consequently, they were the most resistant to influence from the fourth dimension. This was precisely the same population that the Brotherhood had sought to control through religion. Having failed in that endeavor, they arranged to have them slaughtered. Since World War I directly led to World War II, in which an additional forty-three million Europeans were killed, the Brotherhood had succeeded in wiping out an entire generation of that segment of the human population that was most difficult to manage and control, and therefore was the most troublesome. Having achieved that goal, they are presently focused on diluting the European bloodline by an admixture of a hybrid population. They are flooding Europe with a massive immigration from the Middle East, specifically from Syria and Iraq, in which the Reptilian DNA component is much higher. Thus the entire human population, now drastically reduced, becomes even easier to control, as the Brotherhood's plan for world domination proceeds.

16

The Sun God

*Brutality is not a native characteristic of human nature. It
has been forcefully grafted onto our character by a foreign
element, under great protest, and with appropriate revulsion.*

ANONYMOUS

It appears that Reptilian influence in Japanese government and society started in the Meji era, which began in 1867 with the installation of fourteen-year-old Prince Mutsuhito as the emperor Meji. This era was characterized by the ending of Japan's feudal society and the restoration of the emperor's supreme authority. In actuality, Japanese government reverted to an oligarchy of about twenty of Japan's most powerful men, the Genro, who instituted major reforms in all areas of Japanese society using the emperor as a unifying figurehead. It saw the end of Shogun domination and the empowerment of a central government and a national assembly, along with a new constitution. As part of a program of rapid modernization centered around the emperor, Japanese scholars instituted State Shinto, that is, the adoption of the Shinto philosophy as the ruling national religion. The Meji regime lasted until 1945 even though Mutsuhito himself died in 1912, and Emperor Taisho took over until his death in 1926, when his son Hirohito, grandson of Mutsuhito, ascended to the Chrysanthemum Throne as the emperor Showa. This period witnessed the industrial revolution in Japan, the advent of conscription, and the modernization of the military, based on the Prussian model.

Over time, the military assumed more and more power until they essentially ruled the country, answering only to the prime minister. The assassination of Prime Minister Inukai Tsuyoshi in 1932 ended civilian control of the military. Hirohito himself put down an attempted military coup in 1936, thus essentially establishing a military dictatorship under his direct control, although he operated through his figurehead, Prime Minister Fumimaro Konoe. Since Hirohito had been promoted to army colonel and navy captain in 1925, this permitted him to rule over military matters with authority. For Reptilian control, the ideal arrangement was a military dictatorship, which they also achieved in Germany and Italy. Thus the conduct of World War II was easily handled simply by controlling these three men: Hirohito, Mussolini, and Hitler.

The planning was long term and meticulous. Starting in the 1920s, the Japanese developed an astounding array of warships and land battle weapons in large numbers. By 1941 the Imperial Japanese Navy consisted of 10 aircraft carriers, 12 battleships, 25 fleet and escort carriers, 18 heavy cruisers, 25 light cruisers, 169 destroyers, and 184 submarines. The aircraft carriers were the most modern in the world at that time. At the start of hostilities the United States had only 7 aircraft carriers. The Japanese had the most advanced submarines, some of which could carry bomber aircraft. Clearly, this was not a nation contemplating future peace and tranquillity. It was a nation preparing for a world war, confident that it would have no difficulty destroying the U. S. Navy.

RESURRECTING BUSHIDO

As part of the new Meji emperor–centered government, a new "Imperial Rescript" was distributed to all schools, showing a picture of the emperor and requiring students to pledge to offer themselves "courageously to the State" in times of emergency. This was clearly a prelude to preparing them for wartime service. Regarding the early preparation of young Japanese men for warfare, James Bartley says in his article "Understanding the Reptilian Mind":

Plate 1. Reptoid Warrior

Plate 2. Nomoli figures, 19,000 years old

Plate 3. Orion
constellation

Plate 4. Atlantean deluge

Plate 5. The storm clouds gather on Atlantis. The migrations begin.
(Jim Nichols, artist)

Plate 6. Thutmose III

Plate 7. Manna falling from heaven

Plate 8. King Clovis

Plate 9. Morgan Le Fey

MARY MAGDALENE
in the South of France

PAULA LAWLOR

Plate 10. Advertisement for the book A Love Devout:
The True Untold Story of Mary Magdalene *by Paula Lawlor*

Plate 11. Nero's Christian torches

Plate 12. The kaiser as a new Napoleon. Note the crown on the table.

Plate 13. French kamikaze poster

Plate 14. Thule Society emblem

Plate 15. Hitler as a savior knight

Plate 16. Modern-day Berlin Eckart Stadium

Plate 17. Argentina map showing Bariloche (southwest corner)

Plate 18. Bariloche ski resort

Plate. 19. Believed to be TAW-50 antigravity hypersonic fighter

Plate 20. Collage illustrating the ill-fated Operation Highjump

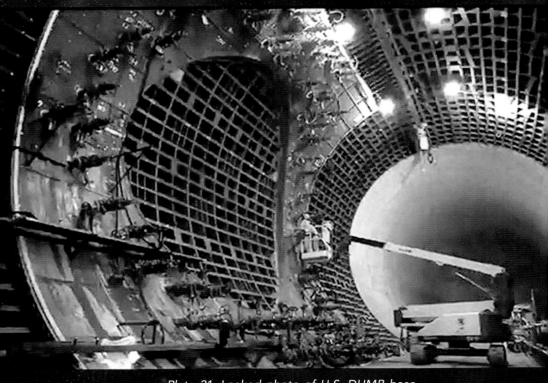

Plate 21. Leaked photo of U.S. DUMB base

Plate 22. The singularity

Plate 23. Transhumanism magazine cover

Plate 24. Alien cave paintings found in Italy, 10,000 BCE

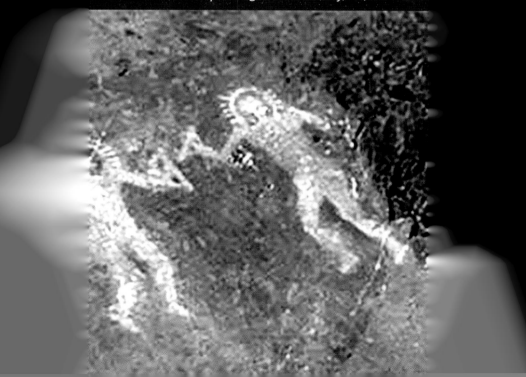

ドウルスの虜。 Zaurus MI-E21

Plate 26. Korean smartphone ad

Plate 27. Representation of Quetzalcoatl

And what exactly happened in those military schools? Individual spirit was ruthlessly stamped out of recruits. Vicious hazing and a relentless pecking order were the order of the day. Recruits were given to understand that they were merely a small cog in a vast machine and that non-conformity of any sort would not be tolerated. This encouraged a hive consciousness within the soldiers and lowered their impulse control vis a vis innocent civilians and captured prisoners of war. Recruits were often savagely beaten for no reason at all. Japanese author Iritani Toshio states that officers frequently justified unauthorized beatings by saying the following: "I do not beat you because I hate you. I beat you because I care for you. Do you think I perform these acts with hands swollen and bloody in a state of madness?"

This last quote was dramatically exemplified in the recent film *Unbroken,* directed by Angelina Jolie, wherein the camp commander at a Japanese prisoner-of-war stockade expresses that precise sentiment

Fig. 16.1. Hirohito on his favorite horse, White Snow

to a young British prisoner as he has him savagely beaten. The reference to "hive consciousness" in this quote is extremely interesting because it betrays the fact that the Reptilians, who do act in group consciousness, were probably somehow involved in this Japanese "educational" curriculum.

Japanese students were also indoctrinated with the concept that they were the only civilized people on the planet and all the rest of the population was barbaric. Bartley says, "The above mentality justified all manner of cruel and inhuman behavior towards humans viewed as subhuman and demonic. Implicit in the belief of the racial and moral superiority of the Japanese was the inferiority and barbarism of other races. This resulted in demonization of 'The Other,' i.e. all other races."

Also, the emperor and the war cabinet were not above the hypocrisy of using concepts they had previously discredited to inspire feverish wartime enthusiasm in the military. They summoned Bushido, which means "the way of the warrior," and the samurai spirit from the past. Then, invoking Shinto myths, all Japanese students were taught that the Japanese emperor Hirohito was descended directly from the sun goddess, Amaterasu, and that, according to Bartley, other Japanese "were considered useful insofar as they may one day purify themselves by sacrificing their life in battle for the Emperor. Indeed, for the Japanese commoner, sacrificing oneself in battle is the best thing a Japanese could ever do." This sacrificial consciousness of the Japanese military became useful for strategic purposes during the final naval encounters of the war when "the divine wind" was invoked, and thousands of kamikaze suicide flyers destroyed about eighty ships and caused heavy American casualties. This is a prime example of the type of mentality that can be imbued into a population in a dictatorship and the reason why all the fascist nations were made into dictatorships. In Germany young boys from the Hitler Youth, as young as eight years of age, were recruited directly by Hitler to defend crumbling Berlin in the last days of the war. They fought with fanatical dedication. In the case of Japan, all that was necessary to influence the thinking of the Japanese Army and Navy were a few words from the emperor!

Fig. 16.2. Kamikaze pilots

Fig. 16.3. Kamikaze attack

THE NANKING HOLOCAUST

The Japanese invasion of China in December 1937 was the opening salvo of World War II. It was the first time Japanese troops, molded by the harsh and brutal training discussed above, were let loose on an opposing army and population. On December 10, 1937, the Japanese 10th Army and the Shanghai Expeditionary Force (SEF), now jointly called the Central China Area Army, attacked the Chinese capital city of Nanking (Nanjing) without a declaration of war.* The Japanese had already fought a bloody battle for Shanghai, and now, with reinforcements from the 10th Army and the SEF, they pursued the Chinese Army westward from Shanghai to Nanking. The atrocities that followed as the Japanese soldiers perpetrated horrors on the Chinese soldiers and civilians in Nanking has never been equaled, either by the Nazis or by anyone else, right up to the present day! Bartley tells us:

> Mass executions of captive Chinese soldiers bound together by ropes began in earnest. The Japanese would execute tens of thousands of Chinese a day by machine gunning them as they stood at the banks of the Yangtze River. Dead bodies clogged the river and the river ran red with blood for days. Mass execution of soldiers or even just young males the Japanese thought were soldiers was not enough. Once again, many Japanese soldiers invented games. Photographs were smuggled out of China showing Chinese being buried alive. Others were buried up to their necks and were then run over by Tanks. Chinese of all ages were huddled together in large groups, sprayed with gasoline and set on fire. Infants were dropped into boiling water. Young boys were sliced in half with swords. German Shepherds were set loose on Chinese and ripped them apart whilst crowds of Japanese enjoyed the spectacle.

The Japanese soldiers continued these sadistic attacks for days. Bartley says further:

---

*The Japanese hesitated to declare war on China to avoid violation of the Neutrality Act, which would have aborted shipments of war materials from the United States.

Fig. 16.4. Japanese soldier enjoying the carnage in Nanking, 1937

Chinese were thrown into the icy river where they would instantly be frozen solid whereupon their bodies would be riddled with machine gun bullets. There are many photographs that have survived which show Japanese soldiers beheading captives or conducting bayonet practice upon them oftentimes with smiling or laughing Japanese soldiers in the background. Mutilations of Chinese were a routine occurrence. In their bloodlust and reptilian madness many Japanese soldiers actually ATE the intestines and genitals from Chinese they had slain. This was observed by European missionaries and members of the International settlement. It was believed by many Japanese that eating the penises of their fallen enemy would increase their virility.

THE RAPE OF NANKING

While the men suffered horrible deaths, the real sadism and cruelty of the Japanese invaders was reserved for the women. Noted Chinese-American writer and journalist Iris Chang, who wrote the book *The*

Rape of Nanking in 1997, received letters from former Japanese soldiers who participated in the Nanking holocaust as part of her research for the book. A former member of the Japanese 114th Division named Takokor Kozo said in a letter to Chang, "Women suffered most. . . . No matter how young or old, they could not escape the fate of being raped. We sent out coal trucks from Hsiakwan to the city streets and villages to seize a lot of women. And then each of them were allocated to 15 to 20 soldiers for sexual intercourse and abuse." Kozo further stated that "after raping, we would also kill them. Those women would start to flee once we let them go. Then we would 'bang' shoot them in the back to finish them up." In his article, Bartley says:

> The reptilian mindset of rape-torture was deeply ingrained within the psyches of these soldiers. Young girls would be literally raped to death, their bodies mutilated by swords or bayonets afterwards. Survivors would be unable to walk for weeks or months after their victimization. Many survivors later died of their wounds or disease. Women would be tied down onto furniture with their legs spread on the sidewalks and would be successively raped by countless soldiers who happened to pass by. Again the concept of "Violent Insertions" played itself out when it came to the raping of females no matter how young or how old. Japanese soldiers took many photographs for keepsakes and souvenirs of the women that were raped and mutilated. There are photos of dead women with rods shoved into their vaginas. Eyewitness described whole streets and alleys full of such victims.
>
> Japanese soldiers invented raping games and contests. Brothers were forced to rape their sisters and sons were forced to rape their mothers. Fathers were forced to rape their daughters. Anyone refusing to participate would be executed on the spot. Young female virgins were especially prized by the Japanese. As in the case of the eating of penises, many Japanese soldiers actually cut out the vaginas of young girls and fashioned keepsakes made out of the victims' pubic hair. It was believed by many Japanese soldiers that the pubic hair of a virgin would make them invulnerable to enemy fire. Many Chinese males were also gang raped and mutilated afterwards.

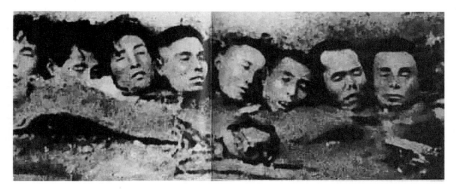

Fig. 16.5. Arranged severed heads in Nanking, 1937

The killing and raping continued for *six weeks!* It has been estimated that more than three hundred thousand Chinese were killed in that period. The book by Chang was the first real chronicle of this "Neronian" orgy of torture and slaughter. Strangely and ironically, Chang, a highly respected author and journalist, was found dead in her car in 2004 on an isolated side road in Los Gatos, California. She had died from a single bullet wound to the head, and her death was pronounced a suicide by the sheriff, who released no further details. She was thirty-six years old. She was survived by her husband, Brett Douglas.

One aspect of the Nanking holocaust that has not been addressed by historians has to do with religion. By the time of the Japanese invasion, Christianity had become widespread in China, especially in the coastal cities like Shanghai, but also in cities not very far inland like Nanking. As the capital of China in 1937, Nanking was highly civilized, with an educated, relatively prosperous middle class. This was largely due to the efforts of Protestant and Catholic missionaries beginning in the sixteenth century. While the Boxer Rebellion at the turn of the twentieth century was a reaction to Christian influence, Christian evangelism and conversion returned quickly and escalated rapidly after the rebellion, so that by the time of the Japanese invasion, Nanking was largely a Christian-dominated city. Scholars refer to that period as the "golden age" of Chinese Christianity. The more that we become familiar with the Reptilians' mind-set, the more obvious it becomes that they harbor a distinctly anti-Christian bias. The Japanese soldiers had been raised in Shintoism and had soaked up the harsh Reptilian values in which veneration of someone gentle and loving like Jesus drew only their contempt. It is logical to conclude that knowing they were mainly killing Christians may have supplied added impetus to the massacre. As we will see, this anti-Christian bias seems to be characteristic of all Reptilian-inspired movements, especially fascism, but now also ISIS. As this is being written, the news reports the massacre of seventy Christians, mostly children, celebrating Easter in a park in Lahore, Pakistan. ISIS took "credit" for the slaughter.

Another flagrant aspect of Reptilian-backed human political and military operations is sexism. Fascism was notoriously and obviously anti-feminine. There was absolutely no respect or even grudging acceptance of any female qualities in wartime Japan or Germany or Italy. The Japanese rapaciousness was clearly based on the degradation of women. The Nazis were notoriously male dominated. Women were used only to bear good little soldiers. And as Freud would certainly have pointed out, even the Nazi "Heil Hitler" salute was transparently symbolic of the erect penis. The goose-stepping soldiers seemed to glory in a proud, tough male attitude. Whereas in the Allied armies, women were employed in important jobs in all branches of the military and were used extensively in previously male-dominated work in munitions and armament factories. The now iconic Rosie the Riveter posters were emblematic of how highly women were regarded by the Western powers. It is known that the Reptilian warrior caste is totally male dominated.

Clearly, the level of brutality and bloodlust on the part of the Japanese Army was unprecedented in modern times, especially as these soldiers came from a relatively civilized country. It would be necessary to go back to Genghis Khan and the Mongol hordes to find anything even approaching it. This was the direct result of Reptilian influence over Hirohito. He authorized the invasion of China and ratified the army's proposal to release Japan from the strictures of international law in the treatment of POWs. Thus, the torture and death of Chinese prisoners was sanctioned directly by him. He also approved the use of toxic gas against the Chinese despite the prohibition against its use by the

League of Nations. According to postwar Japanese historian Yoshiaki Yoshimi, Hirohito personally authorized the use of toxic gas 375 times during the Battle of Wuhan in China in 1938. This was the monumental four-month-long confrontation between the Japanese and Chinese forces in which the Japanese Army suffered 107,000 casualties. While the Chinese losses were double that number, with many deaths presumably from the poison gas, it was definitely a moral victory for the defenders, and it slowed the Japanese advance to a crawl. This prevented the complete conquest of China, and the campaign ultimately ended in a stalemate. And it was the emperor who made the decision to join in the Tripartite Treaty with Germany and Italy on September 27, 1940.

We learn more about Hirohito's character from the imperial edict he issued at the end of June 1944 during the Battle of Saipan, in which he instructed the commander of the Japanese forces to seduce the Japanese civilians living on the island into committing suicide by promising them a happy afterlife equal to that of the soldiers who died in battle. He knew the Americans would take good care of the civilians, and he didn't want to give the United States a propaganda advantage. When the American forces arrived at the north tip of the island in early July, they found that a thousand civilians, including women and children, had already killed themselves by jumping off a cliff, which came to be known as "Banzai Cliff." This incident demonstrates just how concerned Hirohito was with the power of propaganda, as was Hitler. It betrays his Reptilian influence because the Reptilians are masters of mass mind control and persuasion.

Perhaps the most appalling action by Hirohito was his imperial decree of 1936 in which he authorized the expansion of the Army Epidemic Prevention Research Laboratory. This was better known as the infamous Unit 731. The horrors perpetrated by this laboratory under the aegis of defense-related biowarfare experimentation far exceeded anything done by "the Angel of Death," Josef Mengele, and the Nazis at the German concentration camps. Under the command of General Shiro Ishi, this unit was responsible for the deaths of up to twelve thousand men, women, and children used as guinea pigs for grisly biological warfare experiments. The prisoners were subjected to vivisections without anesthesia; removal of organs while the subjects were still alive; amputations to study blood loss; inoculations of diseases disguised as vaccinations, including venereal diseases, plague, cholera, botulism, and anthrax; and deprivation of food and water until death occurred. Men, women, and children were put into high-pressure chambers and centrifuges until they died. Subjects were injected with animal blood and seawater and exposed to lethal x-rays and chemical weapons. The chemical weapons developed from these tests were put into bombs and used in attacks on Chinese cities, farms, reservoirs, and wells. Plague-infested fleas were sprayed from low-flying airplanes on Ningbo in 1940 and Changde in 1941. It has been estimated that between 200,000 and 580,000 people were killed by these attacks in Changde alone. Since it is known that the emperor maintained a hands-on policy for all such military experimentation and attacks, it is inconceivable that he remained uninformed about these actions.

Hirohito made a perfect puppet for the Reptilian overlords because they knew his precise bloodline. Because the Japanese were so diligent in recording ancestry, they were able to trace the bloodlines of the Yamato clan dating back to the sixth century. The Reptilians are master geneticists, so we can be certain that they had access to those records, and they made sure that someone they could totally manipulate ascended to the Chrysanthemum Throne in time for World War II. All three fascist leaders were of bloodlines open to Reptilian overshadowing and influence from the fourth dimension. In his book, *The Biggest Secret,* David Icke has made a persuasive case for the theory that Adolf Hitler was the grandson of a Rothschild, and that the Rothschild family was responsible for his rise to power. Icke informs us that according to the book *The Mind of Hitler,* psychoanalyst/author Walter Langer says that Hitler's grandmother, Maria Anna Schicklgruber became pregnant with the child of Salomon Mayer Rothschild while working as a domestic servant at his mansion in Vienna. Her illegitimate son Alois later became Hitler's father. Icke says, "The Rothschilds and the Illuminati produce many offspring out of wedlock in their secret breeding programs and these children are brought up under other names with other parents." The Rothschilds are strongly suspected to be shape-shifting Reptilian hybrids, which means that Hitler was very likely the same. In the case of Mussolini, not enough

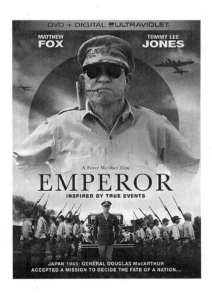

Fig. 16.6. Movie poster for Emperor *(2012)*

is known about his ancestry to make the case for Reptilian overshadowing. But there is strong evidence of his subconscious obsession with having been a Roman emperor, many of whom were Reptilian hybrids. Fascism itself was an attempted re-creation of the Roman Empire.

After the war, General Douglas MacArthur, commander of U.S. forces in the Pacific, was sent to Japan to determine the extent of Emperor Hirohito's responsibility for the prosecution of the war and for war crimes. The film *Emperor* (2012) tells this story. MacArthur designated General Bonner Fellers to research the matter, and Fellers concluded that Hirohito was directly responsible for the war itself and for war crimes.

MacArthur, after consultation with President Harry S. Truman, concluded that the execution of Hirohito would be counter productive and could start a civil war. They decided to bury the report in the interests of rebuilding Japan as a U.S. economic partner. They decided that Hirohito would retain his title as emperor, but would have to give up his divine pretensions and would no longer be considered a god. He lived out his life with respect from his countrymen and died in his palace in 1989 of duodenal cancer. He was given a state funeral in 1990 that was attended by international royalty and world leaders, including the secretary general of the United Nations and the president of the United States.

17
The Antichrist

Reptilian influence in the case of Hitler was much more evident and pronounced than it was with Hirohito. In fact, it appears that unlike Hirohito, Hitler was not a simple pawn. He shared in the Reptilian character so much that it seemed that he was basically a Reptilian in human form. The underground and fourth-dimensional Reptilians apparently selected him as the point of the arrow aimed at Earth civilization. He was prideful, patriarchal, without conscience, ruthless, vastly ambitious, murderous, bullying, massively egotistical, devoid of love, lying, manipulative, vengeful, hate filled, and cunning, and these are just a few of the demonic traits he displayed. These are all character traits attributed to the Reptilians!

It would be very difficult to match Hitler's character with anyone in the annals of history. One could only draw a comparison perhaps with Nero, who killed his own mother and his wife and enjoyed watching Christians torn apart in the Roman "games." This comparison does have some merit since some religious scholars contend that Nero was, in fact, the Antichrist, or would return as the Antichrist, because of his vicious persecution of the Christians. Certainly, if anyone in history could be considered to be the Antichrist, it would definitely have to be Adolf Hitler, and he has been awarded that dubious "honor" by countless researchers and writers over the years. Since they have both been called the Antichrist, this suggests that perhaps Hitler may have been a reincarnation of Nero.

There are some interesting parallels in the lives of both men. Both

Nero and Hitler both had creative pretensions. Hitler was a passable artist and thought he could be an architect. With architect Albert Speer, he never stopped designing imposing Roman edifices for the capital city of his future empire. Nero was a singer and entertainer, accompanying his renditions on the lyre, but also was an artist and would-be architect. Reportedly, his last words were, "What an artist dies in me."

They both began their reigns in power by doing great things for the people. Nero made some much-needed reforms in Roman government. He initiated tax reforms to relieve the financial burdens on the middle class. He eliminated gladiatorial fighting to the death, even if the fighters were convicted criminals. For his first five years, he governed judiciously and prudently through his wise advisor Seneca. Hitler did the same. The economy improved as employment rose and the factories hummed. He brought Germany out of the Depression, and he instituted middle-class perks and vacations. He hosted the Olympic games of 1936, during which visitors from all over the world were impressed with German progress.

Then they both turned ugly. Nero had his mother murdered because she objected to his marriage, and she tried to manipulate his governance, and then he had his wife, Octavia, killed, too. He then began having Christians brutally tortured and killed because he needed

Fig. 17.1. Bust of Nero

a scapegoat for the fire that destroyed most of Rome. Hitler had his niece and lover Geli Raubal killed because the affair threatened his public image. He then began the slaughter of the Jews in Germany and the conquered countries while he ratcheted up his war machine. Both men had assassination plots against them and had the perpetrators viciously put to death. They both committed suicide (at least officially, but see chapter 20) when their personal hatreds and vendettas resulted in the collapse and ruin of their countries.

There is another interesting connection between the two men. In 66 CE Nero had to contend with a revolt in Judea while he was amusing himself at the Olympic games in Greece. This had been precipitated by the slaughter of 3,600 Jewish men, women, and children by the Roman procurator of Judea, Gessius Floras. Gessius also raided their market and their treasury. A Jewish rebellion ensued, led by a contingent of Jewish militants known as the Zealots. They took control of Jerusalem and incited others to join the insurrection. The Syrian governor dispatched the 12th Roman Legion to quell the rebellion. The Zealots, although outnumbered, fought fiercely. They forced the Romans to retreat and slaughtered the entire rear guard consisting of four hundred soldiers. Nero was furious when informed of this royal embarrassment, and he sent his top commander, Titus Vespesian, to put down the revolt. It was during Vespesian's campaign in Judea that Nero committed suicide in 68 CE. It can be speculated that Nero died with an intense hatred of the Jews because the revolt had incited opposition against him within Rome, and that was, in effect, the final straw for the senators, who were crying out for Nero's demise. It was another disgrace for him, added to many others, since it required the intervention of the best Roman general.

If it is true that Hitler was a reincarnation of Nero, this might explain why he was born with such a determination to wreak revenge on the descendants of the people who had brought him such tremendous disfavor in Rome that he was forced to commit suicide. That would be a likely reaction in someone who had a strong vengeful streak in his nature, as Hitler was known to have. So, it seems that the Reptilians had chosen very carefully. It appears that they knew the soul records of the newly born, so they knew about Nero-Hitler's likely racial vendetta. Evidently, they regarded the Jews as a threat to their planned New World Order and planetary takeover.

The Nazis were also anti-Christian and attempted to substitute a newly invented flavor of Christianity that they called Positive Christianity, which effectively separated the Christian faith from the Jewish Old Testament and attempted to repaint Jesus as Nordic and Germanic rather than Jewish. Hitler wanted to change European beliefs to Paganism, but knew that he had to tread carefully to avoid any precipitate denunciation of Christian faiths, which had a history of more than a thousand years in Germany. Pagan-like processions displaying Roman standards and costumes were paraded before the people. The new religion attempted to cast Hitler as the German savior instead of Jesus. The Nazis distributed posters to schoolrooms showing Hitler in armor astride a horse carrying a lance and a swastika flag (see plate 15). They encouraged worship of Hitler as a demigod. Nero had also fashioned himself as a god equal to Apollo. If Hitler had succeeded, it is very likely that he, like Nero, would have begun the incarceration and massacre of those who clung to Christianity. Joseph Howard Tyson says of Hitler in *The Surreal Reich,* "Substituting violent neo-paganism for Judeo-Christian values, he left nothing but destruction and disgrace in his wake." So, as in Japan, the Reptilian anti-Christian bias emerges again.

SEARCHING FOR THE ANTICHRIST

At the age of thirty, Hitler was totally absorbed in politics when he joined the German Workers' Party (Deutsch Arbeiterpartei, DAP) in September of 1919. He was, at that time, a fanatical right-wing revolutionary allied with the so-called White Guards of Capitalism and the Freikorps, the right-wing dislocated and unemployed veterans of World War I. Even though the short-lived Communist government had been overthrown in May of that year, Hitler remained opposed to the Catholic Bavarian government, which was part of the Weimar Republic of Germany.

Hitler had no reason to expect that his joining the DAP would lead to an occult education and an introduction to the philosophy of the Thule Society, whose members dominated the DAP (see plate 14). The Thule Society was an occult/mystical organization whose members conducted regular séances based on the teachings and writings of the "Great Beast," Aleister Crowley, who had inherited the leadership of the Golden Dawn Society in England and had started the Silver Star Society in London. In 1910 Crowley was invited to join the Ordo Templi Orientis (OTO) in Germany by the president, Theodore Reuss. Crowley reformulated the OTO magical workings along the lines of the Silver Star. The Thulists probably had common memberships with the OTO and very likely incorporated Crowley's workings in their black magic sessions. The séance participants communicated with entities they believed to be satanic using Crowleyian rituals, hoping to gain favors and empowerment from the demons. They also attempted to invoke the greatest demonic entity, the Antichrist, to overshadow and influence a new German savior. The Thulists courted evil power and were dedicated to implementing that power to rule over individuals and nations by whatever means necessary. William Bramley says in *The Gods of Eden,* "The Thule was a 'Society of Assassins.' It held secret courts and condemned people to death. It is likely that many victims murdered by the District Command had been condemned earlier in the secret courts of the Thule."

The Thulist who seemed most interested in invoking the Antichrist was Dietrich Eckart. Eckart, who had become wealthy as a playwright, moved in the upper strata of German intellectual and financial society, and owned and wrote for the anti-Semitic newspaper *In Plain German.* He was seeking the man who would become the savior of Germany. He became obsessed with calling down the Antichrist to incarnate in a German leader, giving him superhuman power to lead the German nation to Aryan supremacy in the world. During one séance, Eckart was told by his spirit guide that he would have the honor of training the coming Great One—the incarnation of the Antichrist.

Hitler's membership in the DAP exposed him to the leading figures in the Thule Society. Thule members had created the DAP because they knew they needed an organization to promote a philosophy that would appeal to the workers and the common man. The Thulists themselves were too highbrow and exclusive for that connection. According to Trevor Ravenscroft in *The Spear of Destiny,* the Thule membership included "judges, police-chiefs, barristers, lawyers, university professors and lecturers, aristocratic families, leading industrialists, surgeons, physicians, scientists, as well as a host of rich and influential bourgeois." On the other hand, the DAP members were political brawlers and street fighters. Hitler's fervent leadership in the DAP came to Eckart's attention, and his astral contacts confirmed that Hitler was the one he was seeking. From 1920 to 1923, Eckart undertook a complete occult and black magical education of Hitler, who was a very willing student, having been primed in his drugged-out days on peyote in the flophouses of Vienna. Also, Hitler already had pronounced mediumistic talent and was cognizant of the astral realm. Furthermore, he believed that he had a special destiny to achieve greatness, so he fell in enthusiastically with Eckart's training program.

Some believe that there was a homosexual dimension to this very close relationship between the two men, who were separated by a twenty-year age difference. Hitler was known to have had homosexual encounters while living as a semivagrant in Vienna in his twenties. Eckart, ensconced as he was in the permissive creative community of writers and artists in postwar Leipzig, Munich, and Berlin, has also been suspected of having had gay relationships.

In any case, the commonality of outlook, beliefs, and interests was exceptional. In terms of anti-Semitism, Eckart was even more virulent than Hitler, but on a higher intellectual plane. He gave voice to what he perceived to be outsized Jewish influence in Germany's journalistic, financial, and creative professions. Hitler's relationship with Eckart was essential to his entrance into the higher social and financial circles to which he needed access for his ultimate takeover of Germany. Eckart was the bridge between the rough political world of Hitler and the polite world of high and influential society. And ultimately, Eckart provided the intellectual foundation of the Nazi philosophy.

The critical, defining event of Hitler's rise to power was the

Fig. 17.2. Dietrich Eckart

purchase, on December 18, 1920, by the National Socialist German Workers' Party of the Munich *Volkischer Boebachter* (People's Observer) newspaper, which was brokered by Eckart, who raised the 470,000 marks for the buyout. This gave the Nazi Party a direct voice to the people of Germany, and in the hands of Propaganda Minister Joseph Goebbels, it eventually became their main propaganda vehicle throughout World War II. Hitler oozed gratitude to Eckart for this huge favor. He said in a note, "I want to, dear Eckart, express my warmest thanks for the great help you provided at the last minute. Without your assistance, the matter probably would not have come off." It also provided employment for Eckart. He became the editor in chief in August 1921. This marriage of the bombastic writer Eckart with a powerful propaganda organ accelerated the Nazi takeover of Germany to light speed.

Hitler was not invited to join the Thule Society. He didn't have the right social credentials and graces. Anyway, they really preferred to keep him where he was most effective, as the rabble-rousing political street fighter. However, as a personal friend of Eckart, he was permitted to join in the séances. In those sexual black magic sessions over the three-year period from 1920 to 1923, there is evidence that Hitler's personality changed as he became taken over by a powerful malevolent entity. Eckart believed that it was the Antichrist. According to Ravenscroft in *The Spear of Destiny* regarding the practices of the Thule Society,

"Indulgence in the most sadistic rituals awakened penetrating vision into the workings of evil intelligences and bestowed phenomenal magical powers."

Crowley, while in the Golden Dawn, claimed he had been communicating with the "secret chiefs." Samuel Mathers, the founder of the Golden Dawn, made the first contacts with these entities. In a manifesto to the members in 1896, he wrote:

> As to the secret chiefs with whom I am in touch and from whom I have received the wisdom of the Second Order. . . . They used to meet me physically at a time and place fixed in advance. For my part, I believe they are human beings living on this earth, but possessed of terrible and superhuman powers. . . . I felt I was in contact with a force so terrible that I can only compare it to the shock one would receive from being near a flash of lightning during a great thunderstorm.

Evidently, Eckart resumed that frightening contact and introduced Hitler to those intimidating beings. Hermann Rauschning, the mayor of Danzig, was a friend and confidante of Hitler. In his book *Hitler Speaks,* he reports that in a conversation about the possibility of creating a new, advanced species of human through breeding, Hitler said to him, "The new man is living amongst us now! He is here! Isn't that enough for you? I will tell you a secret. I have seen the new man. He is intrepid and cruel. I was afraid of him." Rauschning says that over the course of many meetings, he obtained the distinct impression that Hitler was a medium possessed of supernatural powers. We are left to speculate that perhaps Hitler was, like Mathers, given "the wisdom of the Second Order" by the secret chiefs. Eckart also passed on to Hitler all of his occult knowledge of ritual and sexual black magic, which was primarily based on the teachings of Crowley. In one of Hitler's personal books in the collection of the U.S. Library of Congress, *Magic: History, Theory, Practice* by Dr. Ernst Schertel (1923), Hitler had double-underlined the passage, ". . . he who does not carry demonic seeds within him will never give birth to the new world."

Fig. 17.3. Aleister Crowley, "The Great Beast"

At the completion of this training, Hitler claimed to be "born anew," filled with the new strength and the resolve he would need to carry out his "mandate." Eckart died in 1923, the year that Hitler entered prison after the Nazis' failed takeover attempt, known as the Beer Hall Putsch. Eckart reportedly said on his deathbed, "Follow Hitler. He will dance, but it is I who have called the tune! I have initiated him into the 'Secret Doctrine'; opened his centers of vision and given him the means to communicate with the powers. Do not mourn for me: I shall have influenced history more than any German." The following year, Hitler dedicated the second volume of his book, *Mein Kampf* (My Struggle), to Eckart. In 1936 he dedicated the amphitheater next to the Olympic Stadium in Berlin (see plate 16) to his former mentor, naming it the Dietrich Eckart Stage. It was modeled after an ancient Greek outdoor theater and remains in use today for concerts and dramatic productions, now called the Waldbuhne, or Woodland Stage.

In 1926, three years after Eckart's death, Hitler continued his pursuit of occult education and training with successful stage performer

Erik Jan Hanussen, whom he had met at a party. Anti-Semitism not-withstanding, Hitler had no qualms about taking instruction from Hanussen, who was Jewish. Hanussen, who had trained himself in telepathy, developed a mind-reading act that was in great demand at theaters and cabarets all over Europe. He wrote the books *The Road to Telepathy: Explanation and Practice* and *Thought Reading: A Primer for Telepathy.* In *The Surreal Reich,* Tyson says, "Hanussen instructed Hitler in autosuggestion, acting, and 'stage presence.' In collaboration with photographer Heinrich Hoffman he showed him how to pose before cameras. . . . He paid special attention to gesture, inflection, gaze, timing, and 'extrasensory attunement.' Sets also played a role in mass hypnosis; colorful banners, music, processions, and lighting all height-ened dramatic spectacles. Above all, Hanussen stressed the importance of self-confidence." Using these techniques, Hitler designed spectacular political rallies and became a powerful speaker, able to mesmerize and excite vast audiences. He learned to start his speeches softly and then build to a peak of pretended frenzied fervor accompanied by animated gesticulations. He also developed a hypnotic power over individuals. Ultimately, Hitler had Hanussen killed at the insistence of the Gestapo.

Fig. 17.4. Hitler practicing dramatic gestures

This rebirth of Hitler into his role as the Führer was clearly engineered by the Reptilians, who masqueraded as the "secret chiefs." His swift rise to power was designed by them beginning in World War I. His miraculous escapes from death, attested to by many who knew him; his very fortunate "training" sessions by accomplices who gave him at least the patina of intellectual acumen and hypnotic theatrical powers; his support by the industrial giants of the period like Thyssen, I. G. Farben, and Krupp; and his endorsement by the powerful Thule Society and the influential financial and journalistic groups that they controlled all made it possible for him to achieve a meteoric rise to dictatorial power.

The manner in which Hitler was coached for his role as the emperor of Europe and Russia by the Reptilians is very instructive. It reveals the thinking and planning of the Reptilian overlords and their techniques, and should be considered a primer for those who now want to eliminate all Reptilian influence and their plan for the creation of the New World Order. It is an invaluable lesson. It should be noted how they were able to bring individuals into Hitler's life to educate and train him in the techniques and methods he would need to succeed. Identifying these people at the soul level and controlling and manipulating their thoughts and actions can only be accomplished by experts in genetics and mind control. The Reptilians are known to be masters of both. This influence can only be exercised from a higher dimension, especially as regards having a view outside of time, thus being able to create timely synchronicities and incidents. As lower fourth-dimensional, or astral, creatures, the Reptilians have that perspective. They use third-dimensional entities like the Greys, hybrids, and the protohuman Illuminati to do their dirty work. It requires too much energy for them to manifest in the third dimension.

The brutalities of the Nazis rivaled, and even exceeded, those of the Japanese in China, all initiated and dictated by Hitler. This fact alone reveals Hitler's Reptilian nature. The Reptilians are known to be merciless and sadistic. Early in the war, Hitler boasted of turning the young men of Germany into "magnificent beasts of prey."

The Hitler Youth movement began in the 1920s, long before Hitler came to power. Originally, in 1922, it was simply the youth brigade of the Nazi Party, intended to train future members of the paramilitary Sturmabteilung (Storm Regiment). It became the Hitler Youth League in July 1926. At that point, Hitler was the head of the Nazi Party and could begin to inculcate Hitlerian values into the membership, consisting of boys age fourteen and older. By 1930 there were twenty thousand members, and a younger group was organized for those ages ten to fourteen. All of these boys were destined to become soldiers in the Wehrmacht because by 1939 even the youngest were old enough to fight. By the time Hitler became chancellor in 1933, there were 2.3 million members. At that time Hitler said, "The weak must be chiseled away. I want young men and women who can suffer pain. A young German must be as swift as a greyhound, as tough as leather, and as hard as Krupp's steel." As in Japan, the Hitler Youth were indoctrinated with the belief that they were "supermen" and other races and nationalities were inferior. Therefore, it would be understandable that it would not be a great loss if the others were to be enslaved or killed. This was precisely how the young Japanese were trained a continent away. It suggests that the philosophies of both fascist societies had a common origin, and that origin was Reptilian.

In his book *Soldiers: German POWs on Fighting, Killing and Dying,* historian Sonke Neitzel reveals casual conversations between German prisoners of war that were secretly recorded at the Trent Park POW Camp in Enfield, England, throughout the war. The English edition was published in 2012. A review of the book was written by Allan Hall in an article in the *Daily Mail* on September 16, 2012. This book leaves no doubt that many of these German Wehrmacht soldiers had absolutely no conscience-stricken moments and had no qualms about executing civilians in cold blood for no reason. In his article, Hall says:

> The overheard conversations not only provided high-grade military intelligence—they also aided their British captors in trying to fathom what made "honourable" warriors into killers no better than the S.S. or Gestapo. What the captured men boasted of was not the betterment of professional soldiers, the thrill of a victory

over fellow men-at-arms in a fair fight. Their conversations betray how deep the Nazi state corrupted the military code, and in doing so, the men who considered themselves honourable men. Decorated war hero Hans Hartigs said, "I used to shoot at everything, certainly not just military targets. We liked to go for women pushing prams, often with children at their sides. It was a kind of sport really. . . ." Sergeant Mueller said, "When I was in Kharkov, everything in the old town was destroyed. It was a wonderful town with wonderful memories. . . . Also in Taganrog, wonderful cinemas and beautiful beach cafes. You saw nothing but women. They were working to repair things, these deadly beautiful girls. We simply drove by them, tore them into the car, lay them down, and then chucked them out when we had finished. Man, did they fly!"

Fig. 17.5. Wehrmacht executions and mass burials

Major General Walter Bruns recalled a "typical Jewish action" that he had been involved in.

> The trenches were 24 metres long and roughly 3 metres wide. They had to lie like sardines in a tin, heads towards the middle. Above, six machine-gunners delivered the neck shots. When I arrived, the trenches were pretty full already and the living had to lie on top before they got the neck shot. They were all arranged beautifully so not too much space was wasted. They had already been robbed before they got here. On this Sunday, I saw a half-kilometre long queue shuffling forward step by step, the line-up for death. As they got nearer, they saw what awaited them. Around about here, they had to give up their suitcases and their sacks of valuables. A little further on they had to strip, and they could only keep on a shirt or a slip. They were mostly women and children, not much older than two years old.

Hall says, "Of remorse, regret or sorrow about what he had seen, there was not an inkling." These were the products of Hitler Youth camps, possibly "tough as leather, and as hard as Krupp's steel," but totally lacking anything that resembled a conscience or the slightest concern or compassion for other members of the human race.

The Japanese and German armies betrayed their Reptilian-backed training, passed on from leaders like Hirohito, Hitler, and Himmler. This "take no prisoners" mentality was reminiscent of that of the Reptilians who committed atrocities in the Lyran wars. But the Reptilians make many mistakes and errors of judgment, especially when dealing with humans, who have access to higher dimensions, the fifth and above. That is why they expend so much energy keeping our consciousness at a low level through the media and mind control. Keeping us "dumb and dumber" through mindless entertainment and games is their number-one priority. Their inability to be successful in that effort is their major weakness. For example, they were not able to predict or to control Hitler's mad conceit that he could out-general his generals! Shouldn't he have learned from Napoleon the blatant stupidity of sending an entire army deep into Russia with winter coming? Hitler's madness eventually overtook his mentality. The Reptilians should have seen it coming, but they did not, while the Russian and American generals remained levelheaded. And then there was the incredible craziness of declaring war on the United States because Hitler believed that the attack on Pearl Harbor would cripple us. And it was so easy for us to dupe him into believing that D-day would be launched at Calais rather than Normandy. He was still asleep in his bed as the Allied soldiers took over the French beaches.

The Reptilians know that the developed human mind and soul are powerful, brilliant, and unconquerable, and they are basically afraid of us. It is only necessary for us to expand our consciousness and to rise above the deceptions and snares they put before us. That is why they need fanatical dolts to carry out their plans. Reasonable and caring individuals would have none of it, at any price. This was made clear at the Nuremberg Trials. Albert Speer was the only defendant who realized with horror how he had been duped and caught up in the Hitlerian madness. The others remained defiant to the end and closed ranks against Speer for his traitorous "capitulation." They had been well chosen by their Reptilian overlords.

IX

The Argentinian Reich

Before Nazi influence in postwar America can be understood, it is first necessary to realize that Hitler survived! Certainly, how could anyone believe that someone so attached to implementing his crazed ideas in the world, someone who was so attached to life, could commit suicide? No, he did not give up so easily. The case for Hitler's escape is meticulously presented in the book *Grey Wolf: The Escape of Adolf Hitler* by Simon Dunstan and Gerrard Williams. This book, written in 2011, was followed by *Hitler in Argentina: The Documented Proof of Hitler's Escape from Berlin* by Harry Cooper (2014) and *The Complete Story of the Planned Escape of Hitler: The Nazi-Spain-Argentina Coverup* by Maximillien de Lafayette (2013). Because *Grey Wolf* is so comprehensive and well researched, it is the best guide to use in telling the story, although both of the other books give the same account of Hitler's escape and his subsequent life.

MARTIN BORMANN

Martin Bormann was indispensable to Hitler. He managed all of the party's finances, as well as Hitler's personal funds. According to information provided in *Grey Wolf,* in 1934 he was responsible for increasing the money flowing into this account controlled by Hitler by 1.4 million reichsmarks in one year, thus permitting many additional Nazi programs and rallies. He augmented Hitler's personal income by imposing a tax of 1.5 percent on the payrolls of the companies that were benefiting the most from German rearmament, like Krupp, Thyssen, and I. G. Farben. This money went directly into the Adolf Hitler Fund. In its first year, it raised 30 million reichsmarks. This alone, made Hitler fabulously wealthy. Bormann was a brilliant businessperson. Huge amounts of personal funds for Hitler also flowed into his treasure chest from royalties on *Mein Kampf,* and as stated in *Grey Wolf,* Bormann devised a system for obtaining royalties for every image of Hitler "be it on a postcard or even a postage stamp." These were paid into another personal fund designated the Adolf Hitler Cultural Fund. Then Bormann arranged with the authorities for Hitler to pay no income tax, thanks to Nazi Party influence. By the outbreak of war in 1939, Hitler's annual income was enormous, thanks to Martin Bormann. Hitler himself found financial dealings burdensome and distasteful.

Fig. 18.1. Martin Bormann in 1934

Bormann was also an organizational genius as well as a masterful diplomat, relieving Hitler of a huge load by taking most of these activities off Hitler's shoulders, essentially acting as his front man, thus freeing Hitler to collect stolen artworks and play at being an architect and a general. In 1933 Bormann was appointed national leader of the party. This made him the fourth most powerful figure in Nazi Germany after Hitler, Hermann Goering, and Rudolf Hess. After the May 1941 departure of Hess on his ill-fated flight to England, seeking on his own to negotiate a peace treaty, Bormann became much closer to Hitler. According to *Grey Wolf,* "He was now entirely responsible for arranging the Fuhrer's daily schedule, appointments, and personal business. He was always at his master's side and never took a vacation for fear of losing influence." One party official said, "Bormann clung to Hitler like ivy around an oak, using him to get to the light and to the very summit."

PINCHED DIAMONDS

The covert infiltration of the United States by the Nazis began in the summer of 1943. At that time Operation Barbarossa, the battle for Russia, had turned around. The Russians had held the Germans in the brutal Battle of Kursk and began their offensive westward. Their destroyed armaments were renewed by the Allies through Murmansk, while the Germans had lost three hundred tanks and hundreds of thousands of men. Also at that time the Allies landed in Sicily and began the inexorable takeover of Italy. The handwriting was now on the wall. Bormann realized that the defeat of Germany was inevitable, and he swung into action. He had already, from the very beginning in 1939, laid a solid transportation, business, and financial foundation for German influence in foreign countries all over the world. From *Grey Wolf,* we learn that first and foremost, he had enriched the coffers of the party by auctioning off many of the very valuable artworks that had been stolen from museums in Berlin, Bremen, Cologne, Dresden, Essen, and Frankfurt, and those "lifted" from Jewish collectors, including works by Braque, Klee, van Gogh, Matisse, and Picasso. This auction, at the Grand Hotel National in Lucerne, Switzerland, in June 1939, netted about half a million Swiss francs, which were deposited in the J. Henry Schroder Bank "for Bormann's exclusive use." Then, the Wehrmacht "pinched" more than a million carats of cut and industrial diamonds from the low countries, which would come in very handy for bribing foreign officials, especially those in Argentina, to grant favors to Nazi emigres and businessmen. Thievery was second nature to Nazi morality, which was basically bankrupt, and testified to their control by the amoral Brotherhood of the Snake. They could, of course, justify it by referral to that ancient maxim, "To the victor belongs the spoils."

PROJECT EAGLE FLIGHT

To prepare for the Argentina venture, Bormann acquired a Spanish shipping company and an Italian airline, Linee Aeree Transcontinentali Italiane, which had an established service from Rome to Buenos Aires via Seville, the Portuguese Cape Verde Islands, Recife, and Rio de Janeiro. This permitted sending people and freight to Spain and Argentina via a civilian cover company without using military aircraft, which would arouse foreign governmental suspicions. To finance the foreign organization, Bormann sent counterfeit British banknotes to the German embassies abroad, estimated to be a total of $4.6 billion by today's U.S. valuation. This was about 10 percent of all British banknotes circulating at that time. According to Dunston and Williams, "The imperative for Bormann was now to transfer monies in every shape and form—counterfeit, stolen, or even legitimate government funds—to safe havens abroad. This was achieved as part of an operation code-named Aktion Adlerflug [Project Eagle Flight]—which involved setting up innumerable foreign bank accounts and investing funds in foreign companies that were controlled by hidden German interests."

In the furtherance of Project Eagle Flight, more than two hundred German companies set up subsidiaries in Argentina between 1943 and 1945. To disguise their control by the Nazi Party, the companies were financed and funded by a money-laundering operation through shell companies in Switzerland, Spain, and Portugal. That way, patents and other assets could also be transferred via that same route. After the war ended, these same companies could hire Nazi war criminals coming to Argentina through the "ratlines," that is, secret escape routes. That is how mega-murderer Adolph Eichmann came to be employed by Mercedes Benz in Argentina. That same technique was used to set up companies in Portugal, Spain, Sweden, and Turkey.

THE FOURTH REICH

Critical to infiltration of the United States was the German/Nazi control of majority shares or outright ownership of major U.S. corporations. According to *Grey Wolf,* by the time Germany declared war on the United States on December 11, 1941, I. G. Farben alone had a voting majority in 170 American corporations and minority holdings in 108. Through Stockholm's Enskilda Bank, the Swedish Wallenberg brothers purchased the American Bosch Corporation on behalf of Bormann. They were very well paid for that acquisition. That same

Fig. 18.2. I. G. Farben, circa 1939

bank bought U.S. stocks and bonds on the New York Exchange for Bormann. *Grey Wolf* says, "By these means, Bormann was able to create some 980 front companies, with 770 of these in neutral countries, including 98 in Argentina, 58 in Portugal, 112 in Spain, 233 in Sweden, 234 in Switzerland, and 35 in Turkey—no doubt there were others whose existence has never been revealed. Every single one was a conduit for the flight of capital from Germany, just waiting for Bormann to give the order when the time was right." Bormann had indeed faithfully observed the charge given to him by Hitler, "Bury your treasure deep, as you will need it to begin the Fourth Reich."

This is a fascinating and revealing quote. It suggests that Hitler ultimately planned to fade into the background and that he expected the advent of a Fourth Reich, which would be led by Bormann. This may explain why Bormann was so motivated to establish the foundation for ultimate Nazi rulership of the world. He was planning his own empire! I think it would be fair to equate the Fourth Reich to the New World Order, which was first officially mentioned by George H. W. Bush in his speech on September 11, 1990, before a joint session of Congress. His precise words were, "Out of these troubled times, our . . . objective—a new world order—can emerge. . . . Today, that new world is struggling to be born, a world quite different from the one we have known."

Could Bush perhaps have been referring to the advent of the Fourth Reich? This may not be so far-fetched when it is realized that his father, Prescott Bush, was a founding member and a director of the Union Banking Corporation (UBC) in New York City prior to and during World War II. The UBC was basically a U.S. front organization for German steel magnate Fritz Thyssen, who donated large sums to the Nazi Party until 1938. It seems very likely that it was Bormann who set up this connection, or at least had a hand in it. Thyssen and his fellow industrialists contributed three million reichsmarks to the Nazis in 1933 to back Hitler, and he sent a letter to President von Hindenberg urging him to appoint Hitler as chancellor. Those actions were probably the precipitant factors that catapulted Hitler to power in 1933. In 1942 the Roosevelt administration seized the assets of the UBC by the authority of the Trading with the Enemy Act. While there is no evidence that

Prescott Bush held Nazi sympathies or that George H. W. Bush agreed with his father's purported sympathies, it is nevertheless interesting that the son first publicly enunciated the New World Order objective on September 11, 1990! And precisely eleven years later, his son, President George W. Bush was in office when that date became emblazoned in America's memory, which, in retrospect, now draws attention to that New World Order date. A conspiricist might point out the Illuminati obsession with dates, and that September 11, 1944 was the date the Allied armies first entered Germany. By the way, according to author Paul Manning, Martin Bormann was still alive in Argentina in 1980.

PROJECT LAND OF FIRE

With the financial pieces in place, Bormann turned his attention to getting Hitler out of Germany. He designed a plan that he called Aktion Fuererland, or Project Land of Fire. This referred to setting up a safe haven in Tierra del Fuego, which means Land of Fire, in sparsely populated Patagonia at the southern tip of South America. Patagonia is the southernmost province of Argentina. It was the ideal location for many reasons. The population was predominantly of German descent. Lieutenant Wilhelm Canaris, an officer in the German Navy during World War I, had found refuge there in 1915 after he escaped from internment in Chile. He was sheltered and protected there by the German community. Most importantly, a military coup in Argentina in 1943 brought in a fascist regime, including Colonel Juan Domingo Peron, who was highly placed in the new government. Peron had been on the German intelligence payroll since 1941. There is evidence that the coup was probably instigated and aided by Nazi Germany in anticipation of the need for Argentinian compliance in tolerating a Nazi colony in exile in Argentina. *Grey Wolf* tells us that General Wilhelm von Faupel, a German military advisor, traveled to Argentina in April 1943 and told Peron that the only way to avoid charges of high treason was to seize power. The coup occurred one month later. Bormann, planning well in advance, had deposited a huge amount of money in Argentine banks, much of which was probably used to finance the coup.

In its final version, the plan, according to *Grey Wolf,* was to "create a secret, self-contained refuge for Hitler in the heart of a sympathetic German community, at a chosen site near the town of San Carlos de Bariloche in the far west of Argentina's Rio Negro province (see plate 17). Here, the Führer could be provided with complete protection from outsiders since all routes in by road, rail, or air were in the hands of Germans." Bormann initiated the execution of the plan in mid-1943 by coordinating with his chief agent in Buenos Aires, Ludwig Freude. That region of Argentina was like a miniature Germany (see plate 18). *Grey Wolf* says, "Today, if you visit Villa General Belgrano, San Carlos de Bariloche, Villa La Angostura, Santa Rosa de Calamuchita, or any of a hundred other German settlements in Argentina, it is still difficult to believe that you are in Latin America. . . . Each of the larger towns has always had its own German school, cultural institute, beer hall, and restaurants. Even at the time of this writing in 2010, Argentines of German descent account for more than three million of the country's population of forty-two million." Joseph Goebbels said in March 1944, "Argentina will one day be at the head of a tariff union comprising the

Fig. 18.3. Nazi organization in Bariloche

nations in the southern half of South America. Such a focus of opposition against the United States of America will . . . form a powerful economic block."

THE LOOT OF CONQUERED EUROPE

Bormann had set up a regular submarine shuttle trip from Cadiz, Spain, to Argentina in August 1942. These trips, made every six to eight weeks between 1943 and 1945, used the latest in U-boat technology, the Type IX. These submarines were able to make the 5,400-mile journey mainly underwater if necessary. This was made possible by the use of the Schnorchel, which presented a barely detectable above-water extrusion, almost invisible to radar. By mid-1943 the Allied ships had taken back the Atlantic waters, and German submarines were being routinely sunk. The Schnorchel was a combination air intake and diesel-engine exhaust pipe that allowed engine cruising at shallow depths at night, and the submarine could travel fully submerged on recharged batteries during the day. This method of travel limited the U-boat to one hundred miles a day, which means it took about sixty days for a one-way trip. These submarines, about the size of small freighters, were loaded to the gunwales with money. *Grey Wolf* puts it this way: "It was the loot of conquered Europe that provided . . . the whole funding for the structure of Bormann's influence in Argentina and the preparation of the future Nazi refuge."

Hermann Goering had a $20 million account in Argentine banks, Joseph Goebbels had $1.8 million, and Nazi Minister for Foreign Affairs Joachim von Ribbentrop had $0.5 million. Unfortunately, these three were not able to enjoy their ill-gotten gains. Goering committed suicide, and Ribbentrop was executed at Nuremberg. Goebbels killed himself and his family in a secret underground bunker in Berlin. But these amounts were nothing compared to the estimated $50 billion in gold, at today's valuation, that Bormann sent to Argentina, along with platinum, precious gems, coins, looted artworks, and stocks and bonds. *Grey Wolf* tells us also that in February 1944, the German Embassy had 47 million pesos in Argentinian banks, along with seven safety deposit boxes stuffed with 115 million pesos in gold and silver coins. Freude revealed that there was an additional $37.66 million in a bank in Buenos Aires in the names of other Nazis. *Grey Wolf* says also, "Many major German companies were implicated in the transfer of assets to Argentina, including Siemens, Krupp, Mannesman, Thyssen, I. G. Farben, and Schroder's Bank, dealing through local or Swiss holding companies."

JUAN AND EVITA:
LOVE STORY OR COLLABORATION?

In January 1944 Juan Peron was the vice president of Argentina. He supposedly met Eva Duarte at a fund-raising event in May of that year. She was already a rising radio star. But, in actuality, they had really met in the summer of 1941, and both were on Bormann's payroll from that time forward. In any case, they now took the opportunity to publicly announce their relationship. Much of the gold and funds smuggled into Argentina in 1945 was deposited to Eva's accounts in three banks. In April 1944 Peron, then still vice president, said, "Hitler's fight in peace

Fig. 18.4. Juan Peron and Eva Duarte

and war will guide us. . . . Once Brazil has fallen the South American continent will be ours. Following the German example, we will instill the masses with the necessary military spirit." With Peron wielding major influence as vice president and Eva installed as his wife, by 1945, all obstacles in the way of Hitler's arrival in Argentina were cleared away. Now it only remained for Bormann to make the arrangements.

THE SECRET DOOR

Bormann's plan for saving Hitler was complex. It involved several linked segments, connected by slim time margins. A failure in any one of the segments, or a missed connection, could sink the whole operation. Furthermore, it would probably be executed against a backdrop of chaotic, war-torn streets and buildings with Allied armies approaching from both directions. But it is a testament to his sharp mind and his ability to anticipate all the possible variables that allowed Bormann to pull it off. Hitler trusted Bormann completely, so if there was a glitch, he probably would not have known what to do. He must have shuddered as he thought about the fate of Mussolini, he and his mistress captured by partisans and executed immediately, their bodies hung upside down from meat hooks in a public square.

There was an old bunker underneath the Old Chancellery Building, called the Vorbunker. This was essentially an enhanced air raid shelter. As the Allied bombs began to shake this shelter, Hitler realized he needed a deeper and more commodious bunker. A new one was then constructed 26 feet beneath the ground, 8.2 feet farther down than the Vorbunker. It contained bedrooms, a kitchen, a conference room, offices for Goebbels and Bormann, and a study for Hitler. This bunker, named the Führerbunker, connected to the Vorbunker by going up one level. The Vorbunker had access to three tunnels, one leading to the Foreign Office, another to the Propaganda Ministry, and the third to the shelters under the New Chancellery Building. But it also had stairs leading directly to the Old Chancellery Building, put in place to allow the workers there to quickly get to the Vorbunker during an air raid. The Führerbunker was not ready for occupancy until October 23, 1944,

Fig. 18.5. Hitler's office in the Old Chancellery Building

when Hitler and his staff moved in to begin their underground life. What Hitler had not revealed to anyone other than Bormann was the fact that his private study in the Old Chancellery Building was connected via a hidden passageway to a third bunker, which was deeper than the Vorbunker. Access to this passageway was through a door disguised by a light concrete sliding panel beside a bookcase.

The hidden tunnel led to the third bunker, which was stocked with food and weapons for up to twelve people for two weeks, as well as a water supply and toilet facilities. This tunnel connected with the Berlin subway system. Once through the sliding door, it was possible to go underground to anywhere in Berlin and to emerge at a subway station entrance.

ESCAPE TO SPAIN

The following sequence of events, as chronicled in *Grey Wolf,* is partly speculative, but it ties in perfectly with the known times of appearances of Hitler and his mistress, Eva Braun, at various points of connection on their journey to Argentina, so it is probably accurate. Just after midnight on April 27, Hitler, Braun, and their German shepherd, Blondi, walked through the Führerbunker and the Vorbunker and ascended the stairs to the Old Chancellery Building. They went through the sliding door and proceeded down the tunnel to the third bunker, where they made final arrangements with Bormann, who remained behind. It was now his job to go back to the Führerbunker and make it appear that Hitler and Braun had committed suicide. Then they walked through the subway tunnel to the Fehrbellina Platz station, where three Tiger II tanks waited for them and took them to an improvised airstrip on Hohenzollerndamm. There, at approximately 3 a.m. on April 28th, they boarded a Junker Ju 52 aircraft, along with Hermann Fegelein, a general in the Waffen-SS, and Wehrmacht General Joachim Rumohr and his wife. Decorated Luftwaffe pilot Captain Peter Baumgart flew the group toward Denmark. Baumgart later testified in a court in Poland about that trip. He also bragged about his flying prowess, telling the court that during the war he had shot down 128 Allied aircraft over Italy and North Africa. This was the most hazardous leg of the journey, flying at night in moonlight, almost at treetop level, to avoid Allied aircraft. They stopped at Magdeburg for a while, and then flew north, trying to dodge Allied fighters. They landed on April 29 at a former German zeppelin base in Tonder, Denmark. Baumgart did not know who his passengers were until they landed, when Hitler shook his hand and pressed a check for 20,000 reichsmarks in his hand. Here, an audience of about one hundred people was gathered to hear the Führer give an ad hoc fifteen-minute speech. He informed the crowd that Admiral Karl Doenitz was now the supreme commander of the German forces. Then he, Braun, and Fegelein boarded a plane for a forty-five minute flight to Travemunde, on the north German coast.

At Travemunde, Lieutenant Colonel Werner Baumbach waited to fly the refugees to Spain in a Junker Ju 252. This would be a relatively comfortable six-hour flight in a pressurized cabin at altitudes of up to 22,500 feet. The old-model Junker had a range of 2,500 miles, almost twice what was needed for the 1,370-mile trip to Reus in Catalonia, Spain. The Junker waited on the runway with the engines running.

Upon arrival at Reus, Fegelein, Hitler, and Braun transferred to a Spanish Air Force Junker Ju 52. The plane in which they had arrived was scheduled for demolition to remove all evidence of the flight. This flight, with a Spanish pilot, stopped at Moron in the south of Spain to refuel, and then continued to a German submarine base on the island of Fuerteventura in the Spanish Canary Islands. Hitler's escape from the utter devastation of Germany that he had caused was now complete. The exiles now waited to board U-518, the submarine that would carry them 5,400 miles across the Atlantic to the eastern shore of Argentina.

With Hitler gone, Bormann and his closest associate, SS General Heinrich Mueller, chief of the Gestapo, went into the Old Chancellery Building and met with the doubles of Hitler and Braun. Hitler's double was Gustav Weber, a nearly identical doppelganger, and Braun's double was absolutely identical. They escorted the doubles back to the Führerbunker under some pretense. Then, two days later Weber was shot in the head, and Braun's double was poisoned, both by Mueller. Then their bodies were cremated outside in the garden. Thus began the myth that Hitler and Eva Braun had committed suicide.

19

The Nazi Infiltration
of the Americas

By July 30, 1945, Hitler and Braun were comfortably ensconced at the Estancia San Ramon near the town of San Carlos de Bariloche, near the far southwestern border of Argentina with Chile. This huge, remote, and isolated ranch, totally fenced in, was owned by German prince Stephen zu Schaumburg-Lippe. The only access was via a dirt road that went by the small local airport and that required permission to enter from trusted Nazi neighbors. Well-known American journalist Drew Pearson said in his syndicated column on July 24, 1945, "It would have been impossible for any non-German to penetrate the area to make a thorough investigation as to Hitler's whereabouts." Bariloche, in the foothills of the high Chilean Andes, could easily be taken for an Alpine ski resort town, so Hitler and Braun must have felt very much at home. They were to remain at San Ramon for nine months, until early May 1946.

Over the course of the war, the Allied code breakers at Bletchley Park in England had broken through even the toughest encryption algorithms of the Germans. Only one remained impenetrable. The British named it "Thrasher." *Grey Wolf* says, "This cypher was employed by Bormann's private communications network built around the top-secret Siemens and Halske encryption machine, the T43 *Schlusselfernsshreibmachine*. . . . Bormann needed to establish a totally secure communications network, one that was capable of reaching

Fig. 19.1. T43 Siemens and Halske encryption machine

U-boats at sea and ground stations in Spain and the Canary Islands and that could relay messages across the Atlantic to Buenos Aires. A modified version of the T43 was the answer to his needs." Three T43s had been used in the Führerbunker. One had been installed somewhere in Buenos Aires. It seems reasonable to conclude that the surviving leader of the Third Reich would have a T43 available to him in Argentina to allow him to continue his control over the now far-flung remnants of his still-loyal regime. Hitler probably had a T43, with an operator, installed at San Ramon, from which he could issue orders to commence the inception and organization of the Fourth Reich. It should not be forgotten that an entire Nazi city, Neu Berlin, really a government in exile, had existed under the ice at Neuschwabenland in Antarctica at least since 1938 (see *Secret Journey to Planet Serpo,* by this author). More than likely, Bormann had seen to it that there were several T43s at that location. And it was really there that the inception of the Fourth Reich would begin. It was only a short submarine ride from Tierra del Fuego to Antarctica, and Hitler had ceded command of the Third Reich to Admiral Karl Doenitz, who was in charge of the submarine fleet.

The Neuschwabenland colony encompassed a highly sophisticated science and technology component. Some of the top Nazi scientists and engineers engaged in antigravity technology had fled there as defeat became inevitable. As this author says in *Secret Journey to Planet Serpo,* "According to noted Third Reich researcher/writer Rob Arndt . . . after the war, the Allies were able to determine that fifty-four U-boats were missing from Nazi Germany. He says also that between 142,000 and 250,000 people were unaccounted for, including the entire SS Technical Branch, the entire Vril and Thule Gesellschafts, 6,000 scientists and technicians and tens of thousands of slave laborers." In short, this was the entire technological and scientific nucleus of the Fourth Reich. So Hitler's empire was still extensive and required that he remain in constant communication with his minions.

After Bormann had arranged for "Gestapo" Mueller to kill the doubles in the Führerbunker, they both set out to escape from Germany. *Grey Wolf* chronicles their adventures. Mueller "disappeared" on the night of May 1, and Bormann left in the early hours of May 2. Bormann was wounded by a shell fragment hitting his foot when a Tiger II tank that he had boarded was hit by a Soviet antitank weapon. Undaunted, he proceeded on foot and picked up civilian clothes, new identity papers, and cash that he had stashed at the Hotel Atlas, and then made it safely through the British lines to the environs of Flensburg. There he met up with Mueller at a safe house and learned from him that Doenitz had already surrendered unconditionally to the Allies. Bormann now headed for Bavaria, where he had previously made arrangements to get to Argentina.

THE GEHLEN ORG

In late summer 1945, with Hitler settled in Argentina and Bormann scrambling to get there, other events were taking place in Europe that had a major impact on the infiltration of ex-Nazis into the United States. Lieutenant Colonel Reinhard Gehlen, a senior intelligence Wehrmacht officer assigned to the Foreign Armies East section of the German General Staff, along with his top aides, surrendered to the Allies on May 22, 1945. They surrendered to Captain John R. Boker of the U.S. Army Counterintelligence Corps in Bavaria. In his wartime position, Gehlen had accumulated a tremendous amount of intelligence about the Soviet Union and the Red Army. Gehlen knew that the war was lost as early as 1942 and had begun organizing and building secret files of his intelligence material, realizing that they would constitute an invaluable bargaining chit in dealings with the United States and Great Britain in their inevitable postwar confrontation with the Soviet Union. To his credit, he had acquiesced immediately to playing a minor role in the plot to assassinate Hitler in 1942, when recruited by Colonel Claus von Stauffenberg. He had also allowed the conspirators to meet in his section, and he was present at Berchtesgaden in the meeting of the group to discuss the final details prior to the bombing attempt on July 20, 1944. In early March 1945, Gehlen had his senior officers packed microfilm copies of all his files into fifty watertight steel drums, which were buried in various places in the Austrian Alps. It is fascinating to learn from the Greyfalcon website that Hitler had decided to send Gehlen to an insane asylum because he believed that he had been fabricating the gloomy forecasts of Russian victories on the Eastern Front. It was then that Gehlen fled to the Alps. The deal he offered to Boker was fifty drums of Soviet intelligence files in return for his release and the release of his senior officers from the POW camps.

On September 20, 1945, Gehlen and three of his officers, on the instructions of General Walter Bedell Smith, President Dwight D. Eisenhower's chief of staff, were free and on a plane to Washington, D.C., to begin working for the U.S. Army's Strategic Services Unit of the War Department! This was the successor organization to the Office of Strategic Services (OSS), the wartime intelligence agency, which was dissolved by Truman on that date. This unique employment of a former Nazi military intelligence officer was unprecedented, but it had been approved by William "Wild Bill" Donovan, former chief of the OSS, and Allen Dulles, former OSS station chief in Berne, Switzerland. It was motivated by the brewing Cold War, just as Gehlen had anticipated three years earlier. What the Americans did not know was that Gehlen had cleared his collaboration with them with Doenitz while he was still a POW in a prison camp in Wiesbaden. So he entered into this arrangement with the full blessing of the new German High Command. Because they knew about his anti-Hitler stance and because he harbored no fanatical racial hatreds and had participated in no atrocities, Gehlen seduced the U.S. intelligence apparatus into

Fig. 19.2. Wild Bill Donovan

*Fig. 19.3. Lieutenant Colonel
Reinhard Gehlen*

believing that he was a recalcitrant Nazi, while really he was secretly attached to the concept of a new and glorious Fourth Reich. To him and to other wiser Nazis, the problem was not Germany; it was Hitler. Since he had no contact with Bormann, it is probable that Gehlen had no idea that Hitler was still alive, which was highly compartmentalized information among the German expatriates.

NOTORIOUS NAZIS

Gehlen was given permission to set up his own organization to constitute a cell within the Strategic Services Unit to focus on Soviet intelligence. Truman and Gehlen's supervisors had required that he hire no former SS or Gestapo men to his organization. He agreed to this restriction "in principle" and gave his official word. He immediately violated this agreement and hired some of the most notorious Nazi war criminals, including Klaus Barbie, the so-called Butcher of Lyon, Franz Six, and Emil Augsburg.

In Lyon, France, in 1942, it is said that Barbie was directly responsible for the deaths of fourteen thousand people. He himself brutally tortured prisoners, breaking limbs, using electroshock, and sexually abusing his victims: men, women, and children! When Jean Moulin, the head of the French Resistance, was captured, he was subjected to unimaginable abuse, personally, by Barbie. A fellow prisoner, Christian Pineau, later described the results. He said that Moulin was "unconscious, his eyes dug in as though they had been punched through his head. An ugly blue wound scarred his temple. A mute rattle came out of his swollen lips." Moulin eventually died in captivity after being used as an example to other prisoners. For his atrocities in Lyon, Hitler himself awarded to Barbie the First Class Iron Cross with Swords!

Six, a highly educated SS commander, was in charge of one of the death squads in Russia. His Vorkommando unit in Smolensk executed 4,600 people who Hitler had decided would be politically troublesome in his "Nazified" Russia. Augsburg was in charge of the murders of Polish Jews in 1940 and 1941. According to the Greyfalcon website, "Six and Augsburg had been members of an SS mobile Death's Head killing squad that hunted down and killed Soviet Jews, intellectuals and partisans wherever they could be found. Six was known as a Streber, or Eager Beaver, for the enthusiastic manner in which he pursued his job. Gehlen also recruited the former Gestapo chiefs of Paris, France, and Kiel, Germany. Then, that not being enough, he hired Willi Krichbaum, the former senior Gestapo leader for southeastern Europe."

The seemingly inbred, cold-blooded brutality of the Nazi military is unique in modern times. Soldiers in all armies follow orders, but most rebel when ordered to carry out grisly atrocities. The wartime Wehrmacht and SS men had no such reservations, but rather carried out their ordered cruelties against anyone, women and children included, frequently with relish. In my first book, *The Secret History of Extraterrestrials,* I made the case for the premise that the underground Reptilians provided Hitler with a cloned army of about one million men. Hitler made reference to that fact in a witnessed remark to Bormann when he became irritated at Bormann's failure to find some domestic help. He said, "I conjure entire divisions out of the earth. It must be an easy task to find a few girls for my Berghof." These robotic men would have had no compunctions about sadistic cruelty because they had no souls and therefore no consciences. It seems unlikely that Hitler would have thrown away these soulless monsters as cannon fodder on the Eastern Front, but rather probably used them in the SS and the Gestapo, where they were required to visit their brutalities against women and children—jobs that human soldiers would hesitate or refuse to carry out.

ODESSA

In September 1946, Gehlen was sent back to Europe to manage his organization, called the Gehlen Org, from Pullach, West Germany, a town near Munich, and continued to report back to the War Department in Washington. He did not report to the Central Intelligence Group, an independent agency created by Truman in April 1946 and the precursor to the current Central Intelligence Agency (CIA). Once back in Germany, the Gehlen Org beefed up its ranks. Gehlen initially hired 350 former German intelligence agents. This eventually grew to more than 4,000. The cover name for the group was the South German Industrial Development Organization. After getting settled back in Germany, Gehlen began a sub-rosa association with a group called Odessa. This organization, created as the curtain descended on the Third Reich, resulted from a meeting at the Maison Rouge Hotel in Strasbourg on August 10, 1944. It was attended by the top industrial leaders, including Gustav Krupp and Fritz Thyssen. According to the online Jewish Virtual Library:

> The Nazis recognized that Germany's assets would fall into the hands of the rapidly approaching enemy if they were not transferred and hidden. The nation's wealth, much of it acquired through the plunder of the nations it invaded and the people the Nazis murdered, had to be transferred so they would be out of judicial reach, but accessible to fund a future movement to resurrect the party and build a new Reich. Leading Nazi officials also feared retribution from the Allies and, rather than face likely punishment for their war crimes, they decided to seek safe havens outside Germany and beyond the reach of justice. . . . The outcome of the meeting in Strasbourg was the genesis of an organization; one well financed and well organized, with the express purpose of helping fleeing Nazis escape justice. This organization was called the "Organization Der Ehemaligen SS-Angehörigen" (The Organization of former SS members)—better known as Odessa. . . . In short order, Odessa, built a large and reliable network geared to achieve its ends and began operations. Routes were mapped and contacts were established. Influential Nazis vanished as they were secretly ushered out of Germany and assisted in starting new lives under false names in foreign countries. At the end of the war, only a handful of high-ranking Nazi officials stood trial. Many who were guilty of war crimes escaped with the help of Odessa.

Bormann played a major role in the creation of Odessa, intending to send most of the escapees to the main Third Reich refuge, Argentina. Conspiracy researcher Carl Oglesby says that the Gehlen Org was "by far the most audacious, most critical, and most essential part of the entire Odessa undertaking." In fact, Oglesby contends, the Gehlen Org was really a cover group for the financially well-endowed Odessa. Gehlen, it turns out, was Germany's spymaster, juggling huge organizations with the skill of a circus performer and setting previous allies at loggerheads in a new cold war that brought the planet to the very edge of nuclear disaster.

ALLEN DULLES

As the OSS station chief in Berne, Switzerland, during the war, Allen Dulles was uniquely positioned to meet important Nazi functionaries. As defeat was staring them in the face, they paraded to his apartment on the Herrengasse, hoping they could arrange a separate peace with the Americans. The prospect of having to surrender to the Russians was too horrible a fate to contemplate. Visions of cracking rocks in Siberia danced in their heads. So, Dulles was sitting in the catbird seat, and he enjoyed every minute of it. First there was Fritz Kolbe, an official with the Foreign Office in Berlin, in the summer of 1943. He opened his briefcase with a key and poured out onto Dulles's desk a cascade of ultra-top-secret documents that any spy would have killed for. Kolbe told him, "You can keep them for a few days and make copies of them." All he wanted in return was to see Hitler and the top Nazis dead. Then there was General Ludwig Beck, diplomat and intelligence office Hans Gisevius, and others, all willing to trade what was left of the Fatherland for any reasonable deal with Uncle Sam. Dulles was inclined to take advantage of these overtures and work something out with the Germans. He thought it would be a great coup. However, he was also very aware that Churchill, Roosevelt, and Stalin had laid down the irreversible ground rules—unconditional surrender to the Allied forces jointly. There could be no separate peace! The heroic defense of Stalingrad had turned the war, and too much blood had been spilled on the soil of Mother Russia. There could be no effort to circumvent the Russians.

Dulles had a long history of sympathy with German causes and strong anti-Bolshevik sentiments. He had first made many friends in the haute social strata of Berlin and Vienna when he was posted there by the State Department in 1919. Then, according to Leonard Mosley in his book *Dulles,* as a member of the U.S. State Department delegation to the Disarmament Conference in 1926, Dulles wrote memoranda that "pleaded for a relaxation of the rigid anti-armament clauses of the Versailles Treaty, to allow the more liberal elements in German democratic government to build some sort of defensive force." Later, as a young lawyer with the firm of Sullivan and Cromwell in New York, still believing that the German reparations for World War I were too onerous, Mosley says, "He connived with one of the company's clients, du Pont, to get munitions through export controls and into Germany."

Dulles knew all about Gehlen before he surrendered. Kolbe had informed him of Gehlen's blowup with Hitler and that he had fled to the Austrian Alps with his files and his staff and was ready to make a deal with the Americans. In fact, Dulles went so far as to brief Colonel William W. Quinn, the intelligence officer with the 7th Army, of a Nazi "Hail Mary" effort to attack Patton's army from a secure Alpine redoubt. He said that this intelligence had come from Gehlen via Kolbe. It embarrassed Dulles when Eisenhower wisely ignored the warning.

After Gehlen surrendered he remained unacknowledged in the POW camp in Wiesbaden for four weeks before Quinn recognized his name on a POW list. He recalled the briefing from Dulles and notified Brigadier General Edwin L. Silbert. By that time, Supreme Headquarters Allied Expeditionary Force knew of Gehlen's importance because the Russians were looking for him and wanted him turned over to them. So Silbert, who had also been briefed by Dulles, was already searching for him when Quinn called. Silbert immediately had Gehlen moved to a more civilized POW camp at Augsburg for special interrogation. Silbert notified General Walter Bedell Smith, the War Department, and the OSS, and all agreed that Gehlen should be hustled out of Germany before the Russians could get their hands on him. And so he was, on the very same date that the OSS was dissolved. Dulles, who was in Washington at that time for a visit, was able to privately question Gehlen when he arrived. It was probably at that first meeting that a bond was established between the two men when Dulles may have discovered that Gehlen was a member of the Sovereign Military Order of Malta. Dulles, although not a Catholic, was also a Knight of Malta.

BIRTH OF THE
CENTRAL INTELLIGENCE AGENCY

Dulles was not brought into the Central Intelligence Group, but remained on the government sidelines, sitting on several committees while returning to work at his old law firm, Sullivan and Cromwell. However, he did sit in on several debriefings of Gehlen, and he recommended, along with others, that Gehlen be returned to Germany as a U.S. intelligence asset reporting on Russian and European activity and be given a budget of $3.5 million. Gehlen continued to report to the Strategic Services Unit under General Lucius Clay in the War Department. During this process Dulles became much better acquainted with Gehlen. It might even be said that they became friends.

Mosley tells us in *Dulles* that while this was happening, Dulles and others "argued eloquently for the creation of an entirely new intelligence organization, with rights, privileges, its own constitution, and funds: freedom to act without interference from the State Department, the Army, Navy, or Air Force departments; and direct access to the President." Truman and the Congress acquiesced and established the National Security Council in July 1947. The National Security Council then set up, under the National Security Agency (NSA), "a Central Intelligence Agency with a Director of Central Intelligence. . . . The Director shall be appointed by the President, by and with the advice and consent of the Senate." Dulles helped to draw up the legislation. But Truman selected Admiral Roscoe H. Hillenkoetter to become the first director of the new CIA. "Wild Bill" Donovan, the erstwhile chief of the OSS, was skipped over for the job because he and Truman

Fig. 19.4. Allen Welsh Dulles

detested each other. This also left Dulles, Donovan's protégé, out in the cold.

Dulles hovered in the shadows, waiting for his opportunity to come to prominence in the new agency that he had helped to create. In the meantime, he was part of a three-man team in 1948, assembled by Truman, to write a report recommending changes in the CIA. The team included William H. Jackson, who was an expert in counterintelligence. The report became known as NCS50 and was filed away by Truman. Dulles's chance came in 1950 when Hillenkoetter was asked to resign his post as director of the CIA. Hillenkoetter had just not been up to the job when the Korean War broke out, and Truman realized that he now needed to have an experienced soldier in charge. He brought in General Smith as the new director. Smith had been Eisenhower's chief of staff during WWII and had been invaluable in planning D-day. He was also one of the key people who had recommended that Gehlen be brought to the United States. Truman instructed Smith to implement the recommendations in NCS50.

Logically, Smith hired Jackson, one of the authors of the report, as his deputy director, while Dulles smoldered. Jackson was completely unsuited for the job, and Smith ushered him out gently and reached for the phone to call Dulles. Two years later when Eisenhower, a Republican, became the president, "Beetle" Smith, Eisenhower's old and loyal friend, resigned from the CIA to take a job in the State Department. His replacement by Allen Dulles was contentious, but it did not hurt Dulles's cause that his older brother, John Foster Dulles, was now the secretary of state and he had Ike's ear. Foster's pro-German sympathies were even more pronounced than his brother's. In the pre-war days, when they were both attorneys at Sullivan and Cromwell, it was Foster who was the most reluctant to cease representing the German industrial clients who were behind the Nazi war machine. A year later, in 1953, Allen Dulles was confirmed by the Senate as the new director of the CIA. Finally, after a ten-year wait, he now had his dream job—America's chief spymaster. At the age of sixty he was still in his prime. If it hadn't been for his gout, acquired after too many elaborate repasts in Berne, he would have been ecstatic.

THE OFFICE OF POLICY COORDINATION

By 1948 it had become obvious that the CIA needed some "teeth." George Kennen, director of the State Department Planning Staff, recommended that it be given the capability for covert operations. This resulted in the creation of a branch within the CIA called the Office of Policy Coordination (OPC), which would have the power to insert intelligence operatives overseas. Dulles managed to get his old friend and OSS associate Frank Wisner appointed as assistant director of policy coordination. Wisner, with the secret help of Dulles, quickly made the OPC into an independent agency reporting only to the State Department and the Department of Defense. By 1949 it had espionage stations in five countries and employed 302 agents, with a central location in Germany. In 1949 the Gehlen Org was on a starvation budget, and Wisner took advantage of the situation to bring the Gehlen Org into the OPC with much improved finances. By the late spring of 1949, the Gehlen Org was an operating arm of the OPC, and Gehlen immediately started producing results. Shortly after Smith took over the CIA, he had the clout to bring the OPC back into the CIA, with Wisner now reporting only to him. Dulles, now deputy director, soon genially shunted his longtime protégé aside and took over control of the OPC, which became the nucleus of the new CIA. Wisner was hurt, but did not object. Dulles was now in control of an efficient spy network established by Wisner, and Gehlen now reported directly to him. Dulles immediately flew out to Germany to renew the relationship with his "old friend." According to *Dulles,* "The years had done nothing to diminish Gehlen's peacock persona, and in thought, manner and braggadocio he was as much, if not more, of a Nazi as ever." But Dulles said, "He's on our side, and that's all that matters." Since they were both Knights of Malta, there was more to this association than was evident.

Martin A. Lee, author of *Acid Dreams* and *The Beast Awakens,* says in "The CIA's Worst Kept Secret," an article on the Internet, "Ironically, some of the men employed by Gehlen would go on to play leading roles in European neo-fascist organizations that despise the United States. One of the consequences of the CIA's ghoulish alliance with the Org is evident today in a resurgent fascist movement in Europe that can trace its ideological lineage back to Hitler's Reich through Gehlen operatives who collaborated with U.S. intelligence. Slow to recognize that their Nazi hired guns would feign an allegiance to the Western alliance as long as they deemed it tactically advantageous, CIA officials invested far too much in Gehlen's spooky Nazi outfit. 'It was a horrendous mistake, morally, politically, and also in very pragmatic intelligence terms,' said American University professor Richard Breitman, chairman of the IWG (Interagency Working Group) review panel."

The Gehlen Org was a fully functional, ready-made intelligence agency with spies in place all over the Soviet bloc, led by a highly experienced master of espionage. With the Cold War starting to perk, it was all too easy to make it the nucleus and the bones of the young CIA, which was not nearly ready yet to find, select, and train effective agents. It would take years to build and duplicate a spy organization such as that, especially for a country like the United States, which really did not have the experience necessary to put it together. And with the Cold War quickly becoming frigid, we really didn't have the time to do that. So the president and the Congress were seduced into letting it happen—letting an organization of ex-SS Nazi thugs, thieves, torturers, and murderers constitute our first national intelligence agency, their sinister and conscienceless values permeating the organization for all time. Perhaps, if the OPC director were not someone who had already shown an admiration of Germanic culture and a covert appreciation of the Nazi philosophy, it could have turned out differently. But Dulles, who eventually became the director of the CIA for ten years, put his stamp on the new organization, and it has not been easy to erase.

20
Project Paperclip

Even as one arm of the U.S. military was working to bring Nazi war criminals to justice after the war, another arm was using whatever means necessary to protect Nazi scientists and give them a safe haven in America. Ultimately this country paid a heavy price for that moral indifference. . . .

It had taken the greatest war in history to put a stop to an unspeakable evil. And now the cutting edge of that nightmare was being transplanted to America.

LINDA HUNT, *SECRET AGENDA:*
THE UNITED STATES GOVERNMENT,
NAZI SCIENTISTS AND PROJECT PAPERCLIP 1945 TO 1990

The hunt for Nazi technicians and scientists who had contributed to the German war effort began immediately after D-day in mid-1944. As the Allied armies pushed forward into France, scientific teams attached to special U.S. Army units called T-Forces combed the conquered territories, seeking the men who had designed the fearsome war machine unleashed on the Allied powers. These teams consisted of Army, Navy, Army Air Force, and OSS intelligence agents who knew precisely who and what to look for. They were controlled by the

Combined Intelligence Objectives Subcommittee (CIOS), headquartered in the United Kingdom. At its peak in early 1945, this organization fielded more than ten thousand operatives, who were scouring England, France, Belgium, Holland, Luxembourg, and Germany. In her book *Secret Agenda: The United States Government, Nazi Scientists and Project Paperclip 1945 to 1990,* Linda Hunt says, "The teams' mission was to capture and interrogate Hitler's scientists, locate and microfilm documents, and confiscate all useful equipment found in laboratories and factories." But as early as December 1944, "Wild Bill" Donovan, the director of the OSS, who also happened to be a Knight of Malta (as were Allen Dulles and Gehlen), asked Roosevelt to offer special privileges for high-ranking German officials working with the OSS, including a haven in the United States and the ability to deposit their money in American banks. Roosevelt said no. But that didn't stop the CIOS agents from cutting private deals with German and Nazi scientists who were wanted for war crimes. About this, Hunt says, "Dazzled by German technology that was in some cases years ahead of our own, they simply ignored its evil foundation—which sometimes meant stepping over and around piles of dead bodies—and pursued Nazi scientific knowledge like a forbidden fruit." This was a troublesome phenomenon that implies that some scientists can be just as amoral as anyone else.

THE GATES OF HELL

Their attitudes may have changed when the 42nd Infantry Division broke through the gates of the Dachau Concentration Camp, which the division's commanding officer, Colonel Walter J. Fellenz, referred to as "the gates of hell." Hunt relates that Major Leo Alexander, a Boston psychiatrist, and the soldiers of the 363rd Medical Battalion "were overwhelmed by the stench when they walked into the building. Parts of human bodies—arms, legs, organs of every type—were lying everywhere. Hundreds of innocent people had been murdered there in the name of science. And some of the men who conducted these experiments were the same respected scientists, university professors, and doctors that the Army Air Force teams would later hire to work under Paperclip." The experiments conducted there were on behalf of Hermann Goering's Luftwaffe. Hunt says:

> The experiments were ostensibly conducted to find ways to save the lives of Luftwaffe pilots who crashed at sea and were forced to live on seawater or parachuted out of airplanes at high altitudes or were exposed to extremely cold weather. Dachau inmates were deliberately infected with disease, force-fed seawater, or starved for oxygen in a chamber. In one experiment a group of Russian prisoners was frozen to death in vats of ice water in the camp yard during the winter. The prisoners endured excruciating pain before they died, as parts of their bodies slowly began to freeze. A Luftwaffe doctor, Sigmund Rascher, and University of Kiel Professor E. Holzlohner were among those conducting the experiments. They wanted to know if frozen flyers' lives could be saved if their bodies were thawed out.

The main German scientist responsible for these horrors was Luftwaffe Colonel Hubertus Strughold, the head of the Institute for Aviation Medicine in Berlin. Strughold denied any culpability when interviewed by Alexander. But after the records of Heinrich Himmler,

Fig. 20.1 Hubertus Strughold

commander of the SS, were found in a cave, Strughold's involvement became clear. But this discovery came too late. Strughold was already in the protective custody of the U.S. Army Air Force. Ironically, the U.S. investigators concluded that what Strughold learned from these horrific experiments was old news. The Allies knew about these things two years previously without torturing innocent prisoners to death. This testifies to the fact that the Nazi scientists were infected with moral atrophy since their first instinct was to torture and kill to draw scientific conclusions that could easily have been obtained otherwise.

Meanwhile, the Nazi rocket scientists were being rounded up at Peenemünde. Wernher von Braun and four hundred other rocket scientists surrendered peacefully and were taken to Garmisch by U.S. Army colonel Holger Toftoy and five Army technical intelligence teams. Hunt says, "One ordnance team member, Major Robert Staver, recalled that he was jubilant when the Army caught up with the Nazi rocket scientists. The most brilliant among them was the chief scientist and designer, who was only thirty-two years old. But Wernher von Braun's rocket career dated back to the 1930s, when he was the protégé of Hermann Oberth, the father of German rocketry."

Fig. 20.2. Von Braun and Nazi officers

* * *

At the same time, an infantry unit led by Colonel James M. Collins was headed toward Camp Dora near Nordhausen when his advance officer called him over the radio. Camp Dora was the "home" for the slave workers at the Mittelwerk V-2 rocket plant at Nordhausen. Hunt tells us that he shouted:

> "Colonel you'd better get up here and see what we've got. It's terrible." By this time, scenes from hell had become part of Collins's daily routine. But his mind reeled with horror at what he found at Camp Dora. As Collins approached the huge, cavelike entrance to the factory on the hill, six thousand bodies covered the ground. As far as he could see, row upon row of skin-covered skeletons were frozen solid in grotesque shapes, bearing bruises and wounds from beatings. "They had been starved to death," Collins recalled. "Their arms were just little sticks; their legs had practically no flesh on them at all." As the soldiers moved through the choking stench of death, they found the smoldering furnaces of Dora's crematory. The doors were still open where the SS had been shoving bodies in and burning them up.

Fig. 20.3. The Camp Dora dead

COMPETITION

The American occupying army had two different goals, one technical and another humanitarian. When they clashed, the humanitarian objectives of identifying and bringing to justice the war criminals frequently took second place. Hunt says in *Secret Agenda:*

> Members of the ordnance technical intelligence team, including Toftoy's aide, Major James Hamill, and Staver, arrived at the scene around the same time as an army war crimes unit. U.S. Army Major Herschel Auerbach had been sent to the site to investigate the crimes committed against the prisoners. His unit went one way, interrogating individuals and searching for evidence against those responsible for the deaths of twenty thousand Dora prisoners, while Hamill and Staver went in a different direction, to load up the V-2 rockets found in the tunnels, track down technical documents, and search the hills for rocket scientists who had worked in the Mittelwerk factory. In the end, however, both groups ended up looking for the same men.

The three men most responsible for the crimes against the Dora inmates were Albin Sawatzki, the Mittelwerk technical director; production director Arthur Rudolf; and Georg Rickhey, the general manager. They essentially escaped justice because they had vital information about V-2 rockets and bombproof shelters. U.S. Army Colonel Peter Beasley sent them all to London for further interrogation.

CHEMICAL WARFARE CRIMES

A team of nineteen American, British, and Canadian chemical warfare experts investigated the major German targeted sites. According to Hunt:

> The team was headed by Commander A. K. Mills of the British Ministry of Aircraft Production. Mills's group tracked down a Wehrmacht experimental station at Raubkammer, a gas defense laboratory, a Luftwaffe chemical warfare experimental station, and

several Luftwaffe and Wehrmacht chemical munition plants. . . .
Mills's team discovered that chemical warfare experiments had been
conducted on both animals and humans in the captured facilities.
At Raubkammer, a main laboratory and nine annexes housed laboratory animals used in experiments, including dogs, cats, guinea
pigs, apes, and horses. He also found four thousand photographs
of mustard gas experiments conducted on men who appeared to
be political prisoners from concentration camps. In some cases liquid mustard had been applied directly to the victims' skin, which
resulted in oozing blisters, burns, and deep scars all over their bodies. At least six of them had died.

The investigators discovered that the Germans had developed three
new nerve gases, Tabun, Sarin, and Soman, all much more deadly than
the mustard gases then possessed by the Allies. The team arrested fourteen chemical warfare scientists and brought them to a detention camp.
Also at that camp was SS Brigadier General Walter Schieber, who had
been in charge of the chemical industry at the Armaments Ministry.
Schieber would eventually work under Project Paperclip in West
Germany for ten years, making nerve gas for the Chemical Division
of the European Command. But surprisingly and uncharacteristically,
it was a fact that Hitler had adhered scrupulously to the prohibition
against chemical weapons established by the Geneva Protocol of 1925.
It has been speculated that this may have been because he himself had
suffered such an attack in World War I.

This so-called exploitation phase of the Allied occupation ended
with the German surrender in early May 1945. Hunt says, "Army
Ordnance, CIOS, and other scientific teams had assessed nearly every
primary technical and scientific target. But jealous rivalries erupted
between the teams and among the four Allied nations, which were competing for the same spoils of war. That competition, particularly with
the Soviets, would heighten when Germany was divided into four occupied zones." At the end of this phase, the Americans had succeeded in
closeting more than fifteen hundred German scientists and technicians
in detention camps in a German zone that was under U.S. control. Most

of them were forced to leave their homes and families while American experts sought to adapt their knowledge and experience to our systems and requirements. There was an urgency to that process because we were still at war with Japan, whereas the other three occupation powers did not have as much at stake.

PROJECT OVERCAST

Colonel Donald Putt was the assistant commanding officer of the Allied Technical Information Service. In that capacity, he was in charge of German scientists brought to a holding center at the Hotel Wittelsbacher Hof in Bad Kissingen. In the summer of 1945, there were about 120 men at that facility; most of them were jet engine, wind tunnel, and rocket fuel experts. Putt was very impressed with the résumés of these men and wanted them brought to the United States. He was not concerned with their Nazi affiliations or their political views. He later said, "The Germans were years ahead of us in aircraft design." Putt obtained the backing of General Hugh Knerr, soon to become the commander of Wright Field Army Air Base in Dayton, Ohio. Putt and Knerr believed that these men could advance U.S. aircraft design and development by ten years. But American interrogators in Putt's group opposed this move because some, if not many, of these captives were ardent Nazis. But other such proposals were stacking up on the desks of the Joint Chiefs of Staff (JCS). Toftoy wanted von Braun and his associated rocket engineers immediately brought to the United States. Undersecretary of War Robert Patterson was dead set against it. Furthermore, Truman had already enunciated a policy of excluding ardent Nazis from entrance into the United States, and von Braun was known to have been in the SS. Also, U.S. immigration laws prohibited members of fascist organizations from coming here. Hunt says:

> The idea also conflicted with JCS policies regarding the pros-
> ecution of Nazi war criminals and denazification of the general
> German population. When Justice Robert Jackson returned from

Europe shortly after his appointment as chief of counsel for the prosecution of war crimes, he told Truman, "I have assurances from the War Department that those likely to be accused as war criminals will be kept in close confinement and stern control." But ultimately the JCS circumvented all of these prohibitions and approved the policy because the ongoing war with Japan trumped all other considerations. This policy became Project Overcast. It was approved with the proviso that the program was to be "limited to those few 'chosen, rare minds' whose skills could not be fully exploited in Europe. Once that exploitation was completed they were to be returned immediately to Germany," and furthermore, "If any specialists who are brought to this country are subsequently found to be listed as alleged war criminals, they should be returned to Europe for trial." Both of these strictures were basically ignored.

Soon after the surrender of Japan in August 1945, German scientists started to enter the United States in numbers, under the auspices of Overcast. These men were hired by U.S. corporations overseas but were supposed to be processed by the military. This was a slipshod operation. Hunt says in *Secret Agenda:*

They entered the country without visas, outside normal immigration procedures, but all had employment contracts in their pockets. Although they were supposed to be under tight military custody, Peenemünde's former guidance department chief, Ernst Steinhoff, wasn't even met at the boat. He ended up hitchhiking to his job at Aberdeen Proving Ground, Maryland. . . . Interrogation centers were set up at Fort Strong, Massachusetts, located on an island in Boston Harbor, where the Germans were supposed to fill out forms and be interviewed. Most escaped close scrutiny. . . . Most officers conducting the interrogations did not even inquire whether the new arrivals were ardent Nazis or wanted for war crimes. . . . It wasn't long before nearly 150 Overcast specialists were working at various military bases across the country under this lax policy.

*Fig. 20.4. Original group of 104 German rocket scientists at Fort Bliss,
Texas, brought in by Project Overcast in early 1946*

Most of these early arrivals were the rocket scientists from
Peenemünde, including Wernher von Braun. One hundred and eigh-
teen of these men were sent to Fort Bliss, Texas, which was near the
White Sands Proving Ground where missiles could be tested. Most of
the others went to the Foreign Technology Division of the Army Air
Force at Wright Field in Dayton, Ohio, where they worked under Putt.
Others went to Long Island to work on torpedo and submarine tech-
nology. Twenty wind-tunnel specialists went to White Oak, Maryland.

PAPERCLIP AND THE
JOINT INTELLIGENCE OBJECTIVES AGENCY

Responsibility for Project Overcast was under the authority of the JCS
and was relegated to the Joint Intelligence Committee (JIC). Linda
Hunt explains on her website:

> The JIC was the intelligence arm of the Joint Chiefs of Staff,
> responsible for advising the JCS on the intelligence problems and
> policies and furnishing intelligence information to the JCS and the
> State Department. The JIC was composed of the Army's director
> of intelligence, the chief of naval intelligence, the assistant chief of

Air Staff-2, and a representative of the State Department. They considered policy questions regarding the German scientist project and recommended procedural changes to the JCS. The Army's director of intelligence always played a key role in the project, since the policy made Army intelligence (G-2) administratively responsible for many aspects of the program, including background investigations. . . . The JIOA was established as a subcommittee of the JIC specifically to assume direct responsibility for running the German scientist program until the JIOA was disbanded in 1962. This agency was comprised of a JIOA Governing Committee, made up of one representative of each member agency of the JIC, and an operational staff of military intelligence officers from the different services. . . .

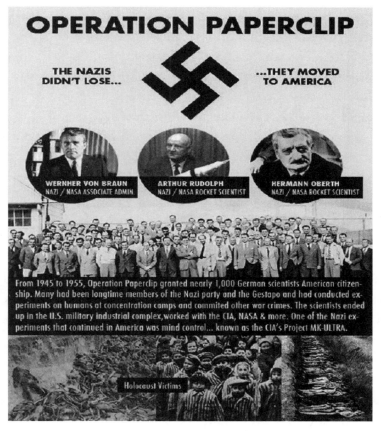

Fig. 20.5. Operation Paperclip poster

JIOA's duties included administering the project's policies and procedures, compiling dossiers, and serving as liaison to British intelligence officers running a similar project in Great Britain. In addition, JIOA took over many of CIOS's activities when that agency was dissolved shortly after Nazi Germany's surrender. JIOA was responsible for collecting, declassifying, and distributing CIOS and other technical intelligence reports on German science and industry.

In the spring of 1946, Project Overcast was dissolved and became Project Paperclip. This name was derived from the practice of attaching a paperclip to the dossiers of scientists who had an "ardent Nazi" affiliation or a demonstrated sympathy and who might be considered war criminals. The empowerment of the JIOA to administer Paperclip had the effect of elevating the status of the director to a position of supreme importance in the selection of German scientists for entrance into the United States. The advent of Project Paperclip in mid-1946 coincided with another important event relative to the penetration of Nazis into the United States. Reinhard Gehlen was sent back to Germany in September as head of the Gehlen Org with a budget of $3.5 million, which would probably equate to around $30 million today. But more significant was the fact that he probably had at his disposal the virtually unlimited funds of the large German banks that were financing the group of former SS members known as Odessa.

THE OSENBERG LIST

The first director of the JIOA, Army Colonel E. W. Gruhn, decided that he needed a list from which to work. Such a list had been compiled by Werner Osenberg, who had been the wartime commander of the Gestapo in charge of the scientific section. There were fifteen thousand names on that list, each one carefully notated by Osenberg as to political orientation and affiliations as well as his evaluation of their scientific credentials and abilities. Since Osenberg worked for Goering, he was looking for the most dedicated Nazis. Hunt says, "Of course, those scientists who held fanatic Nazi views and SS membership were also those whom Osenberg considered to be the best qualified." The list had been saved by an alert POW camp commander, who rescued it from being flushed down a toilet. But Osenberg himself was apprehended in 1945 and placed in a POW camp in Germany. When his importance was recognized by the JIOA, he was sent to Versailles, France, where he was used to recommend the best scientists for American repatriation. One can only imagine the glee that he must have felt as he had some of the worst Nazis in the Third Reich shipped to the shores of victorious America.

Navy Captain Bosquet Wev became director of the JIOA in early 1946. Army Lieutenant Monroe Hagood from G-2, Putt, and Toftoy were all on the JIOA committee at that time. All these men were in favor of more lenient regulations regarding the importation of ex-Nazis. On the other hand, Samuel Klaus, a lawyer from the State Department, also on the committee, took the role of the humanitarian watchdog and frequently clashed with the others. In these clashes, Klaus could hold his own, but the scales became seriously unbalanced when Major General Stephen J. Chamberlin was named the army's director of intelligence in June 1946.

Hunt says, "Hagood's CPM Branch, Army Air Force officers Putt and Knerr, and Army Colonel Toftoy were among eleven officers holding meetings on their own—without Klaus—to work on changes they wanted made in the new project. Their agenda included expanding the category of people to include prisoners of war, militarists, SS officers, and anyone else who they thought would be of use to the military. One proposal would have included 558 German POWs held in the United States since the beginning of World War II." One month later, "Hagood, Putt, and others in the Washington group, *in conjunction with U.S. Army intelligence officers in Germany,* secretly approved a scheme to include SS officers and former high-ranking officials of the Third Reich *who already were employed by Army intelligence in Germany.* They would have to be smuggled into America, since their backgrounds clearly violated U.S. immigration laws" (italics added), Klaus continued to be deliberately excluded from meetings and kept out of the loop. Hunt says, "The intelligence officers quickly forged ahead with the schemes they had hatched in Klaus's absence. On July 30 Chamberlin asked Chief of Staff Eisenhower to approve a plan to smuggle in thirty ex-Nazi experts on the USSR among a thousand 'scientists' in the new project." This proposal was submitted to Dean Acheson, acting secretary of state, for presentation to President Truman. Acheson recommended to the president that it be approved. Truman approved it on September 3. Project Paperclip had now entered new and dangerously un-American territory.

A DEAD NAZI HORSE

Hunt says:

> Paperclip's legacy has its roots in the cold war philosophy espoused by the intelligence officers who ran the operation. Their motives, schemes, and cover-up efforts are a logical focus for this book, since those are what shaped Paperclip from the beginning. Moreover, the military's secret agenda was far different from the one foisted on the American public. At its heart was an unshakable conviction that the end justified the means. The officers who ran Paperclip were determined to use any means necessary to keep Nazi scientists out of Russian hands, even if that meant violating U.S. laws and foreign policy. There may be no better example of the officers' brazen disregard for U.S. policies than the action they took in 1948. As first revealed in an article in the *Bulletin of the Atomic Scientists*, JIOA officers simply changed the records of those scientists they wanted, expunging evidence of war crimes and ardent Nazism. Though this meant directly defying an order given by Truman, JIOA Director Bosquet Wev excused the action by asserting that the government's concern over "picayune details" such as Nazi records would result in "the best interests of the United States [being] subjugated to the efforts expended in beating a dead Nazi horse."

Since Paperclip was indeed being run by intelligence officers, it began to appear that perhaps the Gehlen Org had linked up with the JIOA and that Reinhard Gehlen was calling the shots from his now-secure position in Pullach, West Germany. After all, as we have seen, the Odessa had plenty of money to spread around, and now that the war was over, these poorly paid military men in the JIOA were probably thinking of their financial future. If any sort of financial arrangement could have been established between the Gehlen Org and Wev, it would then have become possible to send known war criminals from Germany through Odessa and the "ratlines" directly to Paperclip with the cooperation of the JIOA. Their dossiers would then be scrubbed or sanitized and their names changed, and these men then could infiltrate the United States in positions of influence and power in our military-industrial complex. That seems to be what happened. The tables had been turned, and the Brotherhood of the Snake was now up to its old tricks, the old fifth column game—infiltration and weakening from within.

Eisenhower tried to warn us about that in his farewell address on January 17, 1961. He said, "In the councils of government, we must guard against the acquisition of unwarranted influence, whether sought or unsought, by the military-industrial complex. The potential for the disastrous rise of misplaced power exists and will persist. We must never let the weight of this combination endanger our liberties or democratic processes. We should take nothing for granted. Only an alert and

Fig. 20.6. President Eisenhower. He warned us about the military-industrial complex. (Bernard Safran, artist)

knowledgeable citizenry can compel the proper meshing of the huge industrial and military machinery of defense with our peaceful methods and goals, so that security and liberty may prosper together." What Ike didn't say, and what he couldn't say, but what he probably knew, was that the military-industrial complex was now riddled with ex-Nazis with an agenda in service to the advent of the Fourth Reich!

A JUGGERNAUT

In the prologue to *Secret Agenda,* Hunt says:

> American soldiers fighting in World War II had barely laid down their guns when hundreds of German and Austrian scientists, including a number implicated in Nazi war crimes, began immigrating to the United States. They were brought here under a secret intelligence project code-named "Paperclip." Ever since, the U.S. government has successfully promoted the lie that Paperclip was a short-term operation limited to a few postwar raids on Hitler's hoard of scientific talent. The General Accounting Office even claims that the project ended in 1947. All of which is sheer propaganda. For the first time ever, this book reveals that Paperclip was the biggest, longest-running operation involving Nazis in our country's history. The project continued nonstop until 1973—*decades* longer than was previously thought. And remnants of it are still in operation today [1991]. (italics added)

At least 1,600 scientific and research specialists and thousands of their dependents were brought to the United States under Operation Paperclip. Hundreds of others arrived under two other Paperclip-related projects and went to work for universities, defense contractors, and CIA fronts. The Paperclip operation eventually became such a juggernaut that in 1956 one American ambassador characterized it as "a continuing U.S. recruitment program which has no parallel in any other Allied country."

21

The Fourth Reich

Adolf Hitler and Eva Braun moved into their permanent residence about sixty miles north of Bariloche in mid-June 1947, after a one-year vacation in Casino, Brazil, a town on the Argentine border. Their new home was in a private estancia called Inalco. The residence was a large rustic mansion fronting on Lake Nahuel Huapi and backed up to a wooded mountainside area in the Andes foothills, very close to the Chilean border. It was built specifically for Hitler in 1943, evidently

Fig. 21.1. Hitler's residence at Inalco

when he recognized, as did others, that the war was basically over. The house was totally secure, accessible only by boat or airplane. According to *Grey Wolf,* Hitler and Braun lived there until 1954, when she took their two daughters and moved to another location, in "Hitler's Valley" about 230 miles distant. Evidently she was now finished with the moldy remnants of the Third Reich and the madman who had ruled it. Hitler himself remained at Inalco, alone, until 1955, when Juan Peron was ousted from power in a coup, and Bormann convinced him that he needed an even more remote refuge. He was moved farther south to the town of La Clara. He was now sixty-six years old and beginning to deteriorate rapidly. His Parkinson's disease symptoms had worsened, and *Grey Wolf* says, "He now spent a large part of his time resting or brooding. Politics was becoming less and less important."

But Bormann, at the age of fifty-five, was very healthy. He was very much alive and was now living in Argentina. Rumors of his death in Berlin were, like Mark Twain's, "greatly exaggerated." *Grey Wolf* tells us that he arrived in Buenos Aires on May 17, 1948, dressed as a Jesuit priest and with a passport in the name of Reverend Juan Gomez. He registered at the Apostolic nunciature in Buenos Aires, and on October 12 was granted, on religious grounds, the ultimate document of residence, the "blue stamp," which gave him the right to remain in Argentina indefinitely.

BORMANN'S EMPIRE

Bormann had been pouring money and valuables into Argentina ever since 1943, in the custodial care of the Perons, to prepare for the eventual arrival of the top Nazi echelon. Bormann had complete control of the fate of Hitler in his exile, and he used Hitler to ensure the fidelity of the other fascists who still revered him and who would become the nucleus of the Fourth Reich. But Hitler had no further real power. He was only a figurehead, and Bormann was now totally in charge. Before he left his secure redoubt in the Austrian Alps to go to Argentina, he met with Eva Peron in Italy in late June 1947. She had come to Europe to deposit Juan Peron's share of the "loot of conquered Europe" that

Bormann had been sending to Argentina in secure Swiss banks in Zurich. *Grey Wolf* estimated the total amount of that deposit to be about $800 million. That would be around $8 billion today. In that meeting she informed Bormann that Juan Peron had decided to keep 75 percent of the German money, instead of the originally agreed on 25 percent. Bormann was furious, but he had to accede. There is no honor among thieves. Hitler was already ensconced in Argentina, and Bormann wanted a smooth transition for himself and his staff. That left him with a paltry $300 million, or roughly $3 billion in 2015 dollars. However, the wily Bormann had stashed much more in the form of corporate investments in Argentina and all over the world.

Bormann quickly doffed his clerical attire and moved into a hotel in Buenos Aires. *Grey Wolf* tells us, "He spent much of his time in Buenos Aires; his front was a company that manufactured refrigerators, behind which he extended his financial dealings across the world." He was now sitting on top of a vast worldwide fascist undercover empire, and he had the immense wealth at his disposal with which to manage that empire. Aracelie Mendez, a young woman from Spain who did some secretarial work for Bormann at his office on Pasaje Barolo, knew him as Ricardo Bauer, one of his several identities. *Grey Wolf* says, "She witnessed many of his financial dealings; he once received a bank transfer for US $400,000 from Europe. He told her that he had shares in a factory in Belgium and another in Holland and that this transfer and many others were part of his profits." He owned his one-quarter share of the 192 pounds of platinum, 2.77 tons of gold, and 4,638 carats of diamonds and other precious gems that he had sent to Argentina. It is known that he sold a diamond in Buenos Aires for $120,000. Bormann's liquid assets were in currencies from different countries. He had at least $4 million on deposit in Argentine banks.

THE FAILURE OF OPERATION HIGHJUMP

In those early postwar days, there was still a lot of pride of country in the United States and an idealistic belief in Christian tolerance and fair-mindedness, especially as Americans contrasted themselves with the Nazis and the horrors uncovered in the concentration camps. The American military was not yet infected by Nazi infiltration. That attitude manifested as an all-out effort to destroy the Nazi base in Antarctica in 1946. Led by intrepid polar explorer Admiral Richard Byrd, one of America's favorite sons, Operation Highjump was planned by war hero Admiral Chester W. Nimitz and commanded by Admiral Richard Cruzen. Task Force 68, comprising a fleet of thirteen ships including an aircraft carrier, thirty-three aircraft and 4,700 marines, departed the United States in December 1946. It was planned to be a six-month campaign through the Antarctic summer. The attack was repelled by German flying disks that came out of the waters of the Southern Ocean and quickly destroyed an American ship and killed sixty-eight men in a twenty-minute engagement. Byrd was forced to retreat and to terminate the operation after only two months. The task force returned to America in February 1947. In his testimony before Congress, an angry Byrd suggested turning Antarctica into a thermo-nuclear test range!

It was after that humbling defeat of the legendary American Navy that the Nazis in Argentina felt confident enough of their technology to begin to advance their long-term agenda. Now they really began to believe that they had the "muscle" to push forward with the Fourth Reich. And so it was in June of that year that Hitler felt secure enough to move into his permanent residence at Inalco, and Bormann, now floating in riches, implemented his move to Argentina, arriving in mid-1948. At that point, with the T43 communications network in place, the Perons in power, and Bormann directing his worldwide Nazi empire from his secure headquarters in Buenos Aires, superficially at least on behalf of the still-living Führer, they could start the wheels in motion. Gehlen was consolidating his spy network in Germany and feeding Nazi war criminals into Operation Paperclip through the ratlines and Odessa. Odessa was also sitting on top of piles of money recovered by the German banks from their accounts in Switzerland and getting con-tributions from the still-functioning large corporations in Germany. The Antarctic colony was now safe from attack and continuing to grow and to manufacture flying disks.

The stage was now set for the primary operations necessary to initiate the Fourth Reich. The Nazis now had to gain control over the U.S. government and economy and to suppress space exploration. In order to implement worldwide fascist control and to enslave the human race, the Brotherhood of the Snake had to keep the human race in a state of isolation and dependence, unable to receive help from friendly and helpful extraterrestrial civilizations. They knew that the Pleiadians and the Andromedans were prepared to offer assistance, if requested. Also, as with Atlantis, it was necessary to begin the hybridization process to dilute the Western European bloodline in the United States and make it more subject to control by the Brotherhood from the fourth dimension.

THE FIFTIES

As the transformational decade of the fifties dawned, the Brotherhood was positioned to take control of the key levers of power in the American government. General Eisenhower's move into the presidency in 1952 brought into power the ultraconservative Republicans who before and during the war had business and banking connections with Nazi Germany and who had been in sympathy with many aspects of the Nazi philosophy. John Foster Dulles became secretary of state, and his younger brother, Allen Dulles, became the director of the CIA in 1953. These two canny veterans of insider Washington skirmishes now had, between them, a lock on American foreign policy and a powerful influence on domestic policy. They were easily able to manipulate the naive but well-intentioned president, who had absolutely no political experience. The Republicans also took over Congress for the first two years of the Eisenhower administration, ensuring conservative control.

The Dulles brothers had been law partners at Sullivan and Cromwell in New York City in the 1930s. Perhaps their most important client was the Rockefeller-owned Standard Oil of New Jersey. They personally brokered the partnership between Standard Oil and the German-based I. G. Farben, which was, at that time, one of the largest chemical combines in the world. Farben produced all the gasoline and other chemicals for the Nazi war machine. Farben later achieved infamy by manufacturing the poison gas Zyklon B, which was used in the mass extermination of the Jewish prisoners at the Auschwitz death camp. Its massive petrochemical plant was adjacent to Auschwitz. When the Allied armies rolled into Germany in 1945, they were astonished to see the I. G. Farben plant completely untouched by Allied bombs, while every building nearby was completely demolished. In fact, since it was still intact, the Americans adopted it as their headquarters.

Sullivan and Cromwell also represented the J. Henry Schroder Bank. The Dulles brothers met with Hitler on January 4, 1933, in Cologne, at the home of Kurt von Schroder. They represented the Kuhn, Loeb Company, which provided the short-term financing for Hitler to run for chancellor of Germany. Schroder guaranteed the funds on behalf of Hitler. Schroder later agreed to pay the bills of the Nazi Party and to guarantee their debts, and he became Hitler's personal banker. Allen Dulles was a director of the London branch of the Schroder Bank. Dulles also represented the affairs in America of Fritz Thyssen, the German steel magnate who helped finance Hitler's rise to power.

Given the friendship that had developed between Reinhard Gehlen and Allen Dulles and given Dulles's history displaying sympathy for Nazi causes, it seems reasonable to conclude that Allen Dulles brought many of the Gehlen Org agents into the CIA. In fact, in those early CIA days, the entire organization was dedicated to anti-Soviet activity and to "fighting" the cold war. Consequently, virtually all of the spies that Gehlen had employed in Europe were brought en masse to constitute the entire early CIA organization. Dulles agreed with the far-right attitudes of the Gehlen network and believed it was patriotic to build a Cold War spy network. Consequently, Nazi attitudes permeated the CIA, and since Allen Dulles remained in power for ten years, those attitudes became embedded in the CIA culture, and they remain in the organization right up to the present day. It is probable that many of the German spies recruited by Gehlen came directly into the CIA with their Nazi affiliations removed from their dossiers. In addition, given their experience with new weaponry, it is likely that some Paperclip technicians and scientists were also recruited into the CIA by Dulles.

Both Dulles brothers were members of the Council on Foreign Relations. The avowed goal of the council is a world government—the New World Order. The ex-Nazis who were infiltrating the U.S. government all sought to advance this globalist agenda. It was covertly understood by the deep insiders that this was really a code phrase for the Fourth Reich. John Foster Dulles apparently supported that basis of that idea when he said in 1941, as the first chairman of the Commission on a Just and Durable Peace, that the commission's first order of business was to pass a resolution proclaiming that "a world of irresponsible, competing, and unrestrained national sovereignties, whether acting alone or in alliance or in coalition, is a world of international anarchy. It must make place for a higher and more inclusive authority." Then, consistently, nine years later, as a founding member of the Council on Foreign Relations, he said in his book *War or Peace* (1950), "The United Nations represents not a final stage in the development of world order, but only a primitive stage. Therefore its primary task is to create the conditions which will make possible a more highly developed organization." As President Eisenhower's secretary of state, he was well positioned to advance this agenda.

Since its earliest days in Egypt, the Brotherhood of the Snake has pushed for a wider and wider inclusion of diverse cultures, states, and nations under a central authority. Whenever possible, they prefer an empire under the leadership of a king, queen, or strongman dictator to dealing with individual countries. This permits their rulership over a single individual rather than over hundreds of individual leaders. They pieced together the Egyptian Empire, the Greek city states, the Roman Empire, the Ottoman Empire, the Holy Roman Empire, the British Empire, and most recently the failed German and Japanese empires. Now, in the twenty-first century, with sophisticated communication systems in place, they seek to establish a world empire under the United Nations, which they can then transform into the New World Order. Since human societies seem to be less and less tolerant of kings, queens, or dictators, the only way the Brotherhood can achieve authoritarian rule is by installing a world religious leader. Their plan is for a charismatic individual of their choosing to emerge to assume this leadership position, much like Ayatollah Ali Khamenei in Iran. No doubt, he has already emerged and is being groomed for this role even as this is being written.

THE NATIONAL AERONAUTICS
AND SPACE ADMINISTRATION

Whatever their motivation, G-2 was instrumental in bringing the ex-Nazis into the United States in those immediate postwar years. Bosquet Wev, as director of the JIOA, was the key individual in that effort. Truman had issued an edict stating that no ardent Nazis were to be admitted into the United States. This order was circumvented by Wev and the other primary intelligence members of the JIOA committee, including Montie Cone, who was G-2's Exploitation Branch chief, his superior, Lieutenant Colonel H. B. St. Clair, and Colonel Thomas Ford. At a meeting of the committee at the Pentagon on February 27, 1947, the list of the investigated Germans was on the table, but Klaus from the State Department was not permitted to see it. Hunt says:

> The JIOA had a good reason for wanting to keep the lists secret, and it had nothing to do with classified information. At the time of the meeting, Wev and Cone were sitting on a powder keg. They had just received 146 investigative reports from Europe and nearly all of them were derogatory. They knew that the Germans' Nazi backgrounds violated the policy that Truman had signed. The *OMGUS* [Office of the Military Governor United States] *Security Report* on the scientists disclosed allegations that Zobel and others had participated in experiments on humans, the Axsters had mistreated foreign laborers, Salmon had torched a synagogue, and SS member Debus had turned a colleague over to the Gestapo. Other men were accused of various crimes including theft and sexual perversion. Many had been early members of the Nazi party, the SS, or the SA. One of the reports showed that von Braun had been an ardent Nazi. He was a major in the SS recommended by Heinrich Himmler in 1940, and a party member since 1937.

The JIOA reacted by launching an intense campaign to discredit the people in the State Department who were opposing the immigration of the ex-Nazis. Ultimately, by May of 1948, all of the incriminating dossiers had been cleaned up, with the "ardent Nazi" remarks expunged. FBI Director J. Edgar Hoover was then converted to change his objections, and he recommended to the Justice Department that the contentious ex-Nazis be given immigration visas and admitted to the United States. That group encompassed the core scientists of the yet-to-be-created National Aeronautics and Space Administration (NASA), including Wernher von Braun; Magnus von Braun (Wernher's younger brother); Walter Dornberger; Anton Beier, a former member of the Death's Head SS; Hermann Kurzweg, a member of the SS Elite Guard; Guenther Haukohl and Hans Friedrich, who had supervised the slave laborers at the Mittelwerk V-2 rocket factory; Herbert Axster, who had been a hated, notorious slave driver at Mittelwerk; Theodor Zobel, a wind-tunnel engineer who had performed experiments on humans; Arthur Rudolph, Mittelwerk production director; Albin Sawatzki, Mittelwerk's technical director, who had beaten Dora slaves mercilessly; Georg Rickhey, the Mittelwerk general manager; and Kurt Debus, a former member of the SS and SA who had turned a colleague over to the Gestapo.

NASA was created on July 29, 1958, by Eisenhower and began operations on October 1 of the same year. Its creation was said to have been triggered by the successful orbital revolution of the Soviet Sputnik satellite on October 4, 1957, thus challenging the United States to match that feat by initiating a space program. Wernher von Braun and the other 117 German rocket scientists at Fort Bliss, who had already been testing rockets at the White Sands Proving Ground, were folded into NASA, along with eight thousand employees of the twelve-year-old National Advisory Committee for Aeronautics (NACA). In view of their V-2 rocket experience, the German scientists were far more important to the new agency than the NACA employees were, and they took the lead in research and experimentation. Von Braun was made the director of the Marshall Space Flight Center in Huntsville, Alabama, in July 1960, and he remained in that position for ten years.

THE FAKE SPACE PROGRAM

It has become increasingly obvious that there is something very wrong with NASA. After fifty-eight years of its existence and an average annual budget of $15 billion, NASA scientists are still depending on rocketry, which is now ancient technology, have sent a few men to jump around on the moon, have failed to develop a manned voyage to Mars after having lost several probes, and have focused almost their entire effort on building and maintaining the International Space Station, of which the agency bears only a part of the cost. Scientists and laymen alike are now getting the distinct impression that NASA has been feeding us pabulum while working on much more advanced programs in secret. This suggests that the ex-Nazi influence in NASA still prevails and that they are carrying out the agenda of the Brotherhood in trying to keep the human race earthbound while they secretly take control of the space program. Millions of people understand this subconsciously and are forced to satisfy their longing for space travel through watching science-fiction films. Richard C. Hoagland came to a very similar conclusion in his most recent book, *Dark Mission: The Secret History of NASA,* coauthored by Mike Bara. In a chapter added to the book in 2009 titled "The End Game," Hoagland says:

> There was a time when I was truly optimistic about the possibility of democratizing space. I, like many Americans, bought into the vision that was sold to us in the 1950s right up through Apollo: the movement of entire industries and people into low earth orbit, and the commensurate migration of hundreds of thousands of employees, suppliers and consumers into a new space economy. I expected, as we all did, that Kubrick's 2001 vision [in 1968] of Pan Am Space Clippers and Hilton hotels in orbit would be easily surpassed by the time that fast approaching new millennium arrived. Instead, fully two generations later, we look back and realize that after conquering the Moon and turning toward Mars, we simply gave up and stayed home. The reason for this exploratory stasis could not be more obvious: For over 50 years space has been the sole monopoly of governments.

Hoagland also notes the strange obsession of NASA with ancient Egypt, the place of the emergence of the Brotherhood of the Snake. He also mentions the strange depiction of the Orion star system, the ancestral home of the Reptilians, on an official NASA shoulder patch.

THE REAL SPACE PROGRAM

According to Captain Bill Uhouse, we have had working antigravity disks since 1962. Uhouse, recently deceased, was an ex-Marine pilot and an aeronautical engineer who worked on constructing the disk simulator at Area 51 for thirty-five years. Our disks were back-engineered from a craft given to us in 1953, as a gift, by the Ebens from the planet Serpo in the star system Zeta Reticuli. The simulator, using two-million-volt capacitors, the largest ever built, was completed in 1958, when we began training pilots to fly the new American "flying saucers." Our friendship with the Ebens began in 1947, when we accommodated the lone alien who survived the Roswell crash at Los Alamos Laboratories, where he lived for five years until his death in 1952 (see *Secret Journey to Planet Serpo* by this author). Using this new technology, we established small outpost colonies on the moon and Mars, jointly with the Russians, in 1962, thus launching the true space era.

We have since developed real spacefaring technology, using a variety of advanced propulsion systems. It has been reported in leaked information that we now have spacecraft that are huge and can accommodate as many as three hundred passengers and crew. This was confirmed in a diary entry made by President Ronald Reagan on June 11, 1985. He wrote, "Lunch with 5 top space scientists. It was fascinating. . . . I learned that our shuttle capacity is such that we could orbit 300 people." These craft were developed by the United States and have become a fleet of eight cigar-shaped "mother ships" believed to be more than 4,000 feet in length, acting as space aircraft carriers and accommodating forty-three scout craft.

Richard Boylan, Ph.D., reports on his website, www.drboylan.com (accessed September 20, 2016) that one of these ships, the *SS Nautilus-X,* operates in deep space propelled by magnetic pulsing. He says, "It makes

Fig. 21.2. Craft believed to be SS Nautilus-X *space exploration vehicles*

twice-a-week trips up to the secret military-intelligence space station, which has been in deep space for the past thirty years, and manned by U.S. and USSR (now CIS) military astronauts." Perhaps the most fearsome craft in the U.S. fleet is the TAW-50 (see plate 19). Boylan calls it a hypersonic, antigravity, space fighter-bomber. Reportedly, it can reach speeds in excess of mach 50, or 38,000 mph! This means it can achieve Earth escape velocity, which is 25,000 mph, with its onboard propulsion, that is, without rockets. It has fourth-generation electrogravitics, which allows it come to a complete standstill in less than two milliseconds and stay stationary for extended periods. The Lockheed X22A two-man antigravity disk fighter is equipped with neutral particle-beam weapons, can achieve optical invisibility, and is deployable all over the world. All these craft are housed at the Space Warfare headquarters in a secret underground facility inside King's Peak in the Wasatch Mountains of Utah, eighty miles east of Salt Lake City.

Herbert Dorsey III says in his book *Secret Science and the Secret Space Program:*

> A huge triangular craft, estimated to be 600 feet long and 100 feet across, was seen by a hiker in a remote region of the high Utah dessert [sic]. The huge craft was silently hovering and gradually losing altitude. Then, the dessert [sic] floor opened up. Or rather, some huge doors camouflaged to look like dessert [sic] opened up. The

craft lowered itself into the opening and the camouflaged doors swung close and the area looked just like dessert [sic] again. So apparently, there was an underground base right there in the middle of the desert. And this base could launch and land these huge air/space craft. It is estimated that a craft that size could carry up to 2,000 passengers.

A retired Defense Intelligence Agency operative called "anonymous," who revealed all the details of the journey of twelve Americans across the galaxy to the planet Serpo, claims he was the editor of the Red Book, which chronicles all our contacts with extraterrestrials. Seemingly high up on the intelligence ladder, he gives details of other contacts. He says on the Serpo website (www.serpo.org) (accessed September 20, 2016), "We did have visitors from nine other star systems. . . . We determined recently that some of the visitors were the same type of race but a 'mechanical lifeform.' They were hybrid beings that were created in a laboratory rather than by natural birth." The U.S. space program is administered by the United States Space Command, created in 1985 by

Fig. 21.3. Publicity for a secret space program conference

the U.S. Department of Defense. The headquarters are at Peterson Air Force Base in Colorado Springs, Colorado. This organization is primarily operated as adjunctive to the U.S. Air Force. The space cadets are trained in separate facilities near the Air Force Academy. The Space Command makes routine trips to our now expanded colonies on the moon and Mars.

All these operations have been tightly contained in above-top-secret categories by MJ-12, the high-level committee formed by Truman in 1947 to control all programs related to our relationships with extraterrestrials. The military has been very adept at keeping these matters under wraps, threatening fines of $10,000, dishonorable discharges, and ten years imprisonment, and dropping unmistakable hints of bodily harm to violators and their families. Several whistle-blowers are known to have been assassinated. The CIA has also perfected the practice of selective erasure of memories using electronic dissolution of memory, hypnosis, and drugs on those working on classified projects. And through the control of the media by the Illuminati, newscasters have been trained to ridicule and snicker at any reports of ETs or secret space activities that might filter through. Thus, the public, and most of Congress, continues to believe that what is reported by NASA is the extent of our space program. Thus, the Brotherhood relegates to itself all the amazing advancements in space travel, making certain that the citizenry cannot escape their control by traveling to the stars.

22

The New
World Order

On or about February 21, 1954, Eisenhower met with an alien contingent at Holloman Air Force Base in New Mexico. That group of aliens has come to be popularly known as the Greys. Out of that meeting came an agreement between the U.S. government and the alien race, now known as the Treaty of Greada. We would allow them to abduct a limited number of humans of their choosing and to perform examinations to allow them to study the physiology and psychology of the human race. In return, they would provide our military with advanced technology, especially as regards biotechnology and antigravity aircraft-propulsion systems. They were to provide us with lists of those who had been abducted. This treaty was necessary because galactic law does not permit an alien species to abduct members of a native planetary population without an invitation. Thus did we open the door to what has become a widespread phenomenon, not limited to the United States, that has ultimately allowed the creation of a hybrid race. Since the aliens arrived at the meeting in spaceships, we assumed that they came from off-planet. But that was not the case. The Greys came from their underground realm. They were the crossbreeds of Reptilians and Sirians that have been the scourge of humanity for millennia. They were representatives of the Brotherhood of the Snake.

The first abduction of this new era took place on September 19, 1961,

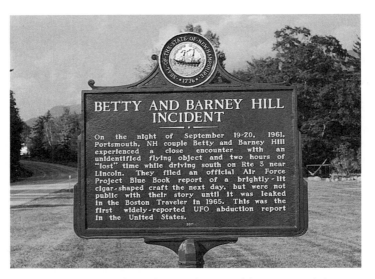

Fig. 22.1. Historical marker at the site of first UFO abduction

on a deserted road near Indian Head, New Hampshire. Betty and Barney Hill were taken out of their car and up into an alien craft hovering over the road and subjected to separate physical examinations by the Greys. The site is now commemorated by a roadside historical marker.

Ironically, that treaty was not really necessary. We had already been given an antigravity disk to back-engineer by our friends, the Ebens from Zeta Reticuli, as a gift. It landed at Kingman, Arizona, on May 21, 1953, and was taken by our military to Area 51. The four Eben crew members were bussed to Los Alamos. But thanks to the hypercompartmentalization of top-secret information, that event may have been known only to MJ-12, and not to the president, at that time. This is not surprising since MJ-12 carried a top-secret code word classification, from which the president was usually excluded. The association of classified groups of our government and military scientists with the Greys and their cousins, the Reptilians, has since grown into a close cooperation that has essentially turned into what could best be termed an alliance. That alliance also includes representatives of large corporations that research and supply classified military equipment, as well as insiders in the intelligence and space community. All together, they constitute the military-industrial complex that Eisenhower warned us about in his farewell address in January 1961. Now that complex, combined with the Bavarian Illuminati, the main Illuminati financial resource, has become referred to colloquially as the Cabal (see plate 28).

HYBRIDIZATION

What the Cabal has permitted to take place is the covert hybridization of the human race, much like what happened on Atlantis. But now the end game is different. Instead of using hybrids to dilute the human bloodline to make humans more susceptible to fourth-dimensional influence, the hybrid creatures are essentially intended to house the souls of aliens because these bodies are not acceptable to human souls due to critical DNA differences. So the hybrids are really no longer humans at the soul level. Since this process has now been progressing for more than fifty years, there are now many millions of alien hybrids walking the streets of our large cities, interacting with humans at every level, and producing second- and third-generation hybrid aliens. The hybrids all have enhanced paranormal capabilities, so they have the advantage of elbowing aside the genuine humans in any competitive situation, as with employment in sensitive governmental jobs, thus gradually taking over those organizations. This situation is analogous to the story line in the prophetic film *Blade Runner,* based on the novel *Do Androids Dream of Electric Sheep?* by Philip K. Dick, wherein it took a very special eye test to differentiate humans from robotic creatures. These hybrids, of course, take their marching orders from the Greys, the Reptilians, and the Bavarian Illuminati. The end game is the gradual replacement of millions, perhaps billions, of humans and the enslavement of the rest, as was intended in World War II.

THE JOINT UNDERGROUND BASES

One of the stipulations of the Treaty of Greada was the agreement that the U.S. government would, jointly with the aliens, construct underground bases for joint research and activity. One such activity was to be the development of advanced spacefaring and biological technology on behalf of the United States. In pursuance of that stipulation, construction of a huge underground facility commenced sometime in the late fifties under the Archuleta Mesa at the Four Corners area of the Southwest near the town of Dulce, New Mexico. That site was selected because it connected with an already existing, ancient, deep-down, multilevel alien colony tied into a complex tunnel system that crisscrosses the underground United States and is connected to a world grid. This was the grid originally developed by the Reptilians when they first went underground thousands of years previously, after the submergence of Lemuria. The tunnels accommodate high-speed maglev trains that can travel at supersonic speeds.

Phil Schneider, a geologist and structural engineer who helped build thirteen deep underground military bases (DUMBs), including the Dulce base, in 1995, estimated the total annual black budget to be around $500 billion (see plate 21). The cost of building the Dulce base was about $20 billion. Schneider claims that he was aware of

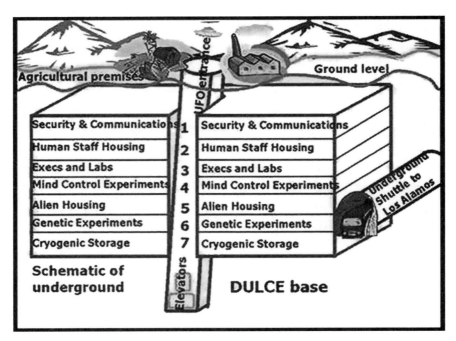

Fig. 22.2. Dulce base schematic

131 DUMB bases in the United States and others in Canada and Mexico. He says that most of the bases are between one and two miles underground. He was involved in an alien firefight when he was lowered into a deep hole that was created for ventilation over the Dulce base. When he encountered the aliens, they tried to kill him, so he fired back with his 9mm pistol. Luckily, another construction worker grabbed his limp body and threw him into an upward-bound basket, which saved his life. Schneider then became angry when he discovered the anti-human attitude of the aliens and started speaking out publicly. His last YouTube video, posted on November 23, 2014, was based on incidents that happened in November 1965. It was recorded in November 1995. Two months later, on January 11, 1996, he was found dead under suspicious circumstances. He had previously said publicly, "If I ever 'commit suicide,' I'll have been murdered."

THE THOMAS COSTELLO REVELATIONS

A man named Bruce Alan DeWalton, who adopted the pseudonym of "Branton," published his book, *The Dulce Book,* online. It offers the most illuminating, thoroughly researched information about the Dulce base available anywhere. Branton speaks of a former security officer at Dulce named Thomas Costello, who escaped from the facility in late 1979 with thirty photos, a video from the control center, and hundreds of incriminating documents. Costello's descriptions of the hellish experiments at Dulce are quoted in a magazine article in the February–March 1991 issue of *UFO Universe,* "The Deep Dark Secret at Dulce," written by Bill Hamilton and "Tal" LeVesque. They say in that article:

> Thomas alleges that there were over 18,000 of the short 'greys' at the Dulce Facility. He has also seen [tall] reptilian humanoids. One of us [Tal] had come face-to-face with a 6-foot tall Reptoid which had materialized [from the fourth dimension] in the [his] house. . . . The security level goes up as one descends to the lower levels. Thomas had an ULTRA-7 clearance. He knew of seven sublevels, but there may have been more. Most of the aliens are on levels

5, 6, and 7. Alien housing is on level 5. The only sign in English was one over a tube shuttle station hallway which read "to Los Alamos." Connections go from Dulce to the Page, Arizona, facility, then to an underground base below Area 51 in Nevada. Tube shuttles go to and from Dulce to facilities below Taos, N.M.; Datil, N.M.; Colorado Springs, Colorado; Creede, Colorado; Sandia; then on to Carlsbad, New Mexico. There is a vast network of tube shuttle connections under the United States, which extends into a global system of tunnels and sub-cities.

Branton says about this in a footnote in chapter 10 in *The Dulce Book,* "This suggests that these DEEPER tunnels may have originally been constructed in more ancient or prehistoric times by beings OTHER than the current reptiloid-draco residents of the deeper levels of the Dulce 'base' itself."

BIO-TECH HORRORS

Hamilton and LeVesque's article continues:

The studies on Level 4 include human-aura research, as well as all aspects of telepathy, hypnosis, and dreams. Thomas says that they know how to separate the bioplasmic body from the physical body and place an "alien entity" force-matrix within a human body after removing the "soul" life-force-matrix of the human . . .

Level 6 is privately called "Nightmare Hall." It holds the genetic labs. Here are experiments done on fish, seals, birds, and mice that are vastly altered from their original forms. There are multi-armed and multi-legged humans and several cages [and vats] of humanoid bat-like creatures (deceased "Mothmen" or those creatures that John Keel refers to in his book *The Mothman Prophecies*? –Branton) up to 7-feet tall. The aliens have taught the humans a lot about genetics, things both useful and dangerous. . . . Level #7 is the worst. Row after row of 1,000's of humans & human-mixture remains in cold storage. Here too are embryos of humanoids in various stages of development. Also, many human childrens' remains in storage vats. Who are [were] these people? [My sources of information include . . .] people who worked in the labs, abductees taken to the base, people who assisted in the construction, intelligence personnel [NSA, CIA, etc.], and UFO-Inner Earth researchers. This information is meant for those who are seriously interested in the Dulce base. For YOUR OWN PROTECTION, be advised to "USE CAUTION" while investigating this complex. . . . The Greys, the Reptoids, the winged Draco species are highly analytical and technologically oriented. THEY HAVE HAD ANCIENT CONFLICTS WITH THE EL-HUMANS and may be STAGING here for a FUTURE CONFLICT . . .

Schneider estimated in a talk he gave in 1996 that about one hundred thousand children and one million adults disappear every year worldwide. He intimated that most, maybe all of these, end up in this and other worldwide chambers of horror!

THE DULCE WARS

As some of the human collaborators began to realize the horrid dimensions of the alien bioengineering in progress, they began to revolt. Branton speaks of "a war" that occurred in a joint facility deep down under Area 51. He says:

This "war" was actually a "massacre" according to MJ12 Special Studies Group [MJ12-SSG] agent Michael Wolf, since the first outbreak of violence in 1975 resulted during a demonstration of an anti-matter reactor within an underground chamber. The Greys operating the demonstration ordered the human security officers to remove the bullets from their weapons. One Security officer questioned this order and just for having the audacity to question, one of the Greys apparently let their true colors show. That is, it prematurely exposed the fact that "they" were not really the "allies" of the American government, but actually an occupational invasion force that had to maintain absolute discipline among its "conquered subjects." This "thing" from out of this world decided that it would make an "example" out of those who questioned their orders, and its comrades followed suit. The Greys commenced to slaughter SEVERAL dozen Security personnel and Scientists, although only one alien Grey died in that initial altercation.

Branton speaks also of a firefight that broke out at Dulce. "Thomas Castello claims that another battle occurred below Dulce four years later in 1979, after several scientists who had discovered the 'Horrible Truth'—of thousands of human abductees in cold storage or imprisoned in cage-like enclosures in the deeper 'Alien' sectors under Dulce—were themselves captured by the aliens following this discovery. These were some of the best minds America had to offer." There were several other such incidents. Collectively they developed into what became known as the Dulce Wars.

Branton cannot suppress his anger and indignation about these alien atrocities. He speaks about when the Telosians, a friendly and humane group of aliens visiting Earth, questioned the rights of the Greys to be present on this planet. They replied that they "have the right to continue their activities since the U.S. Government has authorized their activities on earth and in America." An irate Branton comments:

> Are the *Grays* referring to the *Nazi-backed CIA-NSA "secret government,"* which has infiltrated America through murder and manipulation, and established the *"alien* interaction" projects WITHOUT Congressional consent? It's AS IF these green-blooded, pencil-necked, melon-headed, blood-sucking parasites—who break treaties, violate human will, permanently abduct and even kill humans for scientific or sustenance purposes, lie and deceive, disregard non-intervention ethics, destroy animals and property, manipulate the thoughts of the masses and their leaders against their conscious knowledge, ruin human lives on mental-emotional-physical levels, and literally "feed" off of human LIFE including that of our children—have ANY place to give such excuses!

THE NEW MJ-12

In order to establish the New World Order, the Cabal is planning to implement the necessary social revolution through the United Nations. The Illuminati have already infiltrated the most relevant divisions of the United Nations at the highest levels and are secretly integrating MJ-12 into a UN counterpart organization, which will eventually replace MJ-12. It was internationalized in 1962 under the UN Security Council when it was widened to include the United States, Russia, China, and the European Council (now the European Union). The original MJ-12 then became the U.S. Special Studies Group. The new over-arching organization is called the UN Office for Outer Space Affairs (UNOOSA). The American MJ-12 will eventually become fully integrated into UNOOSA as an executive advisory committee, at which point it will effectively be absorbed by UNOOSA. The new international MJ-12 is currently headed up by astrophysicist Simonetta Di Pippo from Italy, and includes members from Germany, Great Britain, Canada, Thailand, Brazil, Russia, the United States, the Vatican, Australia, and Peru. UNOOSA is now headquartered in Vienna, Austria.

SPACE COMMAND

The United States Space Command is under the jurisdiction of the U.S. Air Force. It was created in 1985 as the responsible agency for all space-related activities of the U.S. military. Michael Salla said in 2007 on his website:

> It has advanced space capabilities far beyond the technology possessed by NASA. This helps confirm what Gary McKinnon discovered when hacking into NASA and Pentagon computers. He claims he was able to eventually hack his way into the Space Command computers where he discovered "a list of officers' names" he said were under the heading "Non-Terrestrial Officers." McKinnon also spoke of "Fleet to Fleet transfers." The Space Command has a

public organization and a top-secret hidden division. This operation is based at the Cheyenne Mountain Air Force Station in Colorado. Ostensibly, its mission is "exceptional support in keeping the space shuttle, International Space Station, and its crews safe from the dangers of orbital debris, spacecraft collisions and other inherent hazards of orbit operations." This implies that it has the technology necessary to destroy these hazards.

According to Ted Tweitmeyer in his online article "The USAF Space Command and What it Does," "It is known that the Space Command has advanced secret spacecraft to exit and re-enter the atmosphere without using rocket technology. This would include but not be limited to vehicles such as the TR-3 made by Lockheed, or also called the black triangle, Black Manta, etc."

SOLAR WARDEN

In a another website article by Michael Salla, from 2009, he says, "If Reagan's comments and whistleblower testimonies are correct, then the operational home of this secret antigravity space fleet . . . is U.S. Strategic Command. The project name of the classified space fleet, according to several whistleblowers, is 'Solar Warden.' The existence of Solar Warden, if true, proves that NASA is a cover program using antiquated rocket propulsion technologies. If so, the 'futuristic' Constellation Program aimed to take astronauts to the moon and Mars is a cover for an existing space program that regularly flies interplanetary missions using advanced antigravity propulsion technologies."

In interviews by Salla with Randy Cramer (Captain Kaye)—who was supposedly part of a supersoldier contingent from Earth sent to bolster human forces on Mars—Cramer claims that Solar Warden has at its disposal eight cigar-shaped spacecraft, at least one of which, the *SS Nautilus,* is about four thousand feet in length and uses advanced propulsion systems that allow it to travel into deep space without rocketry. These "aircraft carriers" of space accommodate forty-three antigravity scout craft that are also capable of advanced propulsion travel into outer space. An anonymous whistle-blower code-named "Henry Deacon," a former physicist at Lawrence Livermore Laboratories, told interviewer Kerry Cassidy on Project Camelot that Solar Warden spaceships routinely supply a large manned base on Mars, thus confirming Cramer's claim.

The fact that the existence of Solar Warden remains top-secret means that it is part of black-ops programs and that the public cannot be informed because it reveals the alliance between the Reptilian-Reptoids and the U.S. military Cabal. It seems very likely that the technology used in Solar Warden was given to us by the aliens as part of the Treaty of Greada and that it is meant to support the advent of the New World Order. Michael Salla says, "NASA's steady decline since its Apollo heyday has nothing to do with the competence and expertise of NASA personnel. The political reality is that highly compartmentalized military programs prevent advanced antigravity technologies [from going] into the public sector for commercial application." In an online article, researcher Doug Yurchey says, "Our *leaders* have been given advanced technology for their silence. THEY cover-up the abductions and alien evidence and are given technology for their participation in the con job. Then, our *leaders* dole out this knowledge in small doses to us. With assistance from the Zeta Reticulans . . . going to the Moon or Mars is simply child's play" (italics added).

THE MARS BASE

Cramer now recalls his entire experience as a U.S. Marine supersoldier inductee into the Mars Defense Force despite having his memory previously erased. Cramer speaks of five domed city-sized human colonies on Mars, manned by supersoldiers from different nations. He was one of an army of one thousand humans living on the surface and underground on the planet and coexisting with a large colony of Reptilians, and another of Insectoids. The Mars Defense Force is a subdivision of the more inclusive Earth Defense Force, which is really a misnomer since it is not really defending the Earth so much as it is defending the elite and the Illuminati, but not the people.

Cramer says that the human base on Mars has periodic clashes with the Reptilian base as they test each other's boundaries by minor

Fig. 22.3. Earth Defense Force logo

incursions. The humans are armed with super weapons not available to the Earth militaries. Cramer spent seventeen years of his twenty-year enlistment at the Mars Base, most of this time living a boring existence but culminating in a military operation in which the Reptilians wiped out almost the entire one-thousand-man detachment, leaving only thirty-five soldiers alive. The main reason for this massacre was entrapment. The human forces were enclosed in an underground tunnel system within the Reptilian base and then surrounded from all directions and slaughtered. This ended the human presence at the Mars base for a long period of time. Cramer was one of the survivors. He was then retrained as a pilot and finished his last three years flying antigravity spacecraft patrolling the inner solar system. The Mars base is governed by the Mars Colony Corporation, an Illuminati organization that has set up mining operations and is being enriched by extracting rare materials from the Martian soil. Just as on Earth, the Mars military is under the control of Earth-based industrialists and bankers. This scenario is exactly as presented in the film from the nineties, *Total Recall.*

ENSLAVEMENT THROUGH DEBT

As they have done since the earliest days, the Brotherhood of the Snake has, in modern times, sought to keep the masses in debt to a central banking system and thus under complete control by the banking elite, who are, of course, the Illuminati. The practices of the Shemsu Hor in ancient Egypt have been repeated in the twentieth century, a tried and true method of enslaving the masses while enriching their hybrid masters. Control of a central banking system allows the Cabal to employ wars wherever necessary to maintain control over the human race. Social psychologist Preston James explores their modern methods in great and illuminating detail in his online article "35 Things the Ruling Cabal Does Not Want You to Know," dated September 2, 2013, in which he says:

> The Nazi faction still exists as a secret, covert Fourth Reich controlling some of the large Wall Street Banks and many of the major oil companies, Big Pharma and defense contractors and some American intel factions. [They] run the Central Banking and [use] pernicious usury to create massive numbers of debt slaves. . . . It seems as if the Cabal and its Cutouts are seemingly under the spell of some evil soulless mind-controlling entity, perhaps best described as a cosmic or demonic parasite that feeds off intense acute or prolonged human suffering and mass death. And it seems as if this suffering is purposefully caused by traumatic harm and death to humans from the intentional social engineering of massive crime, chaos, social breakdown, starvation, and war 24/7 in order to provide a near constant "shedding of blood," which is also alleged to provide energy and life to these parasites who appear to crave their own private near constant mass-human sacrifice.

This control of banking, combined with their control of the media, allows the Illuminati to already exercise almost total dominion over the human race on planet Earth. Their preparations for the advent of the New World Order are now well advanced.

The Nazi expatriates assimilated into the CIA and NASA in the fifties have links to the Bavarian Illuminati, still active in the new Germany. It is that group that is most involved with the Cabal and the construction of the DUMB bases. Allied, as they are, with the megamoney German banking sources, they were able to bring that necessary financial component to America's military-industrial complex, which was responsible for the construction of the underground bases, although most of the money has come from American taxpayers, secretly funneled into black-ops. Speaking about the Nazis, Branton says in a footnote in chapter 4 of *The Dulce Book*. "They were given refuge within the military-industrial complex with the help of members of the Bavarian-based black gnostic—serpent worshipping—lodges in America . . . who control the oil-military-industrial complex. The leaders of the Military-Industrial Complex or M.I.C. not only gave these fascists refuge following the war, but also had financed the Nazi war machine itself during the Second World War."

THE END GAME

Branton goes on to quote a researcher named Jim Bennett, who wrote in a letter, "It is my belief that even if there is a fascist-CIA cabal trying to establish a world dictatorship using the 'threat' of an alien invasion to foment world government, that the 'threat' may be real all the same. It is also possible that the 'Bavarians' may be working with very REAL aliens in an end-game designed to establish a world government using this 'threat' as an excuse to do so, although when the world is under 'their' control the Illuminati may betray the human race by turning much of the global government control-system over to the Grey aliens."

In his article, Branton also says:

> The aliens may have been collaborating with the Bavarians for a very long time as part of their agenda to implement absolute electronic control over the inhabitants of planet earth [see chapter 11 of this book]. One source, an Area 51 worker—and member of a secret Naval Intelligence group called COM-12—by the name of Michael Younger, stated that the Bavarian Black Nobility [secret societies] have agreed to turn over three-quarters of the planet to the Greys if they could retain 25 percent for themselves and have access to alien mind-control technology. The aliens would assist in the abduction, programming, and implanting of people throughout

the world in preparation for a New World Order. . . . Apparently, some top-echelon Bavarians have agreed to this, since they realize that they NEED the alien mind-control and implant technology in order to carry out their plans for world domination."

TRANSHUMANISM

In October 2013, a conference was convened in New York City titled "Global Future 2045: Towards a New Strategy for Human Evolution." Scientists and academicians from all over the world gathered to discuss the future of the human race. Experts in nanotechnology, biotechnology, transbiology, and cybernetics met to trade knowledge and information about a collaborative evolution of humanity into a transcendent era of seamless man-machine merging, now called "the singularity" (see plate 22). According to one astute observer, the esoteric but clearly understood purpose of this convocation was to design "a new model of society that adheres to the globalist ideologies of merging controllable humans with machines to facilitate a new race of human beings that is led by artificial intelligence plugged into the global AI computer system and functions simply to be an autonomous workforce for the global Elite." This is now referred to as the transhumanist agenda (see plate 23). One critic has said, "The goal of transhumanism is to replace all existing laws with the purpose of destroying the essence of humanity for the sake of control. Hybrid humans with robotic implants are expected to be released into the general public by 2014." That has actually begun, more or less on schedule.

Susanne Posel, a globally syndicated independent journalist, says on her website, www.occupycorporatism.com (accessed September 20, 2016), in an article posted on March 8, 2016 titled "DARPA Could Be the First to Connect Man and Machinery," "The government wants to make soldiers into cyborgs that can communicate directly with computers. And while this technology 'is still a long ways away,' DARPA is recruiting 'a diverse set of experts in an attempt to accelerate the project's development' and expedite 'breakthroughs in neuroscience, synthetic biology, low-power electronics, photonics and medical-device manufacturing. . . .'" This is all part of the UN's agenda of population transformation.

The aliens and the Illuminati are well along in their final plans to take over the planet. In addition to creating and cloning millions of hybrids, they are seeking to robotize the human population through the transhumanist agenda so that it can be controlled electronically as well as from the fourth dimension. The goal is to eliminate as many humans as possible who are motivated from spiritual sources. This will be done through another war and subsequent massive depopulation. When the human population that remains is vastly outnumbered by the hybrids and the dehumanized robots and slaves, we will become annexed to the alien empire.

The Story of Bek'Ti
An Excerpt from The Terra Papers:
The Hidden History of Planet Earth

By Robert Morning Sky

I am called "Morning Sky. . . ."

ROBERT MORNING SKY

My grandfather was one of the six young Indian rescuers. When I was young, my grandfather told me the story about his Star visitor. He and his friends called him "Star Elder," a name given out of respect. But as time passed, his name was revealed to the youths. He was called . . . "Bek'Ti."

This is his story . . . and mine.

In the late sixties, I was enrolled at a University in a Religious Studies program. Towards the end of my studies, I submitted a paper that briefly summarized the history of Man and Earth as told by Bek'Ti. I titled the paper, "TERRA, a Hidden History of Planet Earth." I was sure it was a well-presented, well-researched and well-documented work.

It was immediately labeled a work of outrageous, if not blasphemous, distortion of historical records and not of the caliber of a serious student of Religion. The TERRA PAPERS, the story of Bek'Ti, nearly got me thrown out of school.

In frustration, I approached a UFO organization and some UFO researchers reasonably confident that they would be most interested in my story. To my surprise, I was rejected offhand. I was advised by one researcher that UFOs were quite clearly a phenomena of a technology and NOT the works of the mythical beings of primitive peoples. (Curiously, he is now a well-respected UFO author and has recently released a book on the ET/Native American connection.)

For thirty years, I have avoided telling the story. The initial response to my efforts was discouraging. But I have recently been persuaded to try again.

The history of Man and Earth presented by Bek'Ti is both exciting and frightening. The creation of Man and his place in the galaxy is made clear, but in the process his nobility and his pride will be injured. The abduction phenomena and the attending grey beings are revealed to have been integral parts of Man's history but are explained against the framework of the purposes of the Star Beings for Mankind.

The sources of Man's religions and the origins of legendary figures like Zeus, the Minotaur, Osiris and Isis, and a number of other "mythological" beings are explained and also placed into the framework of the History of Planet Earth.

And, so too, upcoming events can be predicted, not from any psychic abilities or channeling, but from patterns of an on-going effort to direct Planet Earth.

Man will soon be surrounded with images of asteroids and falling fiery comets. Dinosaurs will become children's heroes and violence will be the foundation of their play. New airborne diseases, immune to existing treatments, will surface. NASA will be rendered weak and impotent, if not terminated.

A galactic war of conquest rages over our heads. . . .

Earth . . . and Man . . . is the prize.

This is my story. . . .

This is my Grandfather's story . . . and . . . this is the story of Bek'Ti.

* * *

In time, the Star Being would come to trust the six.

By using a small crystal to create images, the Visitor began to communicate with the young men. Calling him the Star Elder, the youths sat at the knee of their Friend, examining all of the crystalline images with great care, piecing together the incredible history of our Solar system and Mankind itself.

Star Elder's message was simple; Star Beings have been here since Earth was a barren rock. They were here when Man was created and have been here throughout his evolution. In some cases their involvement was benevolent, in some cases, it was not. Man has been guided . . . and he has been misled. The Star Beings have been our Gods . . . and our Devils.

They have always been here, and they are still here now.

When pressed to explain his presence on Earth, the "Star Elder" stunned the six. There was a war in the skies above, his ship had been downed by enemy forces!

APPENDIX B

The Story of Stewart Swerdlow

Stewart was born in Long Island, New York, in the late 1950s, and from an early age, remembers encounters with alien beings. In fact, some were not even humanoid. His birth was even more bizarre. The doctors told his mother there was no chance she would ever have children, yet Stewart was born. Even today, his birth is a mystery.

While in high school, Stewart was picked up at night by what he initially thought were extraterrestrials and brought to the underground base at Montauk, Long Island. Later on, he learned that his hijackers were military officials working under the guise of ETs. Because of Stewart's "special" characteristics, he became part of the Montauk genetic experiment program. According to the David Icke website, 'A

Fig. B.1. Stewart Swerdlow

gifted mentalist, Stewart was born clairvoyant and has the ability to see auric fields and personal archetypes as well as read DNA sequences and mind-patterns. His natural abilities were further enhanced by the Montauk experiments. He later learned that only 1 percent of the people in that program ever survived.

Stewart became sort of an anomaly because of his special skills. Based on the skills, he was used extensively as a programmer of the abducted "Montauk boys." While at Montauk, Stewart knew of Al Bielek. He confirms that Bielek was the psychic program manager while he was there. In 1983, when the Montauk Station was destroyed (but later rebuilt), Stewart went into a tailspin. He believes the station had a lock on him and in some sense controlled him. When the lock was released, he lost his identity. Over the last eighteen years, Stewart has been working hard to successfully regain his identity. He was put in federal prisons to persuade him not to talk about his past. What is unique about Stewart is that he never lost the memories of his experiences at Montauk.

Presently, he is teaching others how to use the techniques that were implemented at Montauk for positive purposes. He teaches seminars on how to align and enhance the mental capabilities of his students.

He is the author of *True World History: Humanity's Saga; Blue Blood, True Blood: Conflict and Creation; The Healer's Handbook: A Journey into Hyperspace; Montauk: The Alien Connection* (with Peter Moon); *The Hyperspace Helper: A User-Friendly Guide* (with Janet Swerdlow); *13-Cubed: Case Studies in Mind-Control* (with Janet Swerdlow); and *Stewart Says* (with Janet Swerdlow).

APPENDIX C

The Path to Victory

The reptilians strive to activate that dark serpent seed which is programmed within all of us. The struggle is within. The opposing polarities of Good and Evil are striving to promote certain attributes and behaviors within us. One side wants to corrupt us from within. The other wants us to break out of this spiritual prison. Ultimately it comes down to your own individual choice. I hesitate to use the term "free will" because being an abductee myself I know that I have been manipulated and programmed and it's a constant struggle to overcome all of these hang-ups—but that's what will make the ultimate victory that much greater. I firmly believe in the indomitability of the Human Spirit and I firmly believe that it is in our destiny to achieve Nobility as a race. If we had just been left alone I am sure we would have reached that level of greatness already but alas, that hasn't been the case.

"THE ORIGINAL SERPENT SEED"
BY JAMES BARTLEY

EXTRACT OF A MESSAGE FROM KHYLA,*
A PROCYON INTELLIGENCE AGENT

As collective thought patterns enhance the ability of the Grays to manipulate you, original thinkers acting on their own are more likely to have success than mass movements led by leaders who do everyone else's thinking for them.

In preventing the take-over of your planet as a colony ruled by Gray overlords, you should go back through your own history and learn what you can from the techniques used,

- by the passive resistance used to bring about the independence of India
- by the American Indians and Blacks during their oppression in the United States
- by the Blacks in South Africa at the present time
- by the French Resistance during the Nazi occupation,

. . . and anywhere else in your historical records where there are lessons of this nature to be learned. The point of passive resistance is to endure, to survive until the moment when it becomes possible to switch over to active resistance because outside help has come—being careful to avoid the mistake of the citizens of Budapest, who rose up believing propaganda assurances that the United States would support their uprising, only to be crushed by Soviet tanks when no such help was forthcoming.

---

*A description of Khyla by a contactee: "Khyla looked like a tall handsome human, slender but muscular, masculine yet ethereal. He appeared either naturally or artificially to have black around his eyes, almost like kohl. His face was close to exquisite, but definitely masculine. He had a gaunt face with high cheekbones and piercing cobalt-blue eyes. He had fine blond hair that was almost shoulder-length. He had a muscular neck. His skin was pale flesh color, with a whitish overtone. It is hard to gauge his exact height because of the circumstances under which our encounter occurred, but it was somewhere between six and seven feet." Khyla became a refugee from his planet in Procyon after the Greys took it over by subterfuge and infiltration.

Prematurely triggered active resistance would be a disaster that would enable the Grays to perpetuate their colonization of this planet, exactly the type of situation they would try to bring about.

Beware of zealots with an obsessive hatred of the Grays, who may have been subconsciously programmed by the Grays to act as agents provocateurs. If you get all those sincerely devoted to resistance together into one place, it is much easier to wipe them out. If the resistance remains disseminated among the population at large, it is more difficult to round them up.

Don't add to the superiority of the Gray position by playing into their hands. And remember that although their technology is far in advance of yours, you do vastly out-number them, and can over-extend them. They are already over-extended elsewhere, and unable to commit further forces to this area of the universe, so those already here must operate without reinforcements coming to them.

You are so far outstripped in terms of physical weaponry that you must find a source of strength that transcends the physical—such as techniques of centering consciousness on powerfully motivating imagery, which would be different from one individual to another.

- For the religiously oriented it might be a key event in the life of Jesus, Buddha, Mohammed, Moses, or whoever the appropriate figure would be in the tradition one's belief system is centered around.
- For those who are not religiously oriented, it would be whatever figure that person sincerely admires as representing what is best in humanity, whether it be an artist or inventor or other type of benevolent leader of society.

If the admiration is not wholeheartedly sincere, the intensity with which the attention is focused on the symbolic image in which one wishes to take refuge is not sufficient to be of much use as protection, nor can the attention be maintained for long. The degree of protection given by such imagery depends largely on the intensity and endurance of the single-pointed attention. So it is best to choose whatever figure you genuinely feel spontaneous admiration for, whatever image makes your heart sing and makes you feel at one with the infinite. That will always work, and is all we can do for now.

An example of the type of attitude that the Grays find most confusing is the classic Buddhist discipline of meditating on a bloated corpse until one roars with laughter upon realizing what a complete cosmic joke existence is.

The most likely way to extricate oneself and others from a potentially disastrous situation is to keep the consciousness centered and the heart still, realizing the situation to be the illusion that it is. Do not act out of fear, thereby insuring the victory of the opponent; if one allows oneself to be intimidated, the inevitable result is death. In no matter what type of situation, retain your sense of humor and perspective.

Learn to apply the T'ai Ch'i disciplines in non-physical fashion. Center yourself, then act from that center. Since the Grays have mastered much deeper techniques of hypnosis than humans have, their takeover of human consciousness can only be prevented by strong imagery of a religious or mystical nature. Your contemporary hypnosis works within the mammalian portions of your brain, which in terms of evolutionary development are the more recently acquired portions. Being partially reptilian themselves, the Grays know how to manipulate the reptilian level of your brain, which is the most basic and ancient level.

The only way to counter-act such manipulation is by activating the most high of the highest levels of consciousness accessible to you at your present stage of development. If one is unable to maintain an image evoking that highest level of consciousness firmly in one's thoughts, their hypnosis can bypass the higher levels of your evolutionary development and take control of the deep reptilian level, in this fashion overpowering an individual's true will and obliterating the integrity of the soul. That is how they took over key officials of the CIA, KGB, and other powerful elite groups within your social structure.

* * *

They only need to control the elite at the tip of the top of the social pyramid, the top hundredth of one percent of the population, in order to control us all. A person enslaved in this fashion can be made to do things that your type of hypnosis could not make them do, such as murdering their closest friends or family members. Having gained control over the reptilian level of consciousness, they temporarily paralyze all portions of the mammalian brain higher than the ape level, then activate the ape level's more violent responses, such as territorialism, greed, lust or rage. Humans can be made to respond like apes, unless they are able to resist the attempt to take them over by activating the level of consciousness that corresponds to the crown chakra. Any attempt to fight back at the ape level insures the success of the Grays. The ape-level belligerence, territorialism, and posturing for purposes of prestige and dominance, which are unfortunately so characteristic of the U.S.-U.S.S.R. relationship on both sides, deliver the population of this planet bound hand and foot into the power of the Grays.

After having destroyed approximately three-quarters of the present population through the introduction of viral diseases and the induction of assorted catastrophes, the Grays would not even need to make an overt appearance as saviors from the skies. They could replace humans with hybrids unobtrusively. It could be done so gradually that no one would realize what was happening. The transition from humans to hybrids could be so subtle and seamless that the change-over would never be noticed. It would not even be mentioned in the history books, as scientists would assume that the physical and mental changes were the result of naturally occurring evolution. Human history would become hybrid history without anyone understanding what had actually occurred. The governments might even continue to deny the existence of UFOs.

All that would be needed would be to continue the process that is already in operation. Some researchers are aware of the fact that the hybrids which turn out to resemble the Grays are removed from their mothers and taken elsewhere, but very few are aware that the hybrids which turn out to resemble humans are left to grow up in human society. Before taking hybrids back to their home base to give a much-needed genetic boost to their own ancestral stock, they would want to carry out intensive long-range studies. Certain questions would need to be answered, such as: are the hybrids psychologically stable? Disease-resistant? Productive? Aggressive? They would want to observe the interplay between humans and hybrids, in order to make sure that the hybrids had the qualities necessary to become leaders in human society. In general, Gray/human hybrids would require less food and sleep than terrestrial humans.

They would tend to be more intelligent and slender, but emotionally cold. This does not mean that any human with these characteristics is necessarily a hybrid. As many as 3 percent of the present population may already be hybrids. All the Gray would have to do would be to continue doing exactly what they are doing, to keep boosting that percentage bit by bit, with an occasional sudden jump in the wake of seemingly natural catastrophes, until the original human population has been 100 percent replaced by hybrids.

Why do I know so well how such an operation is carried out? The process is quite similar to that by which the Blonds replaced Neanderthal man with Cro-Magnon man. However, the intelligence of terrestrial humanity has now evolved to the point where it has a choice in the matter. By understanding the long-term hive-mind strategy of the Grays, individual humans who attain multi-dimensional awareness can circumvent and short-circuit it.

If enough individual humans do this, and refrain from quarreling over whether the state of multi-dimensional awareness is to be called Christ-consciousness or any of the other names it has in the different traditions, uniting together from all traditions to liberate the planet, the Grays will be obliged to seek elsewhere in the cosmos for a slave species they can genetically manipulate.

At some point help may come from outside, from my own and/or some of the other space races. There may also be revolt within the ranks of the Grays, based on widespread discontent with their rigid insect-like hierarchical caste system. In the process of infiltrating a species, the Grays cannot avoid being influenced by that species, and some of them who had never thought of questioning authority are beginning to do so, due to the influence of human contact.

The Grays are having problems not only within their own ranks, but also on other planets they have colonized. As a species they are afflicted with severe, perhaps terminal, health problems. They have substantial captive populations of Blond, human and other prisoners of war, eager to join a revolt at the slightest opportunity. There is no reason why one should not send out telepathic appeals for help, in the form of prayer or meditation, or in whatever way is appropriate to the individual, to the higher forces in the cosmos. They do exist, and are sensitive to such signals. There are extraterrestrial and other-dimensional cultures capable of harnessing the innate power of entire galaxies, who could be of immeasurable help in liberating your planet from domination by the Grays, if you could persuade them to intervene. However, they are unlikely to respond until humanity cleans up its own act and stops polluting the planetary environment.

One can also send out telepathic signals of encouragement to those among the Grays who have begun to question authority and acquire a taste for human freedom, but it would be suicidal to attempt to fight the Grays directly with the weapons at present at your disposal. One must be rational in attempting to fight back, and understand the proper way to proceed. Your own consciousness is the most potent weapon that is available to you at the present time. The most effective way to fight the Grays is to change the level of your consciousness from linear thinking to multi-dimensional awareness. Your secret weapon, your ace in the hole, is that you are not hive-mind collective thinkers, though many of you do fall into that category by conforming to conventional group-patterns, and are therefore easily controlled by the Grays.

Collective thought-patterns among humans empower the Grays. It is your individuality, which is your best weapon, because it is the one weapon you have that the Grays do not have. The major weakness of the Grays, their area of vulnerability, their Achilles heel, is their inability to think as individuals. They are an extremely telepathic high-tech society, but as individuals they are not creative thinkers. They take orders well, but they do not conceptualize well.

* * *

They have the technology to throw your planet out of orbit, but there is one key ability that you have and they do not have: the ability to hold in mind imagery that inspires an individual to realize his or her direct personal connection to the source of all that is, which is the ineffable Godhead, no matter what name you may call it.

That is your key to victory.

Recommended Reading and Viewing

BOOKS

Adams, Mark. *Meet Me in Atlantis: My Obsessive Quest to Find the Sunken City*. New York: Dutton, 2015.

Aun Weor, Samuel. *The Revolution of Beelzebub: The Demon Who Renounced Evil and the Man Who Guided Him*. Brooklyn, N.Y.: Glorian Publishing, 2010.

Baigent, Michael, Richard Leigh, and Henry Lincoln. *Holy Blood, Holy Grail: The Secret History of Christ and the Shocking Legacy of the Grail*. New York: Bantam Dell Trade Paperback, 2004.

Bowart, Walter. *Operation Mind Control*. New York: Dell, 1978. (Out of print; e-book available online)

Bramley, William. *The Gods of Eden*. New York: Avon Books, Imprint of HarperCollins Publishers, 1993.

Brown, Dan. *The Da Vinci Code*. New York: Anchor Books Mass-Market Edition, 2009.

Chang, Iris. *The Rape of Nanking: The Forgotten Holocaust of World War II*. New York: Penguin Books, 1998.

Charroux, Robert. *Masters of the World*. New York: Berkley Publishing Corp., 1974.

Delgado, Jose M. R. *Physical Control of the Mind: Toward a Psychocivilized Society*. New York, Harper Colophon Books, 1971. (Out of print)

Donnelly, Ignatius. *Atlantis: The Antediluvian World*. Paperback copy of original 1882 ed., illustrated and indexed. New York: CreateSpace Independent Publishing Platform, 2015.

Gardner, Laurence. *Bloodline of the Holy Grail: The Hidden Lineage of Jesus Revealed*. Illus. ed. New York: Barnes & Noble Books, 2000.

Hall, Allan. Book review of *Soldiers: German POWs on Fighting, Killing, and Dying*. *Daily Mail*, September 16, 2012.

Haze, Xaviant. *Aliens in Ancient Egypt: The Brotherhood of the Serpent and the Secrets of the Nile Civilization*. Rochester, Vt.: Bear & Company, 2013.

———. *The Suppressed History of American Banking: How Big Banks Fought Jackson, Killed Lincoln, and Caused the Civil War*. Rochester, Vt.: Bear & Company, 2016.

Hitler, Adolph. *Mein Kampf* (My Struggle). Unabridged ed. Haole Library online, 2015.

Icke, David. *The Biggest Secret: The Book That Will Change the World*. Scottsdale, Ariz.: Bridge of Love Publications, 1999.

Jacobs, David, Dr. *Secret Life: Firsthand Documented Accounts of UFO Abductions*. New York: Simon and Schuster Fireside Edition, 1992.

———. *The Threat: Revealing the Secret Alien Agenda*. New York: Simon and Schuster Fireside Edition, 1998.

———. *Walking Among Us: The Alien Plan to Control Humanity*. San Francisco, Calif.: Disinformation Books, 2015.

Kasten, Len. *The Secret History of Extraterrestrials*. Rochester, Vt.: Bear & Company, 2010.

———. *Secret Journey to Planet Serpo*. Rochester, Vt.: Inner Traditions International, 2013.

Keith, Jim. *Mass Control: Engineering Human Consciousness*. Kempton, Ill.: Adventures Unlimited Press, 2003.

Mack, John, Dr. *Abduction: Human Encounters with Aliens*. New York: Scribner, 1994.

Malory, Thomas. *Le Morte D'Arthur: The Winchester Manuscript*. New York: Oxford University Press, 2008.

Manning, Paul. *Martin Bormann: Nazi in Exile*. Secaucus, N.J.: Lyle Stuart Inc., 1981.

Martin, Edward T. *King of Travelers: Jesus' Lost Years in India*. 2nd ed. Reno Nev.: Yellow Hat Productions, 2008.

Morning Sky, Robert. *Eden, Atlantis, and the UFO Myth*. Special Release:

Part 1—"Eden Unveiled." Book Two of "The World's Oldest Religion." Publisher and year unknown.

Morning Sky, Robert. *The Terra Papers: The Hidden History of Planet Earth.* The Terra Project, 1980.

Neitzel, Sonke, and Harald Welzer. *Soldiers: German POWs on Fighting, Killing, and Dying.* Reprint ed. New York: Vintage, 2013.

Plato. *The Atlantis Dialogue: Plato's Original Story of the Lost City and Continent.* Translated by B. Jowett. Edited by Aaron Shepard. Friday Harbor, Wash.: Shepard Publications, 2001.

Ravenscroft, Trevor. *The Spear of Destiny: The Occult Power Behind the Spear That Pierced the Side of Christ.* First American paperback ed. York Beach, Maine: Samuel Weiser, 1982.

Salla, Michael E. *Insiders Reveal Secret Space Programs and Extraterrestrial Alliances.* Pahoa, Hawaii: Expolitics Institute, 2015.

Schertel, Ernst, Dr. *Magic: History, Theory, Practice.* Annotated by Adolph Hitler. Edited by J. H. Kelley. Translated by COTUM Research Staff. COTUM, 2009.

Strieber, Whitley. *Solving the Communion Enigma: What Is to Come.* New York: Tarcher Penguin, 2012.

———. *The Super Natural: A New Vision of the Unexplained.* New York: Tarcher Penguin, 2016.

Swerdlow, Stewart A. *Blue Blood, True Blood: Conflict and Creation.* St. Joseph, Mich.: Expansions Publishing Co. Inc., 2002.

———. *True World History: Humanity's Saga.* St. Joseph, Mich.: Expansions Publishing Co. Inc., 2014.

Tompkins, William Mills, and Dr. Robert M. Wood. *Selected by Extraterrestrials: My Life in the Top Secret World of UFOs, Think-Tanks, and Nordic Secretaries.* Self-published by CreateSpace, 2015.

Tyson, Joseph Howard. *The Surreal Reich.* Bloomington, Ind.: iUniverse, 2010.

Valerian, Valdamar. *Defending Sacred Ground: The Andromedan Compendium Volume One.* Edited by Alex Collier. Morrison, Colo.: Leading Edge Research Group, 1997.

Von Daniken, Erich. *Chariots of the Gods? Unsolved Mysteries of the Past.* 2nd ed. New York: G. P. Putnam's Sons, 1969.

Wells, H. G. *The Time Machine.* New York: Marino Fine Books, 2011.

———. *The War in the Air.* New York: Penguin Classics, 2007.

ARTICLES

Bartley, James. "Grand Strategy of the Reptilians." Angelfire. www.angelfire
.com/ut/branton/dracos.html (accessed July 23, 2016).

———. Review of *The Body Snatchers* by Susan Reed. Whale: They Fear Those
with Knowledge and Control Those Without It.
http://whale.to/b/reed_b.html (accessed July 23, 2016).

———. "Understanding the Reptilian Mind." Whale: They Fear Those with
Knowledge and Control Those Without It. www.whale.to/b/bartley3.html
(accessed July 23, 2016).

Begich, Nick, M.D. "Mind Control: The Ultimate Brave New World." *Nexus
Magazine,* February–March 2006.

Montalk. "Discerning Alien Disinformation, Part 2." Biblioteca Pleyades.
www.bibliotecapleyades.net/vida_alien/esp_vida_alien_18zy_02.htm (accessed
July 23, 2016).

———. "Discerning Alien Disinformation, Part 4." Biblioteca Pleyades.
www.bibliotecapleyades.net/vida_alien/esp_vida_alien_18zy_04.htm (accessed
July 23, 2016).

———. "Synopsis of the Alien Master Plan." Biblioteca Pleyades.
www.bibliotecapleyades.net/vida_alien/esp_vida_alien_18zy_00.htm (accessed
July 23, 2016).

Omar, Steve. *Atlantis: History of the Golden Ages.* www.bibliotecapleyades.net
/atlantida_mu/esp_atlantida_5.htm (accessed July 20, 2016).

Stephens, Ian E. "Fluoridation: Mind Control of the Masses." *Nexus Magazine,*
July 9, 2010.

YOUTUBE VIDEOS

"James Bartley—MILAB's and Reptilian Concept of Human Ownership."
https://youtu.be/FHeDtt62PYo (accessed July 23, 2016).

"Japanese World War II Veterans Recall Horrors of Unit 731." https://youtu.be
/Tx7loRv70y8 (accessed July 23, 2016).

"Laura Eisenhower: Reptilian Invasion Has Already Occurred . . ." https://
youtu.be/oek9xsR15g8 (accessed July 23, 2016).

"New World Order Insider Dies after Exposing Entire Agenda." https://youtu
.be/QCAMEeC8BaQ (accessed July 23, 2016).

"Reptilians Caused the Flood." https://youtu.be/qh5W_pF2pQY (accessed
July 23, 2016).

"Reptilians Exist Reasons Why Part 3 (Preston B. Nichols)." https://youtu.be/P1Jxz2DnHck (accessed July 23, 2016).

"Reptilians Exist Reasons Why Part 6." https://youtu.be/-vTi7rie7RE (accessed July 23, 2016).

"Reptilians Live below the Earth and Eat Childrens." https://youtu.be/WJSCGtCm2EE (accessed July 23, 2016).

"The Alien Invasion—Cloning of Celebrities." https://youtu.be/OGTuiT5BlJw (accessed July 23, 2016).

"The Secret Underground Reptilian Cities of Lore." https://youtu.be/Zzq3Vz-tVU0 (accessed July 23, 2016).

Index

Numbers in *italics* preceded by *pl.* indicate colored plate numbers.